S. Hrg. 112-183: Oversight of Dodd-Frank Implementation, Monitoring Systemic Risk and Promoting Financial Stability

U.S. Government Printing Office (GPO)

S. Hrg. 112–183

OVERSIGHT OF DODD-FRANK IMPLEMENTATION: MONITORING SYSTEMIC RISK AND PROMOTING FINANCIAL STABILITY

HEARING

BEFORE THE

COMMITTEE ON BANKING, HOUSING, AND URBAN AFFAIRS UNITED STATES SENATE

ONE HUNDRED TWELFTH CONGRESS

FIRST SESSION

ON

CONTINUING OVERSIGHT OF THE IMPLEMENTATION OF THE DODD-FRANK WALL STREET REFORM AND CONSUMER PROTECTION ACT (DODD-FRANK ACT), FOCUSING ON PROVISIONS RELATED TO MONITORING SYSTEMIC RISK AND PROMOTING FINANCIAL STABILITY

MAY 12, 2011

Printed for the use of the Committee on Banking, Housing, and Urban Affairs

Available at: http://www.fdsys.gov/

U.S. GOVERNMENT PRINTING OFFICE

71–127 PDF   WASHINGTON : 2012

For sale by the Superintendent of Documents, U.S. Government Printing Office
Internet: bookstore.gpo.gov   Phone: toll free (866) 512–1800; DC area (202) 512–1800
Fax: (202) 512–2250   Mail: Stop SSOP, Washington, DC 20402–0001

COMMITTEE ON BANKING, HOUSING, AND URBAN AFFAIRS

TIM JOHNSON, South Dakota, *Chairman*

JACK REED, Rhode Island
CHARLES E. SCHUMER, New York
ROBERT MENENDEZ, New Jersey
DANIEL K. AKAKA, Hawaii
SHERROD BROWN, Ohio
JON TESTER, Montana
HERB KOHL, Wisconsin
MARK R. WARNER, Virginia
JEFF MERKLEY, Oregon
MICHAEL F. BENNET, Colorado
KAY HAGAN, North Carolina

RICHARD C. SHELBY, Alabama
MIKE CRAPO, Idaho
BOB CORKER, Tennessee
JIM DeMINT, South Carolina
DAVID VITTER, Louisiana
MIKE JOHANNS, Nebraska
PATRICK J. TOOMEY, Pennsylvania
MARK KIRK, Illinois
JERRY MORAN, Kansas
ROGER F. WICKER, Mississippi

DWIGHT FETTIG, *Staff Director*
WILLIAM D. DUHNKE, *Republican Staff Director*

CHARLES YI, *Chief Counsel*
LAURA SWANSON, *Policy Director*
COLIN McGINNIS, *Professional Staff Member*
BRETT HEWITT, *Legislative Assistant*

ANDREW OLMEM, *Republican Chief Counsel*
HESTER PEIRCE, *Republican Senior Counsel*
MICHAEL PIWOWAR, *Republican Senior Economist*

DAWN RATLIFF, *Chief Clerk*
LEVON BAGRAMIAN, *Hearing Clerk*
SHELVIN SIMMONS, *IT Director*
JIM CROWELL, *Editor*

(II)

C O N T E N T S

THURSDAY, MAY 12, 2011

OVERSIGHT OF DODD-FRANK IMPLEMENTATION: MONITORING SYSTEMIC RISK AND PROMOTING FINANCIAL STABILITY

THURSDAY, MAY 12, 2011

U.S. SENATE,
COMMITTEE ON BANKING, HOUSING, AND URBAN AFFAIRS,
Washington, DC.

The Committee met at 9:37 a.m. in room SD–538, Dirksen Senate Office Building, Hon. Tim Johnson, Chairman of the Committee, presiding.

OPENING STATEMENT OF CHAIRMAN TIM JOHNSON

Chairman JOHNSON. I would like to call this hearing to order.

Today, as the Committee continues its oversight of the Dodd-Frank Wall Street Reform and Consumer Protection Act, I welcome our witnesses back to talk about systemic risk and financial stability. Last year, when this Committee set out to respond to the worst economic crisis in generations, addressing systemic risk and "too big to fail" were key tasks. Any serious financial reform effort had to include an early warning system that could detect systemic risk before it could threaten to bring down the entire economy. Equally important was creating a new orderly liquidation process to prevent future bailouts and to force large risky financial firms to plan ahead for their own possible failure.

In Dodd-Frank, we accomplished these goals, but those changes cannot just take place at the flick of a switch. Today our witnesses will provide us with an update on the implementation of the provisions related to monitoring systemic risk and promoting financial stability less than 10 months after the legislation was signed into law. Each of these agencies here is part of the Financial Stability Oversight Council, or FSOC, established to be the early warning watchdog for our financial system.

It is important to note that the seats of two voting members of the FSOC remain vacant—the CFPB Director and the independent insurance member. We need to nominate and confirm those members as soon as possible. Any political game plan surrounding these nominees to try to subvert critical Wall Street reforms would be irresponsible and risk our Nation's economic recovery.

One of FSOC's early tasks is to write rules for designating large risky nonbank financial institutions for enhanced supervision. The so-called shadow banking system was one of the key pieces that led to the crisis. And while it is important to provide oversight of the shadow banking system, it is also important that this designation does not become a synonym for "too big to fail."

The Dodd-Frank Act ended "too-big-to-fail" bailouts by establishing the orderly liquidation authority to unwind failing financial firms without putting the financial system or taxpayers at risk. In fact, Ranking Member Shelby worked closely with then-Chairman Dodd to craft an amendment that became the final text of this provision in Dodd-Frank, and I want to thank Ranking Member Shelby for his work.

While we will never be able to anticipate every possible cause of a future crisis, we are much better equipped to deal with the next crisis if and when it occurs. We should never forget the magnitude of the costs of the financial crisis, especially the destruction of millions of jobs and trillions of dollars of household wealth.

Opponents of financial reform may want to use revisionist history, but Americans have not forgotten that the recession was caused in part by excessive risk among some of the largest financial firms. With Dodd-Frank, we have created a new, sound economic foundation that will protect against the entire economy being exposed the next time a large financial firm rolls the dice on a bet it cannot back up. The effective, timely, and well-coordinated implementation of these reforms is critical to our economic security.

I want to remind my colleagues and the witnesses that as soon as we have a quorum present, we will move into executive session to report our six nominees. When finished with the nominees, we will return to our hearing. Given the time constraints today, only the Chairman and the Ranking Member will deliver opening statements.

Ranking Member Shelby.

STATEMENT OF SENATOR RICHARD C. SHELBY

Senator SHELBY. Mr. Chairman, to expedite the hearing, I ask unanimous consent that my opening statement, which is lengthy, be made part of the record, and we can get on with the witnesses.

Chairman JOHNSON. It will be included.

Senator SHELBY. Mr. Chairman, I believe I am right on the number, but you are the counter. I believe we just need one more person to show up to have a quorum.

[Pause.]

Chairman JOHNSON. Mr. Wolin, please proceed—we have a quorum.

[Whereupon, at 9:42 a.m., the Committee proceeded to other business and reconvened at 9:55 a.m.]

Chairman JOHNSON. Before I begin the introductions of our witnesses today, I want to remind my colleagues that the record will be open for the next 7 days for any materials you would like to submit.

Our witnesses today have all been before this Committee numerous times this year, so I will keep the introductions brief.

The Honorable Neal S. Wolin is Deputy Secretary of the U.S. Department of the Treasury.

The Honorable Ben S. Bernanke is currently serving his second term as Chairman of the Board of Governors of the Federal Reserve System.

The Honorable Sheila C. Bair is Chairman of the Federal Deposit Insurance Corporation. Chairman Bair recently announced that she will be stepping down as the Chairman of the FDIC at the beginning of July when her current term expires. Sheila, I would like to thank you for all your work you have done to serve the people of the United States. I will truly miss you come July, and we wish you well in any future endeavors that you pursue.

The Honorable Mary L. Schapiro is Chairman of the U.S. Securities and Exchange Commission.

The Honorable Gary Gensler is the Chairman of the Commodity Futures Trading Commission.

Mr. John Walsh is Acting Comptroller of the Currency of the Office of the Comptroller of the Currency.

I thank you all for being here today. Secretary Wolin, you may begin your testimony.

STATEMENT NEAL S. WOLIN, DEPUTY SECRETARY, DEPARTMENT OF THE TREASURY

Mr. WOLIN. Thank you, Mr. Chairman.

Chairman Johnson, Ranking Member Shelby, members of the Committee, I appreciate the opportunity to update you on the Treasury Department's implementation of the Dodd-Frank Act.

Although our economy and financial markets have made progress toward recovery, we cannot forget why the Congress passed and the President signed the Dodd-Frank Act last year.

In the fall of 2008, we witnessed a financial crisis of a scale and severity not seen in decades. The crisis exposed fundamental failures in our financial system. Our system favored short-term gains over stability and growth. Our system was weak and susceptible to crisis, and our system left taxpayers to save it in times of trouble.

We had no choice but to build a better, stronger system. Enacting Dodd-Frank was the beginning of that process, and as we move forward with implementation, our efforts are guided by broad principles.

We are moving quickly but carefully. Treasury and regulators are seeking public input and are committed to getting the details right.

We are conducting this process in the open, bringing full transparency to implementation. We are consulting broadly, making input on rulemakings publicly available, and posting the details of senior officials' meetings online so that the American people can see who is at the table.

Wherever possible, we are seeking to streamline and simplify Government regulation. Dodd-Frank consolidates organizational structures and oversight responsibilities, updating and rationalizing patchwork regulations built up over decades.

We are creating a more coordinated regulatory process. Regulators are working together to close gaps and to prevent breakdowns in coordination—and within the Financial Stability Oversight Council, we are working across agencies and instilling joint accountability for the strength of the financial system.

We are working to ensure a level playing field. We are working hard internationally to develop similar frameworks on the key issues where global consistency is essential, such as liquidity, leverage, capital, and OTC derivatives.

We are working hard to achieve a careful balance and to protect the freedom for innovation that is absolutely necessary for growth. We are keeping Congress fully informed of our progress on a regular basis.

Treasury has made significant progress in the short time since the Dodd-Frank Act was enacted. In those months, we have stood up the FSOC, which is working to identify risks to U.S. financial stability and promote market discipline, while developing procedures for deciding which nonbank financial institutions and financial market utilities will be subject to heightened prudential standards.

We have made significant progress in creating the Office of Financial Research, which is working to improve the quality of financial data available to policymakers and to facilitate more robust and sophisticated analysis of the financial system.

Dodd-Frank creates, and the Treasury is standing up, the Consumer Financial Protection Bureau, which is working to protect consumers, making sure they have the information they need to understand the terms of financial products.

Treasury is also working to enhance our ability to monitor the insurance sector through the Federal Insurance Office, which, for the first time provides the U.S. Government dedicated expertise regarding the insurance industry.

We have made significant progress in the 10 months since enactment. Continuing to move forward is essential to our country's financial well-being. There is no responsible alternative because if we do not invest in reform now, we run the unacceptable risk that we will pay dearly later. We cannot allow that.

Dodd-Frank Act was enacted to make sure that our financial system is the world's strongest, most dynamic, and most productive.

Thank you, Mr. Chairman.

Chairman JOHNSON. Thank you, Mr. Wolin.

Chairman BERNANKE.

STATEMENT BEN S. BERNANKE, CHAIRMAN, BOARD OF GOVERNORS OF THE FEDERAL RESERVE SYSTEM

Mr. BERNANKE. Thank you. Chairman Johnson, Ranking Member Shelby, and other Members of the Committee, thank you for the opportunity to testify on the Federal Reserve Board's role in monitoring systemic risk and promoting financial stability, both as a member of the Financial Stability Oversight Council and under our own authority.

The Dodd-Frank Act created the FSOC to identify and mitigate threats to the financial stability of the United States. During its existence thus far, the FSOC has promoted interagency collaboration and established the organizational structure and processes necessary to execute its duties.

The FSOC and its member agencies also have completed studies on limits on proprietary trading and investments in hedge funds and private equity funds by banking firms—the so-called Volcker rule—on financial sector concentration limits, on the economic effects of risk retention, and on the economic consequences of systemic risk regulation. The FSOC is currently seeking public comments on proposed rules that would establish a framework for identifying nonbank financial firms and financial market utilities that could pose a threat to financial stability and that, therefore, should be designated for more stringent oversight. Importantly, the FSOC has begun systematically monitoring risks to financial stability and is preparing its inaugural annual report.

In addition to its role on the FSOC, the Federal Reserve has other significant financial stability responsibilities under the Dodd-Frank Act, including supervisory jurisdiction over thrift holding companies and nonbank financial firms that are designated as systemically important by the Council. The act also requires the Federal Reserve (and other financial regulatory agencies) to take a macroprudential approach to supervision and regulation; that is, in supervising financial institutions and critical infrastructures, we are expected to consider the risks to overall financial stability in addition to the safety and soundness of individual firms.

A major thrust of the Dodd-Frank Act is addressing the "too-big-to-fail" problem and mitigating the threat to financial stability posed by systemically important financial firms. As required by the act, the Federal Reserve is developing more stringent prudential standards for large banking organizations and nonbank financial firms designated by the FSOC. These standards will include enhanced risk-based capital and leverage requirements, liquidity requirements, and single-counterparty credit limits. The standards will also require systemically important financial firms to adopt so-called living wills that will spell out how they can be resolved in an orderly manner during times of financial distress. The act also directs the Federal Reserve to conduct annual stress tests of large banking firms and designated nonbank financial firms and to publish a summary of the results. To meet the January 2012 implementation deadline for these enhanced standards, we anticipate putting out a package of proposed rules for comment this summer. Our goal is to produce a well-integrated set of rules that meaningfully reduces the probability of failure of our largest, most complex financial firms and that minimizes the losses to the financial system and the economy if such a firm should fail.

The Federal Reserve is working with other U.S. regulatory agencies to implement Dodd-Frank reforms in additional areas, including the development of risk retention requirements for securitization sponsors, margin requirements for noncleared over-the-counter derivatives, incentive compensation rules, and risk management standards for central counterparties and other financial market utilities.

The Federal Reserve has made significant organizational changes to better carry out its responsibilities. Even before the enactment of the Dodd-Frank Act, we were strengthening our supervision of the largest, most complex financial firms. We have created a centralized multidisciplinary body to oversee the supervision of these firms. This Committee uses horizontal, or cross-firm, evaluations to monitor interconnectedness and common practices among firms that could lead to greater systemic risk. It also uses additional and improved quantitative methods for evaluating the performance of firms and the risks that they might pose. And it more efficiently employs the broad range of skills of the Federal Reserve staff to supplement supervision. We have established a similar body to help us effectively carry out our responsibilities regarding the oversight of systemically important financial market utilities.

More recently, we have also created an Office of Financial Stability Policy and Research at the Federal Reserve Board. This office coordinates our efforts to identify and analyze potential risks to the broader financial system and the economy. It also helps evaluate policies to promote financial stability and serves as the Board's liaison to the FSOC.

As a complement to those efforts under Dodd-Frank, the Federal Reserve has been working for some time with other regulatory agencies and central banks around the world to design and implement a stronger set of prudential requirements for internationally active banking firms. These efforts resulted in the agreements reached in the fall of 2010 on the major elements of the new Basel III prudential framework for globally active banks. The requirements under Basel III that such banks hold more and better quality capital and more robust liquidity buffers should make the financial system more stable and reduce the likelihood of future financial crises. We are working with the other U.S. banking agencies to incorporate the Basel III agreements into U.S. regulations.

More remains to be done at the international level to strengthen the global financial system. Key tasks ahead for the Basel Committee and the Financial Stability Board include determining how to further increase the loss-absorbing capacity of systemically important banking firms and strengthening resolution regimes to minimize adverse systemic effects from the failure of large, complex banks. As we work with our international counterparts, we are striving to keep international regulatory standards as consistent as possible, to ensure both that multinational firms are adequately supervised and to maintain a level international playing field.

Thank you, and I would be pleased to take your questions.

Chairman JOHNSON. Thank you, Chairman Bernanke.

Chairman BAIR.

STATEMENT OF SHEILA C. BAIR, CHAIRMAN, FEDERAL DEPOSIT INSURANCE CORPORATION

Ms. BAIR. Thank you, Mr. Chairman. Chairman Johnson, Ranking Member Shelby, and Members of the Committee, thank you for the opportunity to testify today on behalf of the FDIC.

The recent financial crisis has highlighted the critical importance of financial stability to the functioning of our real economy. While emergency measures taken in the crisis stabilized financial markets and helped end the recession, in its wake, almost 14 million Americans remain out of work and our nation faces a number of other serious economic challenges.

Consistent with historical precedent, a central cause of the crisis was excessive debt and leverage in our financial system. In the fall of 2008, many of the large intermediaries at the core of our financial system had too little capital to maintain market confidence in their solvency. In the period leading up to this crisis, we saw excess leverage of financial institutions and securitization structures and in real estate loans that made our entire system highly vulnerable to a decline in home prices and a rise in problem mortgages. The need for stronger bank capital requirements is being addressed through Basel III and through implementation of the Collins Amendment here in the United States.

One of the most powerful inducements toward excess leverage and institutional risk taking before the crisis was the *de facto* policy of "too big to fail." With the expectation of a Government backstop the largest financial companies are insulated from the normal discipline of the marketplace that applies to smaller banks and practically every other private company. This situation represents a dangerous form of state capitalism, in which the market expects these companies to receive generous Government subsidies in times of financial distress. Unless reversed, the result is likely to be more concentration and complexity in the financial system, more risk taking at the expense of the public, and in due time, another financial crisis.

However, the Dodd-Frank Act does provide the basis for a new resolution framework designed to make it possible to resolve systemically important financial institutions, or SIFIs, without a bailout and without sparking a systemic crisis. Being designated as a SIFI will in no way confer a competitive advantage by anointing an institution as "too big to fail." The heightened supervisory requirements placed on SIFIs, including higher capital requirements and the need to maintain resolution plans, seems to represent a powerful disincentive for large institutions to seek SIFI status.

A key consideration in designating a firm as a SIFI should be whether it could be resolved in a bankruptcy process without systemic impact. Provided we have sufficient information to evaluate the resolvability, it is likely that relatively few non-bank financial companies will ultimately be designated as SIFIs and subject to the heightened supervisory requirements. But we do need the information to make that determination.

The orderly liquidation authority has been called a bailout mechanism by some and a fire sale by others, but neither is true. Instead, it is, I believe, a highly effective resolution framework that greatly enhances our ability to provide continuity and minimize losses and financial institution failures.

Excess leverage is a problem that extends beyond the purview of financial regulators to a broader range of economic policies that encourage the use of debt as opposed to equity, and this is where I hope the Members of the Senate Banking Committee can perhaps play a leadership role in promoting economic policies, including tax measures and fiscal reforms that can reduce or eliminate incentives for excess leverage in our financial system and our economy.

There are two additional risk management issues that I feel should be high priorities for the new Financial Stability Oversight Council under its mandate to identify and address emerging risks to financial stability. First, mortgage servicing deficiencies remain a serious area of concern. Although the FDIC does not supervise the largest loan servicers, over 4 years ago, we began identifying and trying to address these problems using the authorities at our disposal. Problems in mortgage servicing are yet another result of the misaligned incentives in the mortgage process, where fixed compensation provides few incentives to implement the more cost-ly, labor intensive servicing techniques that are necessary to deal with high volumes of problem loans. Not only do these problems represent significant operational, reputational, and litigation risks to mortgage servicers, which we insure, they are also holding back the recovery of U.S. housing markets. The FSOC needs to consider the full range of potential exposure to this problem and the related impact on the industry and the real economy.

We also believe the FSOC needs to actively monitor interest rate risk, or the vulnerability of borrowers and financial institutions to sudden volatile spikes in interest rates. Borrowers and depository institutions may be subject to sudden increases in interest costs when interest rates rise—and they will inevitably rise. This issue takes on particular urgency now in light of the current low level of interest rates and rapid growth in U.S. Federal debt. Developing policies that clearly demonstrate the sustainability of the U.S. fis-cal situation will be of utmost importance in maintaining investor confidence and ensuring a smooth transition to higher interest rates in coming years.

Thank you again for the opportunity to testify about these criti-cally important issues. I would, of course, be pleased to answer your questions.

Chairman JOHNSON. Thank you, Chairman Bair.

Because our Republican colleagues need to leave shortly, I ask that the remaining witnesses' testimony be submitted for the record. We will now move directly to questions.

STATEMENT OF JOHN WALSH, ACTING COMPTROLLER OF THE CURRENCY

Chairman Johnson, Ranking Member Shelby, and Members of the Com-mittee, I appreciate the opportunity to provide an update on the OCC's work to implement the Dodd-Frank Act provisions related to monitoring systemic risk and promoting financial stability, and our perspectives on the functions and operations of the Financial Stability Oversight Council, or FSOC.

The Dodd-Frank Act includes several provisions to address systemic issues that played a role in the financial crisis. These include constraining exces-sive risk taking, instituting stronger capital requirements and more robust stress-testing requirements, and bridging regulatory gaps. The OCC is among the financial regulators that have rulewriting authority for many of these provisions, and my testimony describes our progress in these areas.

One of the key provisions of the Dodd-Frank Act created the Financial Sta-bility Oversight Council, which brings together the views, perspectives, and expertise of the financial regulatory agencies and others to identify, mon-itor, and respond to systemic risk.

FSOC has three major objectives: to identify risks to the financial stability of the United States; to promote market discipline, and to respond to emerging threats to the stability of the U.S. financial system.

In some cases, the Council has direct responsibility to make decisions and take actions. This includes designating certain non-bank financial compa-nies to be supervised by the Federal Reserve and subject to heightened pru-dential standards should the Council determine that material financial dis-tress at such companies would pose a threat to the financial stability of the United States. In other areas, the Council's role is more of an advisory body to the primary financial regulators, such as conducting studies and making recommendations to inform future agency rulemakings.

The varied roles and responsibilities that Congress assigned to the Council appropriately balance and reflect the desire to enhance regulatory coordination for systemically important firms and activities, while preserving and respecting the independent authorities and accountability of primary supervisors.

As detailed in my written statement, FSOC has taken action on a number of items, including the publication of two required studies and proposed rulemakings on the designation of systemically important non-bank financial firms and financial market utilities.

The Council and its committees are also making strides in providing a more systematic and structured framework for identifying, monitoring, and deliberating potential systemic risks to the financial stability of the United States. Briefings and discussions on potential risks and the implications of current market developments on financial stability are a key part of the closed deliberations of each Council meeting.

While I believe FSOC enhances the agencies' collective ability to identify and respond to emerging systemic risks, I would offer two cautionary notes.

First, I believe the Council's success ultimately will depend on the willingness and ability of its members and staff to engage in frank and candid discussions about emerging risks, issues, and institutions. These discussions are not always pleasant as they can challenge one's longstanding views or ways of approaching a problem. But being able to voice dissenting views or assessments will be critical in ensuring that we are seeing and considering the full scope of issues.

In addition, these discussions often will involve information or findings that require further verification or that are extremely sensitive to the operation of either an individual firm or an entire market segment. In some cases, the discussions, if misconstrued, could undermine public and investor confidence and create or exacerbate problems in the financial system. As a result, I believe that it is critical that these types of deliberations—both at the Council and staff level—be conducted in a manner that assures their confidential nature.

Second, even with fullest deliberations and best data, there will continue to be unforeseen events that pose substantial risks to the system, markets, or groups of institutions. We should not expect FSOC to prevent such occurrences. FSOC will, however, provide a mechanism to communicate, coordinate, and respond to such events to help contain and limit their impact.

The issues that the Council will confront in carrying out these duties are, by their nature, complex and far-reaching in terms of their potential effects on our financial markets and economy. Developing appropriate and measured responses to these issues will require thoughtful deliberation and debate among the member agencies. The OCC is committed to providing its expertise and perspectives and in helping FSOC achieve its mission.

Thank you, and I'll be happy to respond to your questions.

Chairman JOHNSON. Senator Shelby.

Senator SHELBY. Mr. Chairman, thank you for yielding to us. We are all, as you know, going down to the White House to meet with the President. I yield my time to Senator Toomey.

Senator TOOMEY. Senator Shelby, thank you very much. I appreciate that as well as all of your cooperation in this process and in many other matters. Thank you.

Mr. Chairman, thank you very much for holding this hearing. I think it is a very important topic and I appreciate your doing this, and to all the witnesses, I know how busy you are and I am grateful that you are here once again to answer our questions.

I would like to zero in, if I could, on the process by which the Council will be designating non-bank financial institutions as SIFIs. I think this is a very, very important issue, and I will confess up front, I am hoping that this Council will cast the narrow net rather than a very broad net, and I think it is vitally important that we have a well defined and very objective process by which we make these designations.

The Notice of Proposed Rulemaking that came out in January, I would suggest, lacked the necessary specificity that we need to understand how this process is going to unfold. As I think everybody knows, it essentially restated the statute and did not provide the kind of guidance on how the statute will be applied.

Now, I think several of you, maybe all of you, have acknowledged in your written testimony the intent to provide additional guidance, and I appreciate that. But I feel very strongly that the form that that additional guidance takes really needs to be a new proposed rule, and that new proposed rule needs to have a comment period, and that comment period needs to be at least 60 days because we just have not had a chance for anybody to evaluate how this is going to be applied.

So I would appreciate it if each of you would confirm that it is your intent to issue a new proposed rule and to provide such a comment period.

Mr. WOLIN. Senator, as our written testimonies have indicated, we will be issuing additional guidance. It will be in the form of some public rulemaking and we will be seeking public comment. I think the Council has not yet landed on precisely how the rule will be styled and exactly what the length of the comment period will be. Obviously, we want to make sure that we get sufficient public input, as we think we have already given a few opportunities for public input. I think as we provide further clarification as to how this process will unfold, we will want to make sure we provide adequate opportunity for people to react and provide their views.

Senator TOOMEY. If I could, just very briefly, I appreciate that. I just would like to underscore there has been really no opportunity to respond yet on how the statute will be applied, and so the President's Executive Order called for all agencies to, as a general matter, provide 60 days. I really think that is a minimum that is necessary, but I am sorry. I am interrupting.

Mr. BERNANKE. Senator, I think more details are necessary. I favor providing more information to the public and getting robust input and comment.

I should say that while I think we can provide more information in terms of the metrics and criteria, I do not think that we could provide an exact formula that will apply mechanically without any application of judgment. I think, ultimately, we are going to have to look at a whole variety of issues which cannot always be put into a numerical metric. That being said, I certainly agree with you that we should get all the input we can from the public on this process.

Ms. BAIR. Yes, we support going out for comment again with more detailed metrics, and the 60-day comment period is something we have tried to adhere to in our rulemaking for major rulemakings. So, I think it is important to get public comment and to provide more clarity and hard metrics.

That said, I would agree with Chairman Bernanke. I do not think we can provide complete bright lines. There will need to be some area for judgment. But clearly, we can do a better job than we have done so far in getting more detailed metrics out.

Senator TOOMEY. And is it your view that the form that that should take would be a Notice of Proposed Rulemaking?

Ms. BAIR. That is a good question, Senator. I would be fine with that. I understand there may be a legal issue with the FSOC's ability to write rules with this kind of criteria versus guidance and I would defer to the Treasury Legal Counsel on the format. If we have legal authority to do it as a rule, I think that would be fine, but I would defer to Treasury on that.

Ms. SCHAPIRO. Senator, I agree with, really, everything that has been said, and particularly with Chairman Bernanke about the need to balance reliance on objective factors with the exercise of reasonable judgment. But that said, I think more transparency and more specificity about this process would be very valuable, and I think a robust comment period will inform the process greatly, so I would be very supportive of that.

Mr. GENSLER. Senator, just concurring, again, I think Chairman Bernanke said it well. I think it is a mixture of judgment and metrics. I think it would be good to put the metrics out to public comment. We at the CFTC have generally used 60 days. I think that is a good period of time. Whether it is guidance or an actual rule, I really have not had an informed view on and largely have to hear from Treasury as to the—the guidance, I think, works very well, often, as well, as long as we get the public input.

Mr. WALSH. Well, going sixth, it would be hard to think of something new to say——

[Laughter.]

Mr. WALSH.——but certainly, going out again with greater detail and greater clarity and seeking views and pursuing a process of review and comment, I think is entirely appropriate.

Senator TOOMEY. Let me just strongly urge that we go with a Notice of Proposed Rulemaking as the mechanism by which we do this and we have at least 60 days. I think this is very important.

I would also like to stress, I think we really have to have this as objective as possible. The implications for a firm being designated are huge, as you know very, very well. It is really profound. And so it is perfectly reasonable for firms to be able to expect to be able to anticipate whether or not they will be brought in by virtue of these objective standards. So I would strongly urge you to pursue that.

If I have time for one quick additional question, Mr. Chairman——

Chairman JOHNSON. Yes.

Senator TOOMEY. Thank you very much. I would like to touch on specifically the question of mutual funds, and again, I will say that by their very nature, their inherent characteristics, I think as a general matter, it is very unlikely that mutual funds are systemically significant to the degree that would justify this designation. I understand certain issues surrounding money market funds that occurred during the crisis are very important, but I also know that the SEC has taken significant steps to address some of these in the rules of last year, in a new set of rules or regulations that are being contemplated now that deal with issues like liquidity and reserves.

So my question is, are money market funds currently under consideration for this designation, and if so, why? Mr. Wolin?

Mr. WOLIN. Senator, I think it is premature for me to be able to answer that question. The deputies of the FSOC have been putting together some preparatory material. I think as we just confirmed to you, we are planning on putting out additional guidance for the public to comment, and until we do that and get the responses from the public and until the FSOC principals have an opportunity to have these kinds of conversations, I think it is hard to know what the right answer to that question is. We will move forward, obviously, with the public's input and with the transparency that the FSOC has been providing to date.

Senator TOOMEY. Would anybody else like to comment?

Ms. SCHAPIRO. Senator, I would just add that I think the SIFI determination is really an institution-by-institution designation and not an entire sector. So under any circumstances, I think we would have to look at individual entities. And we held a one-day roundtable this week exploring the systemic risk issues that are implicated with respect to money market funds and how they invest, and I think that will inform us at the SEC as we go forward in making determinations about what further efforts we might make specifically with regard to the regulation of money market funds. Also, all FSOC members were represented at that roundtable and were able to participate in a very robust discussion directly with the mutual fund industry as well as with European regulators. So I think we will be well informed when we get to the process of thinking about institution-by-institution designation in the money market fund or mutual fund area.

Senator TOOMEY. I see my time has long since expired, so I thank you, Mr. Chairman.

Chairman JOHNSON. Thank you, Senator Toomey.

Secretary Wolin, Chairman Bernanke, and Chairman Bair, Titles I and II are important cornerstones of the Dodd-Frank Act, yet the House Republican budget proposal includes the repeal of Title II. In addition, other legislation has been introduced in both Houses to repeal the entire Dodd-Frank Act. What do you think of these repeal efforts? Should we go back to the system of regulation that existed before the financial crisis?

Mr. WOLIN. Mr. Chairman, as I said in my opening comments, I think that there is no alternative but to move forward with the Dodd-Frank statute as enacted. The idea that taxpayers would continue to be on the hook in these moments of stress is one that is unacceptable and I think the statute clearly puts an end to. We think it is critical that in the areas that you discussed in your opening statement, orderly liquidation authority and the resolution plans that need to be put forward to both the Fed and to the FDIC, that these are critical elements of making sure that we end "too big to fail" and that we make certain that taxpayers are no longer on the hook.

Chairman JOHNSON. Chairman Bernanke?

Mr. BERNANKE. Mr. Chairman, it was clear that the regulatory system that was existing during the crisis was insufficient. There has been a long and thoughtful process about how to reform financial regulation. I would reiterate what Mr. Wolin said about the importance of addressing "too big to fail." Chairman Bair also mentioned this. The new legislation addresses this on a number of levels, including enhanced oversights, tougher capital liquidity requirements, and the resolution regime, which is also very important. Just getting rid of "too big to fail" would be a very important step.

More generally, the philosophy of Dodd-Frank, which is to encourage a systemic or macro prudential approach to regulation where broad systemic risks are taken into account as well as individual firm or market risks, I think is a very important step and one that is being adopted globally as well as by the United States.

Chairman JOHNSON. Chairman Bair?

Ms. BAIR. Yes. I think it would be very harmful to repeal it. There is a lot of work going on now that is moving toward ending "too big to fail." The tools are there. The implementation capability is there. I would not want that work to be diverted. I think repealing and trying to revert back to a bankruptcy process, we know bankruptcy does not work, and so that will be an open invitation to more bailouts if there is no alterative to that.

So we are working very hard to implement this authority, to convince the market that it can and will be used. There were some very highly important and constructive improvements sponsored by Senators Dodd and Shelby during consideration of the Dodd-Frank Act that passed overwhelmingly—I think the vote was 93 in favor—that put in additional important safeguards, like the clawback authority. So I do think it is a very good provision and one that we are taking very seriously to implement and I hope will be getting bipartisan support to continue that process.

Chairman JOHNSON. According to Chairman Angelides of the FCIC, who testified before the Committee on Tuesday, as well as others, the fear of the Federal bank regulators to address the significant consumer protection issues contributed to the financial crisis. Secretary Wolin and Chairman Bair, would you please discuss why we need an independent consumer protection agency and how this new agency can identify and mitigate systemic risks.

Mr. WOLIN. Mr. Chairman, I think that it is clear that failures of consumer protection were very much at the core of what caused the financial crisis we have just been through. The Federal Government was not well equipped to make sure that consumer protection issues were handled well. The responsibility for consumer protection was spread out across a wide range of agencies in the Federal Government. It is absolutely critical, in our view, that there is an agency that focuses very intensely on consumer protection issues. We need to ensure that consumers have the information they need to make responsible choices, to make sure that the kinds of judgments—which contributed in the individual and certainly in the aggregate so mightily to our financial stress—are looked after.

The Consumer Financial Protection Bureau implementation team is off to a very strong start. They are making sure that they put together a set of rules, efficient but nonetheless clear, that consumers can use to make sure they understand the implications of their judgments—to make sure that those rules are adhered to across the financial system, not just amongst banks, but also amongst the non-bank parts of the financial system, which have heretofore not been something that the Federal Government has had authority to focus on.

Chairman JOHNSON. Chairman Bair?

Ms. BAIR. Yes, I think the regulatory arbitrage for consumer protections was a very profound problem leading up to the crisis. We had a Community Banking Advisory Committee meeting yesterday. We have a number of community banks on our Advisory Committee that are mortgage originators and in the years leading up to the crisis, as the craziness continued, they lost significant market share to essentially completely unregulated third-party mortgage originators that had not much in the way of consumer protection requirements. So I think these are good lenders and people who want to do the right thing for their customer and they are regaining market share again in this area.

But as we get farther and farther away from the crisis, a lot of this could startup again and I think we really do need an agency to provide good, strong, common sense standards across the board. I think it will be good for consumers and I think it will also be good for more heavily regulated sectors and for the good players in the industry who are trying to do the right thing.

That said, I think it is important for there to be a market approach to consumer regulation, and the focus is, as I think the current leadership has indicated, on having simpler disclosures and better information to consumers so they can make their own decisions. That is really what we need, and I think that will be a very important value added from the consumer agency.

Chairman JOHNSON. Senator Brown.

Senator BROWN. Thank you very much, Mr. Chairman. I appreciate that.

I have questions for the panel concerning the SIFIs, but I am going to say a couple of things first. Before any institution will be subject to stronger examination and rules for capital risk, it must first be designated as a SIFI, and the Council will soon be missing five full-time members, and I am sorry our colleagues are not here to hear this because I do want to speak pretty bluntly about this. The five are the heads of the FDIC, the CFPB, OCC, FHFA, and the insurance representative, and that will undoubtedly make it harder to designate new companies as systemically important. We need strong nominees who will not be afraid to take bold steps to prevent a new financial crisis.

But if qualified nominees for these important positions are blocked, it will increase the likelihood we have another AIG or Lehman Brothers. I would urge everyone on the Committee to remember what happened to the financial system and the economy 3 years ago and that this is serious business and should not be so politicized that they block nominee after nominee after nominee. I think we all—I am sure people on the panel agree with that. I am, again, sorry my colleagues are not here to at least discuss this and think clearly through what actually can happen.

My question for Deputy Secretary Wolin is about the financial crisis. It was in large part precipitated by shadow banking complex activities initiated by Wall Street firms that typically fell outside the scope of regulation. The designation of systemically important financial institutions is supposed to address this problem.

I want to agree with Senator Toomey's comments and his questions to each of you that the Council-proposed rule seems like a reflection, not an elaboration or road map to determine what is systemically important. It is not clear to me, and I guess from the answers to his questions, from you, at what point a large, highly leveraged hedge fund becomes systemically important. It is impossible to know whether heavily regulated Main Street property and casualty insurers would be systemically important.

And my question, Mr. Secretary, is do you believe that mutual companies engaging in personal lines of insurance, do you think they pose a threat to the financial stability of our economy? Should they be categorized as systemically important?

Mr. WOLIN. Senator, thank you for that question. We are amidst a process under which we are going to provide further elaboration. I think it is, again, premature for me to make judgments about who is in and who is out. It is a firm-specific kind of consideration, as Chairman Schapiro mentioned. The statute obviously lays out the factors that are relevant.

The Council will put out additional guidance and clarification about how we think about those various factors. Firms, in the first instance, will make judgments about whether they think they are of sufficient size, sufficient interconnectedness, sufficient leverage, and so forth. I think until that process reaches a further level of maturity, until the members of the Council have an opportunity to have conversations about how to think about those criteria, I am not in a position to rule any particular firm in or out.

Firms can make judgments based on whether they have those kinds of attributes or not based on the additional guidance that we give, and we will be giving firms an opportunity to be heard on these questions. That is in the statute. We have laid out in our own rulemakings what the process will be. Even before there is a proposal for a designation, they will have an opportunity to come to the FSOC and lay out what they think about the application of these factors to their particular circumstance. So there will be a long process in which individual firms have a very substantial opportunity to be heard and their views be considered before any designations are made.

Senator BROWN. Thank you, and thank you, Mr. Chairman. I just wanted to say to Chairman Bair, thank you for your service the last half-decade. You have served your country well and you have been very helpful to so many of us. Thank you.

Chairman JOHNSON. Senator Bennet.

Senator BENNET. Thank you, Mr. Chairman, and thank you very much for holding this hearing. Thank you to all of you for everything you are doing to try to implement this bill so that we do not have the kind of systemic risk we faced on the front end of the crisis, and I think the oversight of this Committee is a very important part of this.

And it is in that spirit I wanted to ask Secretary Wolin and Chairman Bernanke whether, in your analysis of what we are facing in the economy right now, that there is anything that would create more systemic risk to our economy than the U.S. Congress failing to raise the debt ceiling of the United States.

Mr. WOLIN. Well, Senator Bennet, I think it is absolutely unthinkable that we would not raise the debt ceiling in order to make good on obligations that Congresses and Presidents in the past have made. Secretary Geithner has spoken many times publicly about the wide range of catastrophic implications to failing to raise the debt limit as necessary with respect to, first of all, losing this great national asset that we have, which is that the full faith and credit of the United States has been considered sacred. The real implications with respect to funding rates and interest rates, that will affect not just the U.S. Government, ironically, which has its own set of fiscal implications, but also individuals——

Senator BENNET. Let me just stop you there for 1 second. Has its own set of fiscal implications in the sense that it would actually make our fiscal condition worse rather than better?

Mr. WOLIN. It would, Senator, because it would require us to spend more money to finance the deficit that has already built up. If the interest rates go up, our funding rates go up.

Senator BENNET. And you were headed—I interrupted you, but where you were headed was what the implications were for people living in places like Colorado, so——

Mr. WOLIN. Right. So every American, whether they are buying a house or buying a car or just paying off their credit card bills will have to experience higher interest rates, which will have very real effects on their pocketbooks. But I think more broadly, the effects on wealth and so forth, people's balances in their mutual fund accounts and so forth, all will be put in jeopardy in ways that are unthinkable. The implications are enormous. It is something that we think of as enormous risk.

We have said and we believe that, as has been the case in the past, Congress will increase the debt limit. It is absolutely critical that that happen and that we work through the broader set of fiscal issues, which are obviously enormously important and ones that the President has been very clear need to be addressed, but that we not hold the debt limit as hostage to those critically important discussions.

Senator BENNET. Mr. Chairman?

Mr. BERNANKE. Senator, first, let me say that this is in the context of a broader discussion about fiscal sustainability and fiscal discipline, and I fully support all the efforts of the Congress—and I know they are very difficult challenges—to bring the long-term fiscal situation into something closer to balance. So in no way do I disagree with those objectives.

That being said, I think using the debt limit as a bargaining chip is quite risky. We do not know exactly what would happen if the debt limit was not approved. There are certainly significant operational problems, legal problems associated with making sure that the debt is paid. Even if the debt is paid, there is the issue of market confidence and how the market will respond to the risk of default or even the default on non-debt obligations. So I think it is a risky approach, not to raise the debt limit at a reasonable time.

Again, the costs. At minimum, the costs would be an increase in interest rates, which would actually worsen our deficit and would hurt all borrowers in the economy, including mortgage borrowers and the like. The worst outcome would be one in which the financial system was again destabilized, as we saw following Lehman, which, of course, would have extremely dire consequences for the U.S. economy.

Senator BENNET. Well, I share, obviously, your concern about the fiscal conditions, as well, and I believe that we are going to be able to have a constructive conversation about it.

One thing I would like to say, or ask you, Secretary Wolin, maybe in particular, is the longer this goes on the debt ceiling, is there not risk that the markets will react even before the August date that Secretary Geithner has given us to get this done? Or is there risk?

Mr. WOLIN. Senator, we have not seen it to date, but there is that risk if we get too close and the markets do not see a credible way through this, yes.

Senator BENNET. Thank you, Mr. Chairman.

Chairman JOHNSON. Senator Reed.

Senator REED. Thank you very, very much, Mr. Chairman. Thank you, ladies and gentlemen.

Chairman Bair, let me join my colleagues and thank you for your extraordinary service and wish you well. Your testimony reflects on one of the most pressing economic problems we have throughout the country, and that is the housing crisis. We have taken extraordinary measures to assist the financial sector. We have taken very few effective measures to assist homeowners. Twenty-eight percent of homeowners in the United States are underwater today. That is probably the biggest, in my view, drag on the economic expansion and recovery we face, yet the most recent attempt by the regulators to provide some clarity in my view is woefully inadequate. I wonder if you might comment on that and what we have to do to be as fair to homeowners as we have been to the financial industry.

Ms. BAIR. Well, I do think the regulatory orders are just one step, and the examinations were focused on process issues. They did not really get into broader issues of whether loan modifications were appropriately evaluated and approved or denied.

We have done some broader analysis of banks that service loans under loss share agreements and have found not insignificant error rates in making a net present value determination about whether the borrower should qualify for a mortgage modification.

So, we think in the next phase of this—the third-party lookback that the orders require—it is very important that they view 100 percent of consumer complaints and certainly 100 percent of modification denials, because we are seeing that there are, again, a not insignificant number of errors in these calculations based on the sampling we have done with our loss share acquirers.

I think more broadly we need to be thinking about simplifying the servicing process, the modification process, as well as the relocation process for borrowers who are not going to make it, and there are some out there.

We have also been exploring ways to provide relocation assistance as an incentive when there is not the possibility of a loan modification for the borrower because they simply do not have the income to make an economically viable restructuring. We think that will save us money because the foreclosure process is so backed up now, and this is one of the reasons the housing market is not clearing, and it cannot recover until it clears. The short sales or relocation assistance can shorten the time that it takes to get the property back on the market, and that also can mitigate losses, which we see is in our financial interest to do.

So, yes, I think there needs to be much more aggressive action in terms of looking back for the borrowers that have already been harmed. Looking forward, we need more streamlined processes. We need single points of contact to make sure there is one person, which would be an important quality control on servicing to make sure that the borrower is appropriately dealt with and loss mitigation and loan restructuring efforts occur where they should. So I think that is positive. But there is just a lot more work to be done, and the market is not going to clear until we get this fixed.

Senator REED. You know, what you have said—and I agree with it—has been said repeatedly for the last 2 years, and yet all of you collectively as the Federal regulators had the chance to make these things happen. And essentially what I think you chose to do was to just kick the can down the road a bit further, let the banks appoint an independent evaluator to go in and look again.

Can I ask you, what is the definition of "independent"? Would this be someone who has never done any business with the bank before? Is this a division of a company that has big contracts with all these banks and would be independent in the sense that the rating agencies were independent?

Ms. BAIR. Well, we are not the primary regulator of any of the major servicers, so the representatives of the primary regulators might want to respond to that.

We do have one bank that originates loans for a servicer who has problems, and we put an order on that bank—to tell the bank that the servicer for them needed to take some significant remedial steps. Our view is that the third party does need to be independent, and there also needs to be some validation process done independently by the regulators.

Senator REED. But from your participation, there is no definition of "independence"?

Ms. BAIR. Again, I would defer to Mr. Walsh and Mr. Bernanke, if they want to share thoughts on that, because they are the primary regulators of these servicers. But I agree with you. I think there are a lot of professional banking consultants out there that may be independent in the sense that they do not work for the bank, but they may have other business with them or future business they would like to do with them. So I think this is a huge issue, and there needs to be some validation process——

Senator REED. Let me ask another question, and that is, you indicated that the loan modification process was explicitly excluded from this review. Is that correct?

Ms. BAIR. This review was focused on mortgage document processing.

Senator REED. Again, 2 years of struggling through this, multiple times we have attempted to fix it. The problem is foreclosure and modification together, not one or the other. And this to me is just a way of defining away the problem. And, frankly, it is very disappointing.

My time has expired. If there is an opportunity again, I will raise this with the primary regulators. But, frankly, one of the reasons I raised it with you is that I think you have been very forthright, and the FDIC going back to 2007 has been effective, where the other agencies have been more apologetic than effective.

Thank you.

Chairman JOHNSON. Senator Schumer.

Senator SCHUMER. Well, thank you, Mr. Chairman.

First, Chairman Bernanke, I have a couple of statements that were recently made by the Speaker of the House, John Boehner, and I would like to ask you about them. The first is he said, "We are calling for an end to the Government spending binge that is crowding out private investment and threatening the availability of capital needed for job creation."

Now, several economists have refuted the notion that given particularly now with our current slack in the economy and corporate America having lots of money and still being reluctant to invest it for other reasons, so they have disputed the notion that we are crowding out private investment with Government spending.

Do you agree with Speaker Boehner's statement that Government spending is at this time crowding out private investment?

Mr. BERNANKE. Well, in the near term, I do not think that there is a lot of crowding out. As you point out, interest rates are quite low. There is a lot of excess resources available for firms that need to hire additional workers.

That being said, if we do not address the fiscal trajectory we are on, we are going to be facing increasingly severe crowding out problems and perhaps financial stability problems in the future.

Senator SCHUMER. But it is not occurring now?

Mr. BERNANKE. Not to a substantial extent. I do think that if we had a long-term plan to reduce our long-term fiscal deficit, it might help to lower interest rates and increase confidence today. But under conventional definitions of crowding out in terms of credit markets and labor markets, we are not seeing too much of that.

Senator SCHUMER. Thank you.

The second statement is the inverse of that. Speaker Boehner said, "The recent stimulus spending binge hurt our economy and hampered private sector job creation in America."

CBO's own analysis seemed to contradict that statement. Do you agree with Speaker Boehner's statement that the stimulus spending hurt our economy and hampered private sector job creation in America?

Mr. BERNANKE. Well, again, I would distinguish, Senator, between the short run and the long run.

Senator SCHUMER. Now we are just talking about the stimulus.

Mr. BERNANKE. We have a very significant long-run problem, and to the extent that we are pushing our debt situation further and further into the red, we are taking greater risks.

That being said, I have cited the CBO analysis in the past as being a reasonable analysis of——

Senator SCHUMER. Do you disagree with Speaker Boehner's view that the stimulus, the stimulus we passed last year, hurt our economy and particularly hampered private sector job creation?

Mr. BERNANKE. My best guess is that the stimulus increased employment.

Senator SCHUMER. Thank you. I am glad you disagree.

Next question. This is also for you. This one is not the same type of question.

[Laughter.]

Senator SCHUMER. The Fed, along with other prudent regulators and the CFTC, issued proposed rules relating to when counterparties in derivative transactions are required to post margin, that is, put up cash as security for their obligations. As you know, I had spoken to you about this shortly after the rules were announced, and several members of the New York delegation sent you a letter on this.

I am concerned with the part of the proposal—we all are in the New York delegation—that would apply only to U.S. firms and would result in them facing competitive disadvantages *vis-a-vis* international competitors.

Here is the basic issue as reported last week in the Financial Times: If a German car manufacturer were to do an interest rate swap with a U.S. bank's London arm, it would have to cough up margin; but if the German car maker did a swap with a British bank, it would not have to. That is the Financial Times' summation of this.

So do you agree that this might cause U.S. firms to be at a competitive disadvantage?

Mr. BERNANKE. Yes, I do agree. In transactions with U.S. customers, both foreign and domestic banks have the same rules. In transactions with foreign customers, we have put out margin and capital rules, which have a good purpose, which is increase the safety of our financial system.

Currently, under the Basel agreement, similar capital rules will probably be in effect for foreign banks, but at this point they have not yet done the margin——

Senator SCHUMER. So that leads to my last question with the Chairman's indulgence, since I have 16 seconds left. What is Treasury doing, Secretary Wolin, to ensure that European regulators adopt the same or very similar rules? And would we go forward and enact our rules before they did if it put our U.S. firms at a disadvantage? Because, obviously, I would like to see American institutions do as much foreign business as possible. It creates jobs in New York.

Mr. WOLIN. Senator Schumer, we are working very hard with the Europeans in Brussels and also in individual European capitals to make sure that we have absolutely as much as possible a level playing field. I think we are making good progress on that, but we will have to stay vigilant.

On the question of whether we would put forward rules, I would obviously defer to the Chairman and to the market regulators as to how they would move forward. But I think it is, of course, important, as we have said repeatedly, to have essentially level playing fields so as not to disadvantage U.S. businesses where that is avoidable.

Senator SCHUMER. I assume you are urging the regulators to do just that right here.

Thank you, Mr. Chairman.

Chairman JOHNSON. Senator Merkley.

Senator MERKLEY. Thank you very much, Mr. Chair, and thank you all for your testimony.

I was just downstairs in the gathering of the HELP Committee in a hearing that was wrestling with the impact on the middle class over the last 30 years and essentially the hollowing out of the middle class in America. And I think there is a chart that captures much of the concern. It is a chart that shows how middle-class wages rose with the productivity of the country over the 30 years following World War II, but starting in roughly 1975, 1974, for the next 30 years enormous divergence in which middle-class working wages, inflation adjusted, stayed flat. But we had a tremendous increase in the wealth of the country and the productivity of the country, but working families did not share in that. And it really raises the question of what kind of a country do we want. Do we want a country where families participate in the wealth of this Nation, where they are able to send their children to college, plan for their retirement, own a home, be part of an ownership society, or one in which essentially fewer and fewer families are in a position to access those fundamental instruments related to quality of life? And it is discouraging to see that path over this last 30 years.

In some ways many of the issues that we dealt with in Dodd-Frank Act are related. We have seen basically a doubling of the national debt under the Bush administration and then a tripling of the national debt as a result of the house of cards that was built in the mortgage deregulation by the Bush administration. And now we are seeing the recommendations from the House that say, OK, well, let us dismantle what is left of the programs to provide support for families as a consequence of the debt, even though the debt was created by strategies that were not designed to support the middle class to begin with. The entire picture troubles me.

There is a link between this and the Financial Stability Oversight Council and a couple issues that trouble people in our working communities. One is the ongoing foreclosure crisis, and certainly that is related to financial stability. Another is the speculation driving up the cost of petroleum. And I do not know if you have all addressed either of these, but if you have, feel free to be short. But these are kind of nitty-gritty, on-the-ground economic issues that may not have to do with whether the financial system as a whole collapses, but it is certainly related to the performance of the financial system as it affects families.

So with the anticipated additional wave of foreclosures, almost 5 million on the horizon, the impact of that on the construction industry, which affects almost every aspect of my State economy, and the rising cost of oil, have these been topics that have been wrestled with the Financial Stability Oversight Council? Should they be? And I will just open it up to whoever would care to comment?

Mr. BERNANKE. Senator, first, you talk about a number of broad macro issues, and I cannot do justice to them, but I would just note that the Federal Reserve in its monetary policy is trying to address unemployment, which, of course, is a major source of foreclosures, as well as mortgage interest rates and other factors affecting the foreclosure crisis. So we are addressing it in that respect.

Attempting to address the foreclosure crisis directly, you know, there has been a lot of effort and so far only modest success. It has proven very difficult to find solutions in many cases. In other cases, the process has not, you know, been adequate in the case of banks, and we have already discussed here a bit the recent review of servicing practices. The Federal Reserve and the OCC, with the support of the FDIC, have reviewed those practices. We have issued cease-and-desist orders to try to stop bad practices and to try to require banks to go back and discover who was harmed and to help offset those problems where possible. Going forward, we expect to assess civil money penalties as well.

But you are right that this remains a very, very difficult problem, and at some level it is a problem of regulation and a problem of bank operation. But at some level it is also a macroeconomic problem, and that needs to be addressed in terms of global and national employment and economic conditions.

Senator MERKLEY. Anyone else care to comment on this?

Mr. GENSLER. Well, I just thought I would say the Financial Stability Oversight Council has not talked about some of these matters, about the rising commodity prices, as a council. It may have at staff levels. I think the Dodd-Frank Act has a number of features that helps market regulators like the CFTC have broader oversight that the markets work better for the American public. We are not a price setter, and that is not what Congress or the American public is asking the market regulator to be. But the Dodd-Frank Act gave us broader authority to see the whole market, the whole derivatives market, swaps, stronger anti-manipulation authority in our case, more similar to the SEC's, to actually bring in some of the foreign boards of trade, some foreign exchanges, and also to move forward with what I think Congress said with regard to limiting some of the size of the speculators' positions in these marketplaces.

So we have put proposals out on all of these matters consistent with congressional intent, and we look forward to public comment and trying to finalize the rules.

Senator MERKLEY. Thank you.

Chairman JOHNSON. Senator Tester.

Senator TESTER. Yes, thank you, Chairman Johnson.

I appreciate all of you being here today. I want to talk about debit interchange, of course. Chairman Bernanke, we were here in February. We talked about the serious risk that the Durbin amendment would have on small community banks and credit unions because of the lack of ability to enforce the $10 billion and under exemption. You have gotten more information since then. Do you still feel, with the information you have got on hand, that an exemption can work?

Mr. BERNANKE. Well, to be honest with you, we were agnostic. We still are not sure whether it will work. A number of the networks have expressed their interest or willingness to maintain a tiered interchange fee system, but that is not required. There is no law which says they have to do that.

A suggestion that we got was that we should ask or even require the networks to make public what the interchange fees were that they were charging, and that would be of at least some value in terms of the transparency. But, again, there are market forces that would work against the exemption.

Senator TESTER. OK. You have been in the business for a long time, and you are a very intelligent guy. And I know we are in a political process here, and I know you probably have been getting a lot of pressure from people, or at least one person from the Senate. I am talking about rural America here. I am talking about community banks and credit unions that if they go away, it is another nail in our coffin. It is really important. I think it is really important. Is it going to work?

Mr. BERNANKE. I cannot say with certainty, but I think there is good reason to be concerned about it.

Senator TESTER. Very good reason to be concerned about it. And if it does not work, what are the impacts on rural America?

Mr. BERNANKE. Well, it is going to affect the revenues of the small issuers, and it could result in some smaller banks being less profitable or even failing.

Senator TESTER. OK. Thank you. Wouldn't it seem the prudent thing to do to step back and get more information? Wouldn't you agree the amendment was put in rather quickly?

Mr. BERNANKE. It was put in quickly, but I think I have to defer to Congress on what kind of information you want to get. We have done one review, and we have gotten 11,000 comments.

Senator TESTER. Can you make good decisions with bad information?

Mr. BERNANKE. I——

Senator TESTER. Can you?

Mr. BERNANKE. You cannot, of course, but——

Senator TESTER. Can you make good decisions with little or no information?

Mr. BERNANKE. That is not a problem. We have plenty of information. We have received 11,000 comments, and we have done an enormous amount of surveying of the industry and so on.

Senator TESTER. And you have been able to wade through those comments?

Mr. BERNANKE. That is why we wrote to this Committee that we were going to be late with our rule, but we are making considerable progress, yes.

Senator TESTER. OK. Chairwoman Bair, before I get done, I want to thank you for your service. I very, very much appreciate all the work you have done. As Senator Brown said, you have been very good at what you have done.

The same issue. From your vantage point, do you think it is possible to exempt community banks from the debit interchange?

Ms. BAIR. I think it is questionable. We had suggested that the Fed perhaps could try to use the authority under Reg. E to require that the networks accept two-tier pricing, and our lawyers probably have different perspectives on that, and I think that is obviously the Fed's call because it is the Fed's rule. So if their view is that there is no legal authority to require that, I think it does become even more problematic. And so I do think this is going to reduce revenues at a number of smaller banks, and they will probably have to pass that on to customers in terms of higher fees, primarily for transaction accounts.

So I think that is going to happen, and, again, is that the right result, the result Congress wanted? You need to determine that. But I think that is what will happen.

Senator TESTER. Well, any impact on their safety and soundness? Community banks I am talking about.

Ms. BAIR. In our initial analysis, it does not look like it would, but it would clearly stress some institutions. Putting them to the point of failure, no, we do not think that will happen, but clearly it would stress some, and if there are other challenges that are confronting the community banking sector, it is probably something they do not need to be dealing with right now.

Senator TESTER. OK. So you talked about you did not know if this is what the impact that Congress would have. I trust that this would potentially mean or probably mean or most certainly mean higher fees in other areas for consumers?

Ms. BAIR. Yes, it would have to be passed on in other fees.

Senator TESTER. OK. Mr. Walsh, do you have anything you would like to add to this issue?

Mr. WALSH. Only that we provided a comment letter that did not address particularly this distinction. It dealt more with the flexibility the Fed has to set the overall interchange level. But we have been doing a fair amount of outreach to community bankers, and certainly it has been a key concern for them.

Senator TESTER. The impact on community banks, do you see it very similar to the way—how do you see it? I do not want to put words in your mouth.

Mr. WALSH. Well, I would just say that to the extent that it works out as is suggested where it cuts into revenue for community banks, it is one more stress on them.

Senator TESTER. Right. Do you think an exemption can be implemented?

Mr. WALSH. I have not really studied the issue of whether that can work.

Senator TESTER. OK.

Mr. WALSH. I would defer on that one.

Senator TESTER. All right. Thank you. Thank you all very much.

Chairman JOHNSON. Senator Warner.

Senator WARNER. Well, thank you, Mr. Chairman, and let me say it is great to see you all again. Let me start by adding my comments to so many of my other colleagues in thanking Chairman Bair for her, I think, extraordinary service and lots of help I know personally to me and Senator Corker as we tried to navigate through some of these issues.

I hope, Mr. Chairman, we are going to get—since we are down to the few at this point, maybe we can get a second round of questions because I have got lots of things I would love to raise.

First of all, for Deputy Secretary Wolin, I continue to think the jury is out on whether at least this member's hope and aspiration of what the FSOC would be will be accomplished. I think it is a critically important early warning signal. One of the things that I think will make the FSOC a more informed entity will be the active creation of the OFR, and I was wondering as my first question, Do you have any sense of when we might actually get a nominee for the OFR?

Mr. WOLIN. Senator Warner, we certainly hope soon. I expect, you know, the President will make a nomination for that important job soon. I want to assure you that in the meantime we are working with an awful lot of intensity and focus to stand up the OFR, to make it the important addition to the landscape that it is beginning to be and that it will be.

We have made, I think, very good progress in hiring senior people. We have just now in the last few weeks brought on Dick Berner, a very accomplished individual with lots of experience in the markets and in risk, with impeccable credentials, to lead the stand-up effort. We have hired a chief business officer, someone to run the data center; a chief operating officer and a range of other folks. They are, I think, together beginning the work with the other members of the FSOC in evaluating risk and trying to work through the kinds of debt issues that will be critical for the OFR to work through in order to——

Senator WARNER. I have got a lot of questions, but I would like to—again, I appreciate that, but it has been 11 months. We need a nominee.

I want to also re-echo what a number—Senator Toomey and Senator Brown mentioned as well in terms of the SIFI designation. You know, we have got to give some more clarity here, the sooner the better, and, you know, one of the notions, at least I personally believe, is that if we give guidance to a firm in kind of a quasi-safe harbor, if they can take actions to ensure they are not SIFI designated, I think that inures to the benefit of the system. That means that, in fact, they will be managing—limiting their risk exposure so they do not get this designation. Again, I think that net-net helps us move along in this process, and I concur with Chairman Bernanke's comments. This cannot be done with a strict kind of simple metric of dollars a sense. There has got to be a subjective judgment. But the sooner we can move this forward the better, and the notion of some sense of a safe harbor, whether it is mutual insurance funds, some of the money market funds, I think is helpful.

I would put one other caveat here, that from some of our financial institutions that repeatedly would come and appeal to me—and perhaps Chairman Johnson remembers this as well—during the formation of Dodd-Frank, when they said, "Please, please, do not give us firm guidelines in the legislation. Leave it to the regulators." And now they are coming back and saying, "Oh, my gosh, the regulators have got so much to do." Hopefully those in the audience who were visiting my office when they were saying please do not, Congress, legislate specifics, that you will recall that this is some of what you asked for.

I would also urge that—again, some of our colleagues were not here, and I know one of my other colleagues asked, the point of some of this kind of chipping-away effort, my sense is that there is enormous—while not complete agreement with what we have done, but across the EU, across the UK, around the world, they are glad we went first. And any effort to try to retract that would be, I think, potentially devastating to international implementation. And I wanted to—I know my time is gone, but, Chairman Bernanke, one of the things that you think about with the G–20— and my fear is that as the crisis gets further away, this financial harmonization issue kind of falls down the level a little bit. How do we make sure that on Basel III we really do get there? How do we make sure that as the UK and the EU look at kind of "bail-in" options rather than some of the resolution activities we have gotten—maybe Chairman Bair could address this as well—that we keep this international implementation and international—perhaps slightly different rules, but at least a unified approach on track?

Mr. BERNANKE. Well, that is a major priority of the whole process, and I think on the whole it has gone pretty well. People have joined in in good faith to try to create a level playing field.

So while there are some international differences, at this point I do not see very many. Senator Schumer talked about some aspects of margin requirements and things of that sort. But for banking in general, I do not see many irresolvable differences at this point.

Moreover, a very important part of this is ensuring that the rules are both implemented in a consistent way across countries and enforced in a consistent way across countries. And part of what the Basel Committee and the Financial Stability Board are doing is trying to set up frameworks for looking at those things as well as at the paper rules.

Senator WARNER. Do you or—and my time has expired, but I will stay around for a second round. Do you or Chairman Bair want to comment about potential challenges on resolution, for example, with the UK's bail-in?

Ms. BAIR. Well, I think there has been a lot of work. I think that the international consensus is you do need special resolution regimes for large financial entities. No one is trying to use a bankruptcy process. It is just not suited for it. It should be used as much as it can, but in some instances it is just not suited for it. And I think the G–20 over a year ago approved core principles for resolution regimes. We each co-chaired the Cross-Border Resolution Group at the Basel Committee and played a leading role in devising those. So, there is clearly progress moving forward, and I think bail-in is another tool in the toolkit. I think we have agreement with the UK on that. We think bail-in as one tool in the toolkit is a good thing. They are not suggesting it can replace resolution regimes, because it cannot. You will always need that backstop, I feel.

Also, bail-in as a post-resolution tool, in other words, converting some of the unsecured debt into an equity investment in the new institution, I think there is a lot of progress. Again, it is one of the structures we might pursue in our resolution planning.

So I think there is a tremendous amount of progress. We have entered bilateral agreements already with the UK, China, and have a number in development with other European countries. Also—the EU is moving forward with development of special resolution regimes. So I think there is tremendous progress, both domestically and internationally, and I hope we can continue that forward progress. As I said before, there is good bipartisan political support for it.

Chairman JOHNSON. At the suggestion of Senator Reed, we will proceed with a brief second round.

For all the panelists, currently there are several vacancies at the financial services regulatory agencies. This summer, there will be several more vacancies. I am increasingly concerned about comments by some of my colleagues that any and every nominee will be blocked. Not having strong individuals in place at the agencies as we continue to implement Dodd-Frank seems to me to be detrimental to our fragile economic recovery and financial stability.

What do you believe is the impact of these vacancies?

Mr. WOLIN. Mr. Chairman, these are important roles, and it is important to fill them. The President I think will be making nominations on these open positions soon, those that he has not already made nominations for. I think that it is, of course, important to have leaders in these seats.

Having said that, the work of these various agencies goes on, and the FSOC has been off to a very strong start and has been very effective in its early days and will continue to be so. But that is not to suggest that it is not important to get folks in these various jobs.

Chairman JOHNSON. Chairman Bernanke.

Mr. BERNANKE. Mr. Chairman, while I do think the agencies are continuing to do their work, the leadership does set direction and tone, and I think it is important to have highly qualified people at the heads of these agencies.

That being said, of course, the Senate has to do its duty of advise and consent and ensuring that these are qualified people. But I hope there will not be unnecessary delays and politically motivated blockages that prevent those qualified people from undertaking their duties.

Chairman JOHNSON. Chairman Bair.

Ms. BAIR. Yes, I think this is very important. At my own agency, after I depart on July 8th, our OTS board member will be gone July 21st, which is obviously the transfer date for the OTS. We could rapidly go from five to three directors quickly and actually down to two because one of our internal directors right now is on holdover status and has other opportunities.

So I think that this is very important, and I think having a Presidentially appointed, Senate-confirmed nominee is very important. It is important for the Senate to have their say and their role in the process. It is important for the President to have his prerogatives as the one who is constitutionally charged with nominations and appointments.

So I do think, too, if members want independent thought at an agency, it is important for that Presidential appointment and Senate confirmation process. I look back on my last 5 years and all the tough decisions I had to make, and if I had been in an acting capacity, it would have been inhibiting to me in making some of the tough decisions I had to do. So I hope the process can move forward.

Chairman JOHNSON. Chairman Schapiro.

Ms. SCHAPIRO. I think, Mr. Chairman, for five-member commissions such as the Securities and Exchange Commission, it is really critical that we have, and always maintain, our full complement of Commissioners. I think it is particularly true right now given the huge volume of work that the agency is facing, both with respect to our law enforcement activity but most particularly with respect to the rule-writing responsibilities that we have taken on under Dodd-Frank.

We have no vacancies at the moment, although we do have one Commissioner whose term expired a year ago and has been holding over in that position.

Chairman JOHNSON. Chairman Gensler.

Mr. GENSLER. Like the Securities and Exchange Commission, we are a five-person commission and we are fortunate to have five very able and thoroughly engaged Commissioners, but we do have a term that comes up. Commissioner Dunn, after serving two terms, will be up in June, and yesterday, the President did forward, or at least announced that he is forwarding a nomination to the Senate. So I was glad to see that and I would look forward to maintaining a full Commission—I think it is very helpful to always have five Commissioners who are actively and thoughtfully engaged.

Chairman JOHNSON. Comptroller Walsh?

Mr. WALSH. Well, as the one acting agency head here at the table, I guess I would add the thought that Secretary Geithner invited me to do this job and certainly encouraged me to do the job as if it was my job, but the fact is that I have said to him and said repeatedly that I do think it is very important for independent supervisory agencies to have nominated and confirmed heads in place. It is important for that independence and for the perception of independence, and I think it is obviously the right way to proceed since that is the structure that exists. So I would join others in support of that thought.

Chairman JOHNSON. Senator Merkley, do you have any follow-up questions?

Senator MERKLEY. You bet. First, I want to join my colleagues in thank you, Chairman Bair, for your hard work during an incredibly difficult time in America's financial picture, so I wish you well in the next chapter of your life and will continue to, I am sure, many of us, look to your insights and advice.

One of the things I wanted to pursue, and Deputy Secretary Wolin, I think it is probably appropriate to ask you about this, and that is if we turn the clock back a year and a half, there was and there continues to be a real challenge in terms of lending capacity at a lot of our community banks and often our healthy community banks. In wrestling with this and talking to many, many experts and stakeholders, we have produced a plan called Small Business Lending Fund which was to essentially counter the irrational fear that had followed the irrational exuberance as that fear related to capitalizing community banks. And that capitalization, as leveraged, could provide up to $300 billion in community bank lending. That was something that was amended into the small business jobs bill in a bipartisan fashion.

And I have banks coming to me now who are applying and saying there is no sign that Treasury is ever going to respond to our applications. It just seems like the process is absolutely frozen. What is wrong and how is Treasury going to fix it? This is an important issue to putting our economy back on track.

Mr. WOLIN. Thank you, Senator, for that question. The Small Business Lending Fund is a critical element of getting credit flowing again to small businesses. We support it very strongly and are spending a lot of energy implementing it. We have now received lots of applications. I think you can expect that we will start making announcements very quickly in response to those applications.

Senator MERKLEY. That is great news, and I thank you, and I will not have the same stream of folks coming and asking me what is going wrong.

The second question I wanted to ask, and let me turn to Chair Schapiro, is related to follow-up to the flash crash from a year ago. The SEC, I believe, has had the ability to address greater audit trail for about 20 years and the flash crash kind of put an exclamation point on the need to both develop a real-time audit trail and to develop other issues related to preferential treatment for high volume, high speed trading. Maybe you can update us on where the SEC process is and your personal perspectives on how important this is in terms of the confidence of small investors and others.

Ms. SCHAPIRO. I would be happy to, and let me start with the last part first. I think it is absolutely essential to the confidence of small investors that we have a market structure that is resilient and capable and perceived by all market participants to be fair and that is fair.

Coming off of May 6, we very quickly made a number of changes to the market structure to deal specifically with the extraordinary volatility we saw on that day. We instituted single stock circuit breakers so that if the price of a stock moves more than 10 percent in a five-minute period, trading is halted. It gives time for people to catch their breath, contraside interest in trading the security to come back into the marketplace.

We also eliminated the rules that would permit stub quotes, those executions at one cent and $100,000 that we saw on that day. The exchanges clarified the rules of the road for when they would break trades that were clearly erroneous or were not valid trades in the marketplace, because about 20,000 trades were broken on that day in May last year.

And finally, we banned naked access to the market so that customers and broker-dealers' orders must go through a risk management system and cannot directly enter the marketplace. So important things have been done.

Our next step with respect to May 6 is to move to a limit up, limit down proposal, proffered by the exchanges, that would actually limit the ability to even put into the marketplace an order that was out of a reasonably tight range around the current trading, and I think that will be an important improvement, as well.

But we have broader issues that we are very focused on. Many of them were raised in our concept release of about 14 months ago, 15 months ago, and they focused a lot on high-frequency trading and the strategies that are used by algorithmic traders. We are moving forward with that in pieces and hopefully will begin to take some action in that area.

Two of the most important pieces are the consolidated audit trail and the large trader reporting system that were specifically proposed by the agency a year ago, or almost a year ago, and it is my hope that those will come back to the Commission for final approval in the next couple of months. They are absolutely essential to our ability to reconstruct trading after an eventful day like May 6, but also for us to be able to determine whether people are manipulating the markets or taking advantage of other market participants in any way. And so the consolidated audit trail, which brings together the data from the many trading venues that exist in the U.S. markets, is really a critical regulatory tool. It simply has not been done and we are going to move ahead and try to get it done in the next couple of months.

Senator MERKLEY. I appreciate that it remains something that you are hard at work on, and thank you.

Ms. SCHAPIRO. I am absolutely committed to it.

Chairman JOHNSON. Senator Warner?

Senator WARNER. Thank you, Mr. Chairman.

I want to pick up where Senator Merkley left off just as kind of a quick comment. I appreciate the actions that the SEC has taken. I still have some concerns that can you keep up with the technological challenges, collocation, the sniffing techniques, some of the other technology aspects. And one of the things, Mr. Chairman, I find a little curious is that there are—some of our colleagues on the other side have attacked the new Consumer Bureau because of its ability to have a funding source, and I think we all, as we were trying to get this bill in place, wanted to make sure that the prudential supervisors were in at least parity if not a preeminent role *vis-a-vis* the new consumer entity, and it is curious that one of the ways you do that, particularly with the SEC, would have been to make sure they had adequate funding so they could upgrade their technology, so when they deal with flash crash technology challenges, when we are thinking about perhaps loading on a new challenge to the SEC in terms of reporting back as major publicly traded companies are subjects of cyber attacks, we keep layering on additional challenges, and if we are going to maintain that parity and keep the prudential supervisor, I think, appropriately in the preeminent role, they have got to have the resources to do it.

And that brings me now to one of the areas that I want to ask both Chairman Schapiro and Chairman Gensler on. We are seeing as, I guess, normally through this process on some of the swap execution challenges the difference between the SEC's approach to and the notion that Chairman Gensler has of trying to, let us get five quotes. I have got—I am not sure where this should all play out, but I am anxious to see how we, between the two entities, have that reconciliation and whether at some point, you know, is this where we will—ultimately it will be bumped up to an FSOC—recognize you have got different markets, but at some point having some type of clarity and will this ultimately end up at the FSOC, on swap execution facilities.

Ms. SCHAPIRO. Let me begin and then I will turn it over to Gary. I think it should not be a surprise that we have some different approaches with respect to specific rules. Some of those are a result of our having different statutory foundations and different traditions of how we regulate, but also because there are differences in some of the products based on their liquidity characteristics and how they trade, and that really argues for, in some instances, a different regulatory approach.

But I will say we are working together extremely closely. We are still at the proposing stage for all of these rules. We have sought cross comment. So if the CFTC took a different approach, for example, SEFs, as they did, then we sought cross comment. We asked questions about whether that was a better approach or whether the SEC approach was better or was there an entirely different way to go. We continue to review each other's comment letters on our proposals, so we have a good understanding, and we continue to meet with industry and other interested parties to talk about what is the optimum approach for fulfilling the statutory mandate to bring these products under a regulatory regime, but to do it in a way that is cost efficient and effective and does not have institutions in particular subjected to different sets of regulations where that would be silly and unnecessarily costly.

So we are very focused on all of these issues and our staffs continue to do really fabulous work together to try to narrow those differences, and I expect as we get to the stage where we begin to adopt rules, you will see differences continue to narrow.

Mr. GENSLER. If I could just come back to the one core piece, transparency is a key part of how markets work best. I truly believe that open and competitive and transparent markets are what helps the American public and lowers the systemic risk of a future crisis.

In terms of our working relationship, it has been remarkably close in a dozen or 15 joint roundtables and sharing all the comment letters, as Chairman Schapiro said, and asking cross comments.

More particularly, on the swap execution facility rule, one of the challenges that we have is that the futures regime, the regime for trading futures, was mandated in the 1930s that all of it is on a central exchange. One hundred percent of it has to be transparent and out there for the public to see. That is a good thing, I think, for the American public. The securities laws are a bit different. So there are gaps when we start between securities and futures.

So as we come up with rules for swaps, like interest rate swaps, we have to be mindful that they are not so far off from the futures market that we start to undermine even our futures markets that worked very well in this country, even through the crisis. So we are focused not just on the gap between security-based swaps and swaps, but we are also focused on are we creating something that undermines the futures markets when we do this rule writing for something called swap execution facilities. So it is trying to marry that up.

Senator WARNER. I just want to make sure that we do not have an indirect result of, for those non-exchange-traded swaps, that if we have too high a threshold in terms of additional quotes, that we push it into some——

Mr. GENSLER. Well, actually, Senator Warner, this only relates to something that is cleared. It has to be cleared. It has to be made available for trading. And third, it cannot be a block. The way that both of us looked at this rule, it was this is for the smaller trade.

This is for the $5 or $10 million interest rate swap, not $250 million or $500 million interest rate swap——

Senator WARNER. Right.

Mr. GENSLER.——and it is not for the bilateral swaps. It is not for those swaps done with corporate America as opposed to—or the non-financial corporate America. This is just financial entity to financial entity, a transaction that is cleared, made available for trading, and is not a block. So it is that.

Senator WARNER. Two last questions, very briefly, and I appreciate the Chairman's granting me this. One is, and I am not—we clearly need to move as many of these transactions as possible onto clearinghouses. I just raise a question, not a critique, but we want to have an open access, to not just create such a limited number of clearinghouses. I do have some questions whether your $50 million capital base—I sure want to make sure that $50 million capital base requirement for any clearinghouse is true capital and we get that right. I think trying to have robust competition among clearinghouses is good, but we have got to make sure that they really have the ability to give that counterparty assurance.

Mr. GENSLER. This is important to ensure robust competition amongst dealers. What has happened in this world right now, it is a very closed, concentrated group of dealers.

Senator WARNER. Right.

Mr. GENSLER. In the futures world and in the securities world, there are many members of clearinghouses, and that is allowed. There are 60 to 70 members of the Chicago Mercantile clearinghouse, for instance. In the swaps world, it is very closed, and I think there were high and, I believe, arbitrary limits, that you had to have $5 billion of capital and a $1 trillion swap book, and I think that was in part done to keep a barrier to entry, frankly.

And I think Congress addressed that by saying that clearinghouses have to have open access. We have put a proposal rule out for comment to hear from the public. But it is also for pension funds and asset managers to have more choices as to who is going to be their clearing member, who is going to represent them on the buy side. So I think this is actually a rule that helps pension funds, the asset managers of America, the financial entities who are not swap dealers, have access to this clearing and not be constrained and have to go through a handful of big Wall Street firms.

Senator WARNER. And finally, just again, Secretary Wolin, I do hope that, and it sounds like the SEC and the CFTC are working well together, but at some point, it was at least this member's hope that so that we would not have this patchwork and siloed approach and duplicative sets of regulations, the FSOC was hopefully that place that would help resolve these issues. At some point there needs to be that umpire, and I hope Secretary Geithner will realize, not just in this particular case, but in a series of others, if you have any closing comments. And again, I thank the indulgence of the Chair.

Mr. WOLIN. Senator Warner, as you heard from the two Chairmen, I think they are still early in their process and will move forward. I think while respecting the independence of the regulators, obviously, the FSOC does have a responsibility to look at things that have systemically important implications and to try to bring to bear consistency across the system where those issues are systemically relevant. That is something we have been focused on. There is also, of course, from Treasury's perspective, a need to worry about the international dimensions so that not only do we have consistency where we can here within the United States, but also what is going on elsewhere in the G–20 and beyond, again, for the sort of level playing field kinds of implications that we think are important.

Chairman JOHNSON. Today's hearing has been very helpful and given us all a better understanding of the important provisions in the Dodd-Frank Act to promote financial stability in our nation's economy going forward. We cannot afford to go back to the old financial system that destroyed millions of jobs and cost the economy trillions of dollars. The creation of the FSOC and the other new tools given to our Federal regulators to monitor systemic risk and to unwind failing financial institutions address many of the weaknesses in the old system and this will help the regulators better manage future crises.

Thanks again to my colleagues and our panelists for being here today.

This hearing is adjourned.

[Whereupon, at 11:32 a.m., the hearing was adjourned.]

[Prepared statements and responses to written questions supplied for the record follow:]

PREPARED STATEMENT OF SENATOR RICHARD C. SHELBY

Thank you, Mr. Chairman.

Today's hearing will examine the difficult task of defining and regulating systemic risk. Dodd-Frank established the Financial Stability Oversight Council and charged it with monitoring risk in the U.S. financial system. The Council is also responsible for designating firms for special, systemic risk regulation by the Federal Reserve.

Unfortunately, Dodd-Frank provides little guidance on exactly which firms should be designated for systemic risk regulation and what that regulation should involve. Instead, these decisions were left to the discretion of the regulators through broad delegations of authority. Accordingly, before regulators move forward, they will need to devise a well-considered and transparent regulatory scheme that limits adverse consequences.

So far, regulators appear to be divided on what the final rules should look like and what entities should be designated as systemically significant financial institutions. It is not surprising that regulators are having difficulty determining how to regulate firms for systemic risk. Many commentators have questioned whether it is even possible to make such a determination with any degree of accuracy. Indeed, Secretary Geithner recently told the Special Inspector General for TARP: "You won't be able to make a judgment about what's systemic and what's not until you know the nature of the shock."

Despite the divergent views of its members, the Council is moving forward with its framework for designating nonbank financial entities for extra regulatory scrutiny. Unfortunately, the Council has not yet released for public comment the detailed rules on how they will designate firms. Instead, the Council has issued proposed rules that merely restate the broad statutory parameters. As a result, there is a great deal of confusion about how the Council will proceed with its rulemaking. This has created uncertainty in our markets as firms are unsure which types of activities will cause them to be subject to systemic risk regulation.

Accordingly, I want to hear more details from our witnesses about how they envision systemic risk regulation will function in practice. I am particularly interested in hearing how they will address the potentially adverse consequences that could arise. Most importantly, how will regulators ensure that selecting a handful of firms for enhanced regulation will not increase moral hazard if markets believe that regulators will never allow a designated firm to fail?

As we saw during the recent financial crisis, regulators may go to great lengths to rescue a firm in order to cover up their mistakes. In other words, does the Council's designation responsibility threaten to undermine one of the Council's other responsibilities—the promotion of market discipline by eliminating expectations that the Government will bail out financial institutions if there is a crisis?

In addition, I am interested in hearing how regulators believe designating firms will impact the competitiveness of our markets. In the lead up to the financial crisis, our regulators failed on a grand scale to monitor the activities of individual institutions. There is good reason to doubt whether our regulators can effectively monitor the risks posed system-wide.

Thus, the burden is on our regulators to demonstrate that they know exactly what they are doing before they begin to implement this new form of regulation. The last thing our fragile economy needs is a far-reaching Government experiment that destabilizes the financial system it is intended to protect.

Thank you.

PREPARED STATEMENT OF NEAL S. WOLIN
DEPUTY SECRETARY, DEPARTMENT OF THE TREASURY

MAY 12, 2011

Chairman Johnson, Ranking Member Shelby, and Members of the Committee, I appreciate the opportunity to provide an update on the Treasury Department's implementation of the Dodd-Frank Act.

Last year, the President signed into law the most sweeping financial reforms since the Great Depression. Although our economy and our financial markets have made important progress on the path toward recovery, we cannot forget why we enacted this legislation.

In the fall of 2008, we witnessed a financial panic of a scale and severity not seen in decades. The crisis was brought about by fundamental failures in our financial system. The failures were many and they were varied. The crisis erased trillions of dollars of wealth, put Americans out of work across the country, and shook the foundations of our entire economy. And the crisis exposed the fundamental flaws in our financial system.

There was no alternative to reform. The system we had favored short-term gains for individual firms over the stability and growth of the economy as a whole. The system we had was weak and susceptible to crisis. And the system we had left taxpayers to save it in times of trouble.

We had no choice but to build a better, stronger system. That's why we proposed, Congress passed, and the President signed into law a sweeping set of reforms to do just that.

But enacting this law was just the beginning.

We are now undertaking the difficult and complex process of implementation, and today I'd like to discuss some of our accomplishments and our next steps as we approach the 10 month mark since enactment.

Before I describe how we are implementing the Dodd-Frank Act, I want to detail the broad principles guiding our efforts. First, we are moving as quickly and as carefully as we can.

Wherever possible, we are quickly providing clarity to the public and the markets. But the task we face cannot be achieved overnight. We are writing rules in some of the most complex areas of finance; consolidating authority that was previously spread across multiple agencies; setting up new institutions for consumer protection and for addressing systemic risks; and negotiating with countries around the world. In getting this done, we are making sure to get it right.

After the Dodd-Frank Act was signed into law, many who criticized the legislation said that it lacked details, and that the uncertainty of the shape of final regulations made it difficult for businesses to plan for the future. These critics called for clarity without delay.

Now many of these same critics suggest that the pace of implementation, as prescribed by law, is moving too fast.

Treasury and regulators have consistently indicated—then and now—that we would move quickly but carefully to implement the legislation, that we would seek public input into the process, and that it was critical to get the details right. Over the past 10 months, Treasury and regulators have been doing just that—implementing the statute in a careful, considered, and serious manner.

Second, we are conducting this process out in the open, bringing full transparency to implementation activities.

As new rules have been proposed, we have consulted with a broad range of groups and individuals. The American people are able to see who is at the table. Comments have been made publicly available. Treasury has made public the topics of meetings on Dodd-Frank implementation and the names of the attendees.

In addition to providing transparency across Treasury's activities, the studies and rulemaking processes conducted at Treasury or through the Financial Stability Oversight Council (FSOC or Council) have benefited from significant public outreach and comment, often through both Advanced Notice of Proposed Rulemaking and Notice of Proposed Rulemaking. This process allows interested parties the opportunity to provide input, as well as understand the evolution of rules.

The Office of Financial Research (OFR), Federal Insurance Office (FIO) and Consumer Financial Protection Bureau (CFPB) have all provided transparency and sought public input in their efforts to implement Dodd-Frank reforms.

Third, wherever possible, we are seeking to streamline and simplify Government regulation.

Over the years, our financial system has accumulated layers upon layers of rules, which can be overwhelming. That is why alongside our efforts to strengthen and improve protections through the system, we seek to avoid duplication and to eliminate rules that do not work. For example, Dodd-Frank exempts small companies from complying with certain internal control rules of Sarbanes-Oxley.

The Dodd-Frank Act recognizes the need to update and rationalize the patchwork regulatory framework that was built over decades. Consolidation of organizational structures and oversight responsibilities are a critical part of the statute's reforms.

In addition, the statute requires many joint rulemakings, and even where rules are not required to be issued jointly, agencies must often coordinate to adopt comparable rules for functionally or economically similar products or entities. Through this process we seek to avoid overlapping and inconsistent rules.

These efforts build on a core priority of President Obama. In January, the President issued an Executive Order relating to streamlining and simplifying regulations, seeking to ensure cost-effective, evidence-based regulations that are compatible with economic growth, job creation, and competitiveness. Among other things, the Order requires that agencies: consider costs and benefits and choose the least burdensome path (to the extent consistent with law); encourage public participation in rulemaking; attempt to coordinate, simplify, and harmonize regulations to reduce costs and promote certainty; and conduct retrospective analyses of rules, on a periodic basis, to identify rules that "may be outmoded, ineffective, insufficient, or excessively burdensome."

We are following these priorities as we implement Dodd-Frank. Indeed, we believe that the enactment of Dodd-Frank provides a historic moment for all of the affected agencies to pause and take stock: an opportunity to ensure that future regulation is consistent with these priorities, and that rules currently on the books are serving their intended purposes. Properly applied, these priorities and guidelines can help strike the right regulatory balance: ensuring that regulations protect our financial system and improve the performance of our economy, without imposing unreasonable costs on society.

Fourth, we are creating a more coordinated regulatory process.

Dodd-Frank requires regulators, more than ever before, to work together to close gaps in regulation and to prevent breakdowns in coordination—this is a central change brought about by the law. Beyond joint rules and consultation required on specific rulemakings, the statute requires working together where issues cut across multiple agencies, to make the pieces of reform fit together in a sensible, coherent way.

While our financial regulatory system is built on the independence of regulators—and given the importance of Dodd-Frank implementation, independent regulators will have different views on complicated issues—working through differences is an important part of getting the substance right.

The Dodd-Frank Act preserves agency independence, while providing a new forum for collaboration and consultation among regulators. The Financial Stability Oversight Council, which is a key component of Dodd-Frank, has a mandate to coordinate across agencies and instill joint accountability for the strength of the financial system.

Already, we have worked through the FSOC to develop an integrated roadmap for implementation, to coordinate an unprecedented six-agency proposal on risk retention, and to develop unanimous support for recommendations on implementing the Volcker Rule. As Chair of the FSOC, the Secretary of the Treasury will continue to make it a top priority that the work of the regulators is well-coordinated.

Fifth, we are working to ensure a level playing field.

We are working hard at the international level to make sure that others put in place similar frameworks on the key issues where international consistency is essential—such as OTC derivatives, and financial institutions' liquidity, leverage, and capital.

The details of these rules governing complex markets and institutions are critical and when different jurisdictions implement commonly agreed-to international principles, disagreements may arise. That is why in addition to dialogue in international fora like the G–20 and the Financial Stability Board, we work every day with our foreign counterparts, especially in Europe, through our financial market and regulatory dialogue.

But as we work in the international sphere to promote a level playing field, we must not fail to implement our reforms at home. U.S. leadership on reform is essential to making sure that a level playing field is in place. Ultimately, if we fail to do what is necessary to reform and protect our system, we put at risk its fundamental strength and resilience.

Detailed rules of financial regulation will always vary among sovereign nations. What's important, what we have made good progress on—and what we are committed to—is closing regulatory gaps, ending opportunities for geographic arbitrage, and preventing a global race to the bottom.

Sixth, we are working to protect the freedom for innovation that is absolutely necessary for growth.

Before the crisis, our financial system allowed too much room for abuse and excessive risk. But as we put in place rules to correct those mistakes, we have to achieve a careful balance and safeguard the freedom for competition and innovation that is essential for growth.

For example, as enhanced capital requirements are introduced, we will work to achieve a balanced regime that strengthens firms so they can withstand stress, but that also allows U.S. firms to compete effectively on a global basis.

Moreover, new provisions in Dodd-Frank will increase transparency and reduce risks in the derivatives markets. These electronic trading and central clearing provisions will tighten spreads, reduce costs, and increase understanding of risks for market participants. These new transparent structures will promotes efficient markets, capital formation, and growth in the broader economy, while reducing the risk and potential costs of another destabilizing financial crisis.

Implementation of Dodd-Frank will result in a strong, stable financial system, which is the foundation needed to foster competition, innovation and economic growth.

Seventh, we are keeping Congress fully informed of our progress on a regular basis.

Guided by these principles, we have made significant progress since Dodd-Frank was enacted almost 10 months ago. I'd like to update you on a few of the institutions at the heart of this legislation—the Financial Stability Oversight Council, the Office of Financial Research, the Federal Insurance Office and the Consumer Financial Protection Bureau.

FINANCIAL STABILITY OVERSIGHT COUNCIL

The Dodd-Frank Act created the Financial Stability Oversight Council to coordinate across agencies and instill joint accountability for the stability of the financial system. The Council is mandated to identify and monitor risks to U.S. financial stability, respond to any emerging threats in the system and promote market discipline. The Act also provides the Council with a leading role in several important regulatory decisions, including which nonbank financial institutions and financial market utilities will be designated for heightened prudential standards.

The Council has made significant progress in the short time since the Dodd-Frank Act was signed into law. Since enactment, the Council has: (1) built its basic organizational framework; (2) laid the groundwork for the designation of nonbank financial companies and financial market utilities; (3) initiated monitoring for potential risks to U.S. financial stability; (4) carried out the explicit statutory requirements of the Council, including the completion of several studies; and (5) served as a forum for discussion and coordination among the agencies implementing Dodd-Frank.

COUNCIL STRUCTURE AND OPERATIONS

We have built a structure for the Council that is designed to promote accountability and action. Every 2 weeks, a Deputies Committee comprised of senior officials from each of the member agencies meets to set the Council's agenda, and to direct the work of the Council's Systemic Risk Committee and five functional committees. The functional committees are organized around the Council's ongoing statutory responsibilities: designations of nonbank financial companies, designations of financial market utilities, heightened prudential standards, orderly liquidation and resolution plans, and data.

In the 10 months since Dodd-Frank was enacted, the Council's principals have met four times and plan to meet again later this month—significantly more often than the statutorily required quarterly meetings.

At each meeting to date, the Council has held a public session. This exemplifies a commitment to conduct its work in as open and transparent a manner as practicable given the confidential supervisory and sensitive information that is at the heart of the Council's work.

DESIGNATIONS

For the first time, Dodd-Frank requires consolidated supervision of and heightened prudential standards for the largest, most interconnected nonbank financial companies that could pose a threat to the financial system. The statute also authorizes heightened standards be applied to designated financial market utilities and payment, clearing and settlement activities.

The Council is engaging in two parallel rulemakings to establish a process and define criteria for these designations that are robust and transparent. While the statute carefully outlines the considerations and process requirements for making these designations, the Council is conducting rulemakings to ensure transparency and to obtain input from all interested parties.

For its nonbank designations work, the Council issued an Advanced Notice of Proposed Rulemaking or "ANPR" in October 2010 and a Notice of Proposed Rulemaking or "NPRM" in January 2011 providing guidance on the statutorily mandated criteria and defining the procedures that the Council will follow in considering the designation of nonbank financial companies. For designations of financial market utilities, public comments from last November's ANPR informed an NPRM released in March. The comment period for that NPRM is 60 days and closes on May 27. The Council's member agencies continue to work in close collaboration, having received significant input from market participants, non-profits, academics, and members of the public to develop an analytical framework for designations that will provide a consistent approach and will incorporate the need for both quantitative and qualitative judgments. We plan to provide additional guidance regarding the Council's approach to designation and we will seek public comment on it.

It is important to understand that the Council needs to retain flexibility to exercise judgment as it considers both quantifiable metrics and the unique risks that a particular firm may present to the financial system. Moreover, flexibility is needed because financial markets are dynamic and the designation process must take into account changes in firms, markets and risks. That is one of the key reasons that the statute mandates an annual reevaluation of any designation made by the Council.

The Council's commitment to a robust designations process goes beyond transparency during the rulemaking process. Every designation decision will be firm-specific and is subject to judicial review. Moreover, even before the Council votes on a proposed designation, a company under consideration will have the opportunity to submit written materials to the Council on whether, in the company's view, it meets the standard for designation. Only after Council members have reviewed that information will they vote on a proposed designation, which requires the support of two-thirds of the Council (including the affirmative vote of the Chair) and requires the Council to provide the company with a written explanation of the basis of the proposed designation to the firm. If challenged, the proposed designation is subject to review through a formal hearing process and a two-thirds final vote. Upon the final vote approving the designation, the Council must then submit a report to Congress detailing its final decision.

MONITORING THREATS TO FINANCIAL STABILITY

Monitoring threats to financial stability is the cornerstone of the Council's responsibilities. This macroprudential role demands coordination, collaboration and information sharing among each of the members of the Council. We are working together to bring the best information to bear, while protecting the security and confidentiality of sensitive information.

The Council has established a committee structure to support its monitoring function. The structure is intended to balance the need for an interdisciplinary and cross-cutting approach with the need to leverage existing expertise and experience, and is the locus of accountability for systemic risk monitoring.

Through this structure, the FSOC focuses on identifying and analyzing cross-cutting risks that may affect financial institutions and financial markets in the medium and longer term. With respect to financial institutions, the FSOC focuses on structural issues such as trends in leverage or funding structure, new products, or exposures to particular risks. With respect to financial markets, the FSOC focuses on issues such as trends in volatility or liquidity, market structure, or asset valuations.

In addition, the FSOC serves as a forum for agencies to discuss emerging issues of immediate importance as well as share information about issues that arise in the course of their supervisory and oversight work that could impact financial stability.

The Dodd-Frank Act provides for a public report to Congress detailing this monitoring in the form of an annual report on the activities of the Council and the health of the financial system. As stated in the statute this report will: outline the activities of the Council, including any designations or recommendations made with respect to activities that could threaten financial stability; detail significant financial market and regulatory developments, including insurance and accounting regulations and standards; and, describe potential emerging threats to the financial stability of the United States. The statute also requires that the report provide recommendations to enhance the integrity, efficiency, competitiveness, and stability of United States financial markets; promote market discipline; and maintain investor confidence.

Staff at each of the member agencies is hard at work preparing the Council's first annual report.

STUDIES

On January 18, the Council released a study and recommendations on the implementation of the Dodd-Frank Act's "Volcker Rule." The Council sought input from the public in advance of the study on issues associated with the statutory required considerations and received more than 8,000 comments. The study recommends principles for implementing the Volcker Rule and suggests a comprehensive framework for identifying activities prohibited by the Rule. That framework includes an internal compliance regime, quantitative analysis and reporting, and supervisory review.

Also, at its January meeting, the Council approved a study of the effects of the Dodd-Frank Act's limits on the concentration of large companies on financial stability and released the study's recommendations for public comment. The Council's study found that the concentration limit will reduce moral hazard, increase financial stability, and improve efficiency and competition within the U.S. financial system. The study also made largely technical recommendations to mitigate practical difficulties likely to arise in the administration and enforcement of the concentration limit, without undermining its effectiveness in limiting excessive concentration among financial companies. The Council received six comments and is currently reviewing those comments to determine whether any of the recommendations should be modified.

The Council continues to have specific responsibilities to study key issues outlined in Dodd-Frank. For instance, the Council must complete a study regarding the treatment of fully secured creditors in the context of the Act's orderly liquidation authority by July and a study regarding contingent capital instruments by July 2012.

INTERAGENCY REGULATORY COORDINATION

The Council also has served as a forum for discussion and coordination among the agencies implementing the Dodd-Frank Act. For the Council's first meeting in October 2010, the staff of member agencies developed a detailed, public road map for implementation of the legislation. This integrated roadmap outlined a coordinated timeline of goals, both for the Council and its independent member agencies, to fully implement the Dodd-Frank Act.

As Chair of the Council, the Treasury Secretary is required to coordinate several major rulemakings under the Dodd-Frank Act. For example, to facilitate the joint rulemaking on credit risk retention, Treasury staff held frequent interagency discussions beginning shortly after the Dodd-Frank Act was passed to develop the rule text and preamble. This joint rulemaking required reaching consensus among six rulemaking agencies. The proposed rule, released on March 31, demonstrates our ability to promote effective collaboration, and it is a significant step toward strengthening securitization markets. Treasury staff is currently engaged in a similar process with the staff of member agencies tasked with drafting the Volcker Rule.

The Council's regulatory coordination role is greater than the specific statutory instances where coordination is required. Deputies meetings have served as a forum for sharing information about significant regulatory developments, particularly those that impact the work of more than one member agency and relate to financial stability. For example, the Federal Reserve recently briefed deputies on the results of its Comprehensive Capital Analysis and Review. Treasury has provided updates on housing finance reform.

OFFICE OF FINANCIAL RESEARCH

In order to constrain systemic risk effectively, the Council and its members must have the ability to effectively monitor it.

The Dodd-Frank Act established the Office of Financial Research (OFR) to improve the quality of financial data available to policymakers and facilitate more robust and sophisticated analysis of the financial system.

In the lead-up to the financial crisis, financial reporting failed to adapt to a rapidly evolving financial system. Supervisors and market participants lacked data about the increasing leverage in the rapidly growing shadow banking system. Policymakers and investors responded to the crisis with inadequate information about the interconnectedness of firms and associated risks to the financial system.

The Dodd-Frank Act established two complementary centers within the OFR—one focused on data, and one focused on research and analysis—to help ensure that, going forward, regulators' understanding of the risks within the financial system can keep pace with innovation and with market developments.

The OFR will standardize and provide data and analytical tools for OFR researchers, the FSOC, its members, and the public. In collecting information, the OFR will minimize the reporting burden on industry by, whenever possible, relying on data already in the regulatory system, and by assisting Council members in standardizing information collected by those members. The OFR is already working to accomplish both goals and its staff is working closely with the regulatory community to catalog data already collected to help ensure duplication will not occur. And the OFR is collaborating with the SEC and CFTC to standardize reporting of parties to swap transactions.

More broadly, the OFR is exploring ways in which it can help make Government more efficient. For example, the OFR is investigating how it might act as a central warehouse of data for the regulatory community and other ways in which it could facilitate data sharing. The OFR has also been soliciting input from FSOC member agencies to find ways to support their efforts.

The OFR's Research and Analysis Center, will measure and analyze factors affecting financial stability and help to develop policies that promote it. The OFR will also report to the Congress and the public on its analysis of significant financial market developments, potential emerging threats to stability and policy responses. The combination of better, more granular data, and new analytic capabilities focused on systemic threats can help all market participants—industry as well as regulators—better understand risks within the financial system.

Attracting and hiring top quality senior leadership is critical to OFR and in guiding its mission.

The search for an OFR Director is ongoing and a high priority for the Administration. The Administration is evaluating candidates based on a combination of strong analytical ability, experience in financial services, management experience, and communication skills. In the meantime, key personnel have been hired.

Richard Berner recently joined the Treasury Department as Counselor to the Secretary with the responsibility to oversee the implementation of the Office of Financial Research. Mr. Berner is a well-respected economist who will bring judgment and leadership to the OFR implementation team, along with critical risk management and financial industry expertise.

The OFR also is filling senior personnel roles including its Chief Operating Officer, Chief Data Officer and Chief Business Officer. The OFR is hiring top-tier talent with deep industry experience in data management, technology, and risk management. Industry experience will help ensure that the organization will collect data in a systematic, structured, and non-duplicative way, with clear benefits to industry and regulators.

The OFR is also making progress in establishing its research team and network, which will include academics from across the country and in a variety of disciplines. The interdisciplinary research team will add significant capacity to the FSOC's ability to measure and analyze the many dimensions of financial stability.

We project that by the end of September, the OFR will have over 60 full-time employees. Treasury is committed to providing this implementation team with needed support and guidance, and I, along with other senior Treasury officials, are meeting with the team weekly to make sure priorities are identified, progress is measured and that the stand-up of the OFR is well executed.

As the OFR continues to recruit highly qualified individuals to lead and support its work, current staff is already working with regulators and industry to standardize financial reporting. This will improve the ability of policymakers and private industry to aggregate information-critical to risk management. It will also facilitate more efficient processing by private firms and markets.

The OFR's first step in this direction has been to promote the establishment of a global standard for identifying parties to financial transactions: a legal entity identifiers (LEI). During the financial crisis, a LEI could have given policymakers and private institutions a clearer understanding of the interconnections among financial institutions.

The LEI initiative is moving forward quickly. The OFR is working closely with U.S. and foreign financial regulators to define consistent requirements, and is using established international forums, such as the Financial Stability Board, to engage in multilateral discussions. The OFR already published a framework in its November Policy Statement, consistent with the requirements set forth by the SEC and CFTC in their Notices of Proposed Rulemakings for swap transaction reporting. Meanwhile, various financial trade associations and their members formed a global coalition to produce a common set of requirements for such a standard. Last week they published a white paper that lays out draft requirements, and they are seeking input from public and private entities. The International Organization for Standardization—which has deep expertise in this area and representation from industry and regulators—is moving quickly to define a new standard that it intends to be consistent with public and private requirements.

In addition to these efforts, OFR staff is supporting the work of the Financial Stability Oversight Council. This includes data and analysis in support of the FSOC's evaluation of nonbank financial companies for designation and its report on systemic risk.

The OFR is also establishing forums and networks to allow experts within and outside the regulatory system to contribute to the Council's mission. This year, the OFR will host along with the National Science Foundation, a conference that brings together top academics in finance, economics, and computer science, and members of industry and the regulatory community on systemic risk monitoring and potential responses. OFR staff also will be participating in the academic community through its publications.

CONSUMER FINANCIAL PROTECTION BUREAU

While the Council and the Office of Financial Research are designed to help us monitor and address risk in the broader financial system, the Consumer Financial Protection Bureau was created to address a specific gap in our regulatory structure—the need for a single agency dedicated to consumer protection.

The CFPB, which will assume existing authorities of seven Federal agencies on July 21, 2011, will work to make sure that consumers have the information they need to understand the terms of their agreements with financial companies. It will also work to make regulations and guidance as clear and streamlined as possible in order to ease the burden on providers of consumer financial products and services.

The CFPB will consolidate existing Federal rulemaking authorities with respect to consumer financial products and services, have enforcement and supervision authority for depository institutions with over $10 billion in assets and their affiliates, as well as supervise the consumer financial services activities of many non-bank financial firms that sell consumer financial services.

The Act charges the Secretary of Treasury with standing up the CFPB until a director is appointed. Under his leadership we set up an implementation team with a clear mandate shortly after enactment.

Elizabeth Warren, as Special Advisor to the Secretary, is leading Treasury's effort to build the CFPB. The CFPB implementation team, now consisting of over 200 staff members, is focused on setting up key functions of the bureau such as bank supervision, fair lending and enforcement programs and research, markets, and regulation teams. In order to do this, CFPB is making major investments in infrastructure and human capital. The CFPB implementation team has reached agreement with the six agencies transferring staff with regards to a process for transferring staff to CFPB that will minimize disruption to existing agencies while allowing CFPB to gain from existing expertise.

The CFPB implementation team has made a concentrated effort to reach out to the public, industry, and other concerned groups during the initial stand up of the CFPB. As an example of this extensive outreach, Elizabeth Warren has made it a priority to meet with community bankers and credit unions from all 50 States. She has also met with dozens of CEOs and other executives of the largest financial institutions and consumer advocates. The CFPB's office of servicemember affairs, led by Holly Petraeus, is actively working with the Department of Defense to help inform and protect servicemembers from financial tricks and traps.

The CFPB is well on track to meet the statutory deadlines for reports mandated by Dodd-Frank, and the CFPB implementation team is planning and preparing for the promulgation of certain rules mandated by the Dodd-Frank Act. For example, the CFPB implementation team is actively working to complete initial steps toward the consolidation of the TILA/RESPA mortgage disclosure forms. This consolidation will allow us to reduce the regulatory burden on industry and provide consumers with more of the information they need to make the right decision.

There has been significant progress toward standing up core elements of the CFPB by the designated transfer date of July 21, 2011. In addition to its bank supervision program, the CFPB will stand up components of its consumer response system and be prepared to take over rule writing projects that will transfer over to the bureau.

And the agency will be accountable in executing these tasks. Dodd-Frank includes several provisions to ensure the agency's accountability.

The CFPB must submit annual reports to Congress, the Director must testify multiple times each year on the agency's budget and activities, and the GAO audits the CFPB's expenditures annually. Furthermore, the CFPB is currently subject to the oversight of the inspectors general of Treasury and the Federal Reserve. And, most importantly, there is direct oversight of the agency's rulemaking: the FSOC can review and even reject the CFPB's rules, and, as with any other regulator, Congress has the ability to overturn any of the CFPB's rules.

The goal of the CFPB is to make markets for consumer financial products and services work for Americans—whether they are applying for a mortgage, choosing among credit cards, or using any number of other consumer financial products. The CFPB implementation team is on track to standing up an agency capable of accomplishing this goal.

FEDERAL INSURANCE OFFICE

In addition to providing for new regulatory protections and oversight for consumers, the Dodd-Frank Act enhances the Federal Government's ability to monitor the insurance sector and coordinate and develop Federal policy on major domestic and international insurance issues. The crisis highlighted the lack of expertise within our Federal Government regarding the insurance industry. In response, the Act establishes the Federal Insurance Office (the "FIO"), which will provide the U.S. Government—for the first time—dedicated expertise regarding the insurance industry.

The FIO will monitor for problems or gaps in insurance regulation that can contribute to a systemic crisis in the insurance industry or the financial system; gather data and information on the industry and insurers; and coordinate Federal policy in the insurance sector.

The Act does not provide the FIO with general supervisory or regulatory authority over the business of insurance. The States remain the functional regulators. Through the FIO, however, the Federal Government will work toward modernizing and improving our system of insurance regulation.

Secretary Geithner announced at the March FSOC meeting that Michael McRaith has been selected to become the Director of the FIO. Mr. McRaith is currently the Director of the Illinois Department of Insurance, and will bring significant experience and judgment to the FIO.

Treasury also recently announced that the Department will establish a Federal Advisory Committee on Insurance. The objective of the Committee is to present advice and recommendations to the FIO to assist the Office in carrying out its duties and authorities. The Advisory Committee will reserve half of its membership for the State insurance commissioners so that the FIO will benefit from the knowledge and regulatory experience of our functional regulators. The remaining members will represent a diverse set of expert perspectives from the various sectors of the insurance industry (life, property and casualty, reinsurance, agents and brokers), as well as academics, consumer advocates, or experts in the issues facing underserved insurance communities and consumers.

The FIO has served an important consultative role in advising on several Dodd-Frank studies, rule writing processes and ongoing responsibilities. These include providing expert advice on the Volcker Rule study and rule writing, Orderly Liquidation Authority rule writing and participating in the FSOC insurance working group.

The Federal Insurance Office has become a provision member of the International Association of Insurance Supervisors (IAIS), where it will represent the United States, and it is expected to be voted-in as a full member in the fall. The FIO is also leading the U.S. delegation for the insurance and pensions committee of the Organization for Economic Co-operation and Development.

The Secretary of the Treasury, supported by the FIO, together with the United States Trade Representative, is now empowered to negotiate certain international agreements regarding prudential insurance measures. We anticipate that the FIO will be actively involved, for example, in working with the representatives of other countries on reinsurance collateral and U.S. equivalence under Solvency II.

CONCLUSION

The Dodd-Frank Act builds a stronger financial system by addressing major gaps and weaknesses in regulation. It puts in place buffers and safeguards to reduce the chance that another generation will go through a crisis of similar magnitude. It protects taxpayers from bailouts. It brings fairness and transparency to consumers of financial services. And it lays the foundation for a financial system that is pro-investment and pro-growth. The Act and its successful implementation will help ensure that our financial system becomes safer, stronger and, just as in the past century, the world leader.

Thank you very much.

PREPARED STATEMENT OF BEN S. BERNANKE
CHAIRMAN, BOARD OF GOVERNORS OF THE FEDERAL RESERVE SYSTEM

MAY 12, 2011

Chairman Johnson, Ranking Member Shelby, and other Members of the Committee, thank you for the opportunity to testify on the Federal Reserve Board's role in monitoring systemic risk and promoting financial stability, both as a member of the Financial Stability Oversight Council (FSOC) and under our own authority.

Financial Stability Oversight Council

The Dodd-Frank Wall Street Reform and Consumer Protection Act (Dodd-Frank Act) created the FSOC to identify and mitigate threats to the financial stability of the United States. During its existence thus far, the FSOC has promoted interagency collaboration and established the organizational structure and processes necessary to execute its duties.[1] The FSOC and its member agencies also have completed studies on limits on proprietary trading and investments in hedge funds and private equity funds by banking firms (the Volcker rule), on financial sector concentration limits, on the economic effects of risk retention, and on the economic consequences of systemic risk regulation. The FSOC is currently seeking public comments on proposed rules that would establish a framework for identifying nonbank financial firms and financial market utilities that could pose a threat to financial stability and that therefore should be designated for more stringent oversight. Importantly, the FSOC has begun systematically monitoring risks to financial stability and is preparing its inaugural annual report.

Additional Financial Stability-Related Reforms at the Federal Reserve

In addition to its role on the FSOC, the Federal Reserve has other significant financial stability responsibilities under the Dodd-Frank Act, including supervisory jurisdiction over thrift holding companies and nonbank financial firms that are designated as systemically important by the council. The act also requires the Federal Reserve (and other financial regulatory agencies) to take a macroprudential approach to supervision and regulation; that is, in supervising financial institutions and critical infrastructures, we are expected to consider the risks to overall financial stability in addition to the safety and soundness of individual firms.

A major thrust of the Dodd-Frank Act is addressing the "too-big-to-fail" problem and mitigating the threat to financial stability posed by systemically important financial firms. As required by the act, the Federal Reserve is developing more-stringent prudential standards for large banking organizations and nonbank financial firms designated by the FSOC. These standards will include enhanced risk-based capital and leverage requirements, liquidity requirements, and single-counterparty credit limits. The standards will also require systemically important financial firms to adopt so-called living wills that will spell out how they can be resolved in an orderly manner during times of financial distress. The act also directs the Federal Reserve to conduct annual stress tests of large banking firms and designated nonbank financial firms and to publish a summary of the results. To meet the January 2012 implementation deadline for these enhanced standards, we anticipate putting out a package of proposed rules for comment this summer. Our goal is to produce a well-integrated set of rules that meaningfully reduces the probability of failure of our largest, most complex financial firms, and that minimizes the losses to the financial system and the economy if such a firm should fail.

The Federal Reserve is working with other U.S. regulatory agencies to implement Dodd-Frank reforms in additional areas, including the development of risk retention requirements for securitization sponsors, margin requirements for noncleared over-the-counter derivatives, incentive compensation rules, and risk-management standards for central counterparties and other financial market utilities.

The Federal Reserve has made significant organizational changes to better carry out its responsibilities. Even before the enactment of the Dodd-Frank Act, we were strengthening our supervision of the largest, most complex financial firms. We created a centralized multidisciplinary body called the Large Institution Supervision Coordinating Committee to oversee the supervision of these firms. This committee uses horizontal, or cross-firm, evaluations to monitor interconnectedness and common practices among firms that could lead to greater systemic risk. It also uses additional and improved quantitative methods for evaluating the performance of firms and the risks they might pose. And it more efficiently employs the broad range of skills of the Federal Reserve staff to supplement supervision. We have established a similar body to help us effectively carry out our responsibilities regarding the oversight of systemically important financial market utilities.

More recently, we have also created an Office of Financial Stability Policy and Research at the Federal Reserve Board. This office coordinates our efforts to identify and analyze potential risks to the broader financial system and the economy. It also helps evaluate policies to promote financial stability and serves as the Board's liaison to the FSOC.

International Regulatory Coordination

As a complement to those efforts under Dodd-Frank, the Federal Reserve has been working for some time with other regulatory agencies and central banks

---

[1] The FSOC's internal structure consists of a Deputies Committee—composed of personnel from all of the voting and nonvoting members—and six other standing committees, each with its own specific duties. The Deputies Committee, under the direction of the FSOC members, coordinates the work of the six committees and aims to ensure that the FSOC fulfills its mission in an effective and timely manner.

around the world to design and implement a stronger set of prudential requirements for internationally active banking firms. These efforts resulted in the agreements reached in the fall of 2010 on the major elements of the new Basel III prudential framework for globally active banks. The requirements under Basel III that such banks hold more and better-quality capital and more-robust liquidity buffers should make the financial system more stable and reduce the likelihood of future financial crises. We are working with the other U.S. banking agencies to incorporate the Basel III agreements into U.S. regulations.

More remains to be done at the international level to strengthen the global financial system. Key tasks ahead for the Basel Committee and the Financial Stability Board include determining how to further increase the loss-absorbing capacity of systemically important banking firms and strengthening resolution regimes to minimize adverse systemic effects from the failure of large, complex banks. As we work with our international counterparts, we are striving to keep international regulatory standards as consistent as possible, to ensure that multinational firms are adequately supervised, and to maintain a level international playing field.

Thank you. I would be pleased to take your questions.

PREPARED STATEMENT OF SHEILA C. BAIR

CHAIRMAN, FEDERAL DEPOSIT INSURANCE CORPORATION

MAY 12, 2011

Chairman Johnson, Ranking Member Shelby, and Members of the Committee, thank you for the opportunity to testify today on behalf of the Federal Deposit Insurance Corporation (FDIC) on issues related to monitoring systemic risk and promoting the stability of our financial system.

The recent financial crisis has highlighted the critical importance of financial stability to the functioning of our real economy. In all, over eight and a half million jobs were lost in the recession and its immediate aftermath, and over half of these were lost in the 6-month period following the height of the crisis in September 2008. While the economy is now in its eighth consecutive quarter of expansion, to date only about 20 percent of the jobs lost in the recession have been regained, and the number of private sector payroll jobs stands at the same level it did 12 years ago, in the spring of 1999.

A central cause of this crisis—as has been the case with most previous crises— was excessive debt and leverage in our financial system. At the height of the crisis, the large intermediaries that make up the core of our financial system proved to have too little capital to maintain market confidence in their solvency. The need for stronger capitalization of our financial system is being addressed in part by strengthening bank capital requirements through the Basel III capital protocols and implementation of the Collins amendment. We also learned in the crisis that leverage can be masked through off-balance-sheet positions, implicit guarantees, securitization structures, and derivatives positions. The crisis showed that the problem with leverage is really larger than the bank balance sheet itself. Excessive leverage is a general condition of our financial system that is subsidized by the tax code and lobbied for by financial institutions and borrower constituencies alike, to their short-term benefit and to the long-term cost of our economy.

The ability of many large financial institutions to operate with relatively thin levels of capitalization was enabled by the market's perception that they enjoyed implicit Government backing; in short, they were "too big to fail." This market perception was ratified in the heat of the crisis when policymakers were faced with the dilemma of providing this assistance or seeing our economy endure an even more catastrophic decline.

As a consequence, the Dodd-Frank Act mandates higher prudential standards for systemic financial entities. Importantly, the Act authorizes the creation of a new resolution framework for systemically important financial institutions (SIFIs) designed to ensure that no institution is too big or too interconnected to fail, thereby subjecting every financial institution to the discipline of the marketplace. My testimony will summarize the progress to date in implementing the elements of this framework and will highlight specific areas of importance to their ultimate effectiveness.

In addition to discussing FDIC efforts to implement provisions of the Dodd-Frank Act that address key drivers of the recent financial crisis, I will also discuss future risks to our system which I believe must be proactively addressed by the Government. These include deeply flawed servicing practices which have yet to be corrected and the resulting overhang of foreclosures and looming litigation exposure which is further depressing home prices. Also of concern is interest rate risk and the impact sudden, volatile spikes in interest costs could have on banks and borrowers who rely upon them for credit.

Excessive Reliance on Debt and Financial Leverage

A healthy system of credit intermediation, where the surplus of savings is channeled toward its highest and best use by household and business borrowers, is critically important to the modern economy. Without access to credit, households cannot effectively smooth their lifetime consumption and businesses cannot undertake the capital investments necessary for economic growth. But a starting point for understanding the causes of the crisis and the changes that need to be made in our economic policies is recognition that the U.S. economy has long depended too much on debt and financial leverage to finance all types of economic activity.

In principle, debt and equity are substitute forms of financing for any type of economic activity. However, owing to the inherently riskier distribution of investment returns facing equity holders, equity is generally seen as a higher-cost form of financing. This perceived cost advantage for debt financing is further enhanced by the standard tax treatment of payments to debt holders, which are generally tax deductible, and equity holders, which are not. In light of these considerations, there is a tendency in good times for practically every economic constituency—from mortgage borrowers, to large corporations, to startup companies, to the financial institutions that lend to all of them—to seek higher leverage in pursuit of lower funding costs and higher rates of return on capital.

What is frequently lost when calculating the cost of debt financing are the external costs that are incurred when problems arise and borrowers cannot service the debt. As we have witnessed so many times in this crisis, the lack of a meaningful commitment of equity capital or "skin in the game" feeds subpar underwriting and imprudent borrower behavior that ultimately results in defaults, workouts, repossessions, or liquidations of repossessed assets in order to satisfy the claims of debt holders. These severe adjustments, which tend to occur with high frequency in economic downturns, impose very high costs on economic growth and our financial system. For example, foreclosures dislodge families from their homes, create high legal costs, and, when experienced *en masse,* tend to lower the values of nearby properties. Commercial bankruptcies impose losses on lenders and tend to remove assets from operating businesses and place them on the open market at liquidation prices. When financial institutions cannot meet their obligations, the result can be, at best, an interruption in their ability to serve as intermediary and, at worst, destabilizing runs that may extend across the financial system.

As demonstrated in the recent financial crisis, the social costs of debt financing are significantly higher than the private costs. When a household, business or financial company calculates the cost of financing its spending, it can no doubt lower its financing costs by substituting debt for equity—particularly when interest costs on debt are tax deductible. In good economic times, when few borrowers are forced to default on their obligations, more economic activity can take place at a lower cost of capital when debt is substituted for equity. However, the built-in private incentives for debt finance have long been observed to result in periods of excess leverage that contribute to financial crisis.

As Carmen Reinhart and Kenneth Rogoff describe in their 2009 book *This Time Is Different:*

> If there is one common theme to the vast range of crises we consider in this book, it is that excessive debt accumulation, whether it be by the Government, banks, corporations, or consumers, often poses greater systemic risks than it seems during a boom.[1]

This is precisely what was observed in the run up to the recent crisis. Mortgage lenders effectively loaned 100 percent or more against the value of many homes without underwriting practices that ensured borrowers could service the debt over the long term. Securitization structures were created that left the issuers with little or no residual interest, meaning that these deals were 100 percent debt financed. In addition, financial institutions not only frequently maximized the degree of on-balance-sheet leverage they could engineer; many further leveraged their operations by use of off-balance-sheet structures. For all intents and purposes, these off-balance-sheet structures were not subject to prudential supervision or regulatory capital requirements, but nonetheless enjoyed the implicit backing of the parent institution. These and many other financial practices employed in the years leading up to

---

[1] Reinhart, Carmen and Ken Rogoff. *This Time Is Different: Eight Centuries of Financial Folly.* Princeton: Princeton University Press. 2009. p. xxv.

the crisis made our core financial institutions and our entire financial system more vulnerable to financial shocks.

One important element to restraining financial leverage and enhancing the stability of our system is to strengthen the capital base of our largest financial institutions. The economic costs of the crisis were very much on the mind of the Basel Committee on Bank Supervision (BCBS) when it published the December 2009 paper that ultimately led to the Basel III capital accord.[2] Basel III is not perfect, but it is a great improvement over what came before. The accord not only addresses the insufficient quality and quantity of capital at the largest banks, but also requires capital buffers over and above the minimums so that the macroeconomy is not forced into a deleveraging spiral as banks breach these minimums during a period of high losses. Importantly, Basel III includes an international leverage requirement, a concept that was met with derision when I proposed it in 2006 but has now been embraced by the Basel Committee and the G–20. Finally, the Basel Committee has committed to additional capital and liquidity requirements for large, systemically important institutions that are higher, not lower, than those applicable to small banks. I firmly believe that this extra capital requirement must result in a meaningful cushion of tangible common equity capital. Moreover, I believe we should impose even higher capital charges on systemic entities until they have developed a resolution plan which has been approved as credible by their regulators. This would help ensure that large institutions in all BCBS member countries take seriously their obligation to demonstrate that they can be unwound in an orderly way should they fail.

As the Basel Committee has considered ways to strengthen capital requirements, the financial industry has repeatedly warned of economic harm if it is required to replace debt financing with equity. A 2010 report by the Institute of International Finance argued that the new, higher capital requirements and other reforms will raise bank funding costs, raise the cost of credit in the economy, and have a significant adverse impact on the path of economic activity.[3] But the bulk of credible research shows that higher capital requirements will have a relatively modest effect on the cost of credit and economic activity. These studies, conducted by economists at Harvard, Stanford, the University of Chicago, Bank of England and the Bank for International Settlements, account for not only the private costs and benefits of funding through equity capital, but also the social costs and benefits.[4] As we saw in 2008, when a crisis hits, highly leveraged financial institutions dramatically contract credit to conserve capital. FDIC-insured institutions as a group have reduced their balances of outstanding loans during nine of the last 10 quarters, and their unused loan commitments have declined by $2.5 trillion since the end of 2007. As we have seen, these procyclical lending policies can have a devastating impact on the real economy. As we move forward with important regulatory changes to improve institutional structures in finance, we must do so with an eye to what is in some ways a larger, built-in distortion in our financial system—excessive reliance on debt as opposed to equity.

Under the provisions of Section 941 in the Dodd-Frank Act, the FDIC and other agencies recently issued proposed rules to address the excessive risk-taking inherent in the originate-to-distribute model of lending and securitization. These rules require originators of asset-backed securities to retain not less than 5 percent of the credit risk of those securities, and define standards for Qualifying Residential Mortgages (QRMs) that will be exempt from risk retention when they are securitized. The proposal sets forth a flexible framework for issuers to achieve the 5 percent risk retention requirement. Together, the risk retention and QRM rules will help to limit leverage and better align financial incentives in asset-backed securitization, and give loan underwriting, administration, and servicing much larger roles in credit risk management. They are an important step in restoring investor confidence in

---

[2] See *http://www.bis.org/publ/bcbs164.htm.*

[3] See: "Interim Report on the Cumulative Impact on the Global Economy of Proposed Changes in the Banking Regulatory Framework," Institute of International Finance, June 2010. *http://www.iif.com/press/press+151.php.*

[4] See: Admati, Anat, Peter M. DeMarzo, Martin R. Hellwig and Paul Pfleiderer. "Fallacies, Irrelevant Facts, and Myths in the Discussion of Capital Regulation: Why Bank Equity is Not Expensive." Stanford Graduate School of Business Research Paper No. 2065, March 2011. *http://www.gsb.stanford.edu/news/research/Admati.etal.html.*

Hanson, Samuel, Anil Kashyap and Jeremy Stein. "A Macroprudential Approach to Financial Regulation." Working paper (draft), July 2010. *http://www.economics.harvard.edu/faculty/stein/files/JEP-macroprudential-July22-2010.pdf.*

Marcheggiano, Gilberto, David Miles and Jing Yang. "Optimal Bank Capital." London: Bank of England. External Monetary Policy Committee Unit Discussion Paper No. 31, April 2011. *http://www.bankofengland.co.uk/publications/externalmpcpapers/extmpcpaper0031revised.pdf.*

a market where the volume of issuance remains depressed in the aftermath of the crisis.

Ending Too Big to Fail by Facilitating Orderly Resolutions

One of the most powerful inducements toward excess leverage and institutional risk-taking in the period leading up to the crisis was the lack of effective market discipline on the largest financial institutions that were considered by the market to be "too big to fail." The financial crisis of 2008 centered on the so-called shadow banking system—a network of large-bank affiliates, special-purpose vehicles, and nonbank financial companies that existed not only largely outside of the prudential supervision and capital requirements that apply to federally insured depository institutions in the United States, but also largely outside of the FDIC's process for resolving failed insured financial institutions through receivership.

Several large, complex U.S. financial companies at the center of the 2008 crisis could not be wound down in an orderly manner when they became nonviable. Major segments of their operations were subject to the commercial bankruptcy code, as opposed to bank receivership laws, or they were located abroad and therefore outside of U.S. jurisdiction. In the heat of the crisis, policymakers in several instances resorted to bailouts instead of letting these firms collapse into bankruptcy because they feared that the losses generated in a failure would cascade through the financial system, freezing financial markets and stopping the economy in its tracks.

As it happened, these fears were realized when Lehman Brothers—a large, complex nonbank financial company—filed for bankruptcy on September 15, 2008. Anticipating the complications of a long, costly bankruptcy process, counterparties across the financial system reacted to the Lehman failure by running for the safety of cash and other Government obligations. Subsequent days and weeks saw the collapse of interbank lending and commercial paper issuance, and a near complete disintermediation of the shadow banking system. The only remedy was massive intervention on the part of governments around the world, which pumped equity capital into banks and other financial companies, guaranteed certain non-deposit liabilities, and extended credit backed by a wide range of illiquid assets to banks and nonbank firms alike. Even with these emergency measures, the economic consequences of the crisis have been enormous.

Under a regime of "too big to fail," the largest U.S. banks and other financial companies have every incentive to render themselves so large, so complex, and so opaque that no policymaker would dare risk letting them fail in a crisis. With the benefit of this implicit safety net, these institutions have been insulated from the normal discipline of the marketplace that applies to smaller banks and practically every other private company.

Having recently seen the nation's largest financial institutions receive hundreds of billions of dollars in taxpayer assistance, the market appears to expect more of the same going forward. In February, Moody's reported that its ratings on the senior unsecured debt of eight large U.S. banking organizations received an average "uplift" of 2.2 ratings notches because of the expectation of future Government support. Meanwhile, the largest banks continue to enjoy a large competitive advantage over community banks in funding markets. In the fourth quarter of last year, the average interest cost of funding earning assets for banks with more than $100 billion in assets was about half the average for community banks with less than $1 billion in assets. Indeed, I would also argue that well-managed large banks are disadvantaged by "too big to fail" as it narrows the funding advantage they would otherwise enjoy over weaker competitors.

Unless reversed, we could expect to see more concentration of market power in the hands of the largest institutions, more complexity in financial structures and relationships, more risk-taking at the expense of the public, and, in due time, another financial crisis. However, the Dodd-Frank Act introduces several measures in Title I and Title II that, together, provide the basis for a new resolution framework designed to render any financial institution "resolvable," thereby ending the subsidization of risktaking that took place prior to these reforms.

The new SIFI resolution framework has three basic elements. First, the new Financial Stability Oversight Council, chaired by the Treasury Secretary and made up of the other financial regulatory agencies, is responsible for designating SIFIs based on criteria that are now being established by regulation. Once designated, the SIFIs will be subject to heightened supervision by the Federal Reserve Board and required to maintain detailed resolution plans that demonstrate that they are resolvable under bankruptcy—not bailout—if they should run into severe financial distress. Finally, the law provides for a third alternative to bankruptcy or bailout—an Orderly Liquidation Authority, or OLA, that gives the FDIC many of the same trustee powers over SIFIs that we have long used to manage failed-bank receiverships.

I would like to clarify some misconceptions about these authorities and highlight some priorities I see for their effective implementation.

SIFI Designation It is important at the outset to clarify that being designated as a SIFI will in no way confer a competitive advantage by anointing an institution as "too big to fail." The reality is that SIFIs will be subject to heightened supervision and higher capital requirements. They will also be required to maintain resolution plans and could be required to restructure their operations if they cannot demonstrate that they are resolvable. In light of these significant regulatory requirements, the FDIC has detected absolutely no interest on the part of any financial institution in being named a SIFI. Indeed, many institutions are vigorously lobbying against such a designation.

We believe that the ability of an institution to be resolved in a bankruptcy process without systemic impact should be a key consideration in designating a firm as a SIFI. Further, we believe that the concept of resolvability is consistent with several of the statutory factors that the FSOC is required to consider in designating a firm as systemic, those being size, interconnectedness, lack of substitutes and leverage. If an institution can be reliably deemed resolvable in bankruptcy by the regulators, and operates within the confines of the leverage requirements established by bank regulators, then it should not be designated as a SIFI.

What concerns us, however, is the lack of information we might have about potential SIFIs that may impede our ability to make an accurate determination of resolvability before the fact. This potential blind spot in the designation process raises the specter of a "deathbed designation" of a SIFI, whereby the FDIC would be required to resolve the firm under a Title II resolution without the benefit of a resolution plan or the ability to conduct advance planning, both of which are so critical to an orderly resolution. This situation, which would put the resolution authority in the worst possible position, should be avoided at all costs. Thus, we need to be able to collect detailed information on a limited number of potential SIFIs as part of the designation process. We should provide the industry with some clarity about which firms will be expected to provide the FSOC with this additional information, using simple and transparent metrics such as firm size, similar to the approach used for bank holding companies under the Dodd-Frank Act. This should reduce some of the mystery surrounding the process and should eliminate any market concern about which firms the FSOC has under its review. In addition, no one should jump to the conclusion that by asking for additional information, the FSOC has preordained a firm to be "systemic." It is likely that, after we gather additional information and learn more about these firms, relatively few of them will be viewed as systemic, especially if the firms can demonstrate their resolvability in bankruptcy at this stage of the process.

The FSOC issued an Advanced Notice of Proposed Rulemaking (ANPR) last October and a Notice of Proposed Rulemaking (NPR) on January 26, 2011 describing the processes and procedures that will inform the FSOC's designation of nonbank financial companies under the Dodd-Frank Act. We recognize the concerns raised by several commenters to the FSOC's ANPR and NPR about the lack of detail and clarity surrounding the designation process. This lack of specificity and certainty in the designation process is itself a burden on the industry and an impediment to prompt and effective implementation of the designation process. That is why it is important that the FSOC move forward and develop some hard metrics to guide the SIFI designation process. The sooner we develop and publish these metrics, the sooner this needless uncertainty can be resolved. The FSOC is in the process of developing further clarification of the metrics for comment that will provide more specificity as to the measures and approaches we are considering using for designating non-bank firms.

SIFI Resolution Plans A major—and somewhat underestimated—improvement in the SIFI resolution process is the requirement in the Dodd-Frank Act for firms designated as SIFIs to maintain satisfactory resolution plans that demonstrate their resolvability in a crisis.

When a large, complex financial institution gets into trouble, time is the enemy. The larger, more complex, and more interconnected a financial company is, the longer it takes to assemble a full and accurate picture of its operations and develop a resolution strategy. By requiring detailed resolution plans in advance, and authorizing an onsite FDIC team to conduct pre-resolution planning, the SIFI resolution framework regains the informational advantage that was lacking in the crisis of 2008.

The FDIC recently released a paper detailing how the filing of resolution plans, the ability to conduct advance planning, and other elements of the framework could have dramatically changed the outcome if they had been available in the case of

Lehman.[5] Under the new SIFI resolution framework, the FDIC should have a continuous presence at all designated SIFIs, working with the firms and reviewing their resolution plans as part of their normal course of business. Thus, our presence will in no way be seen as a signal of distress. Instead, it is much more likely to provide a stabilizing influence that encourages management to more fully consider the downside consequences of its actions, to the benefit of the institution and the stability of the system as a whole.

The law also authorizes the FDIC and the Federal Reserve Board to require, if necessary, changes in the structure or activities of these institutions to ensure that they meet the standard of being resolvable in a crisis. In my opinion, the ultimate effectiveness of the SIFI resolution framework will depend in large part on the willingness of the FDIC and the Federal Reserve Board to actively use this authority to require organizational changes that promote the ability to resolve SIFIs.

As currently structured, many large banks and nonbank SIFIs maintain thousands of subsidiaries and manage their activities within business lines that cross many different organizational structures and regulatory jurisdictions. This can make it very difficult to implement an orderly resolution of one part of the company without triggering a costly collapse of the entire company. To solve this problem, the FDIC and the Federal Reserve Board must be willing to insist on organizational changes that better align business lines and legal entities well before a crisis occurs. Unless these structures are rationalized and simplified in advance, there is a real danger that their complexity could make a SIFI resolution far more costly and more difficult than it needs to be.

Such changes are also likely to have collateral benefits for the firm's management in the short run. A simplified organizational structure will put management in a better position to understand and monitor risks and the inter-relationships among business lines, addressing what many see as a major challenge that contributed to the crisis. That is why—well before the test of another major crisis—we must define high informational standards for resolution plans and be willing to insist on organizational changes where necessary in order to ensure that SIFIs meet the standard of resolvability.

Orderly Liquidation Authority (OLA) There also appear to be a number of popular misconceptions as to the nature of the Orderly Liquidation Authority. Some have called it a bailout mechanism, while others see it as a fire sale that will destroy the value of receivership assets. Neither is true. While it is positioned as a backup plan in cases where bankruptcy would threaten to result in wider financial disorder, the OLA is actually a better-suited framework for resolving claims against failed financial institutions. It is a transparent process that operates under fixed rules that prohibit any bailout of shareholders and creditors or any other type of political considerations, which can be a legitimate concern in the case of an ad-hoc emergency rescue program. Not only would the OLA work faster and preserve value better than bankruptcy, but the regulatory authorities who will administer the OLA are in a far better position to coordinate with foreign regulators in the failure of an institution with significant international operations.

The FDIC has made considerable progress in forging bilateral agreements with other countries that will facilitate orderly cross-border resolutions. In addition, we currently co-chair the Cross Border Resolutions Group of the Basel Committee. It is worth noting that not a single other advanced country plans to rely on bankruptcy to resolve large, international financial companies. Most are implementing special resolution regimes similar to the OLA. Under the OLA, we can buy time, if necessary, and preserve franchise value by running the institution as a bridge bank, and then eventually sell it in parts or as a whole. It is a powerful tool that greatly enhances our ability to provide continuity and minimize losses in financial institution failures.

While the OLA strictly prohibits bailouts, the FDIC could use the authority to conduct advance planning, to temporarily operate and fund the institution under Government control to preserve its value as a going concern, and to quickly pay partial recoveries to creditors through advance dividends, as we have long done in failed-bank receiverships. The result would be a faster resolution of claims against the failed institution, smaller losses for creditors, reduced impact on the wider financial system, and an end to the cycle of bailouts.

The history of the recent crisis is replete with examples of missed opportunities to sell or recapitalize troubled institutions before they failed. But with bailout now off the table, management will have a greater incentive to bring in an acquirer or new investors before failure, and shareholders and creditors will have more incen-

---

[5] "The Orderly Liquidation of Lehman Brothers Holdings under the Dodd-Frank Act," *FDIC Quarterly*, Vol. 5, No. 2, 2011. *http://www.fdic.gov/regulations/reform/lehman.html.*

tive to go along with such a plan in order to salvage the value of their claims. These new incentives to be more proactive in dealing with problem SIFIs will reduce their incidence of outright failure and also lessen the risk of systemic effects arising from such failures.

In summary, the measures authorized under the Dodd-Frank Act to create a new, more effective SIFI resolution authority will go far toward reducing leverage and risktaking in our financial system by subjecting every financial institution, no matter its size or degree of interconnectedness, to the discipline of the marketplace. Prompt and effective implementation of these measures will be essential to constraining the tendency toward excess leverage in our financial system and our economy, and in creating incentives for safe and sound practices that will promote financial stability in the future. In light of the ongoing concern about the burden arising from regulatory reform, I think it is worth mentioning that none of these measures to promote the resolvability of SIFIs will have any impact at all on small and midsized financial institutions except to reduce the competitive disadvantage they have long encountered with regard to large, complex institutions. There are clear limits to what can be accomplished by prescriptive regulation. That is why promoting the ability of market forces to constrain risk taking will be essential if we are to achieve a more stable financial system in the years ahead.

Macroprudential Supervision

Beyond the regulatory steps to ensure that the core of our financial system is more resilient to shocks, we also need a regulatory process that is much more attuned to developing macro risks and how they may affect systemically important institutions. This task, generally referred to as macroprudential supervision, has been assigned collectively to the FSOC. Among other things, the Dodd-Frank Act directs the FSOC to facilitate regulatory coordination and information sharing among its member agencies regarding policy development, rulemaking, supervisory information, and reporting requirements. The FSOC is currently working on a number of fronts to better identify and respond to emerging risks to our financial system. The Dodd-Frank Act requires that the FSOC produce annual financial stability reports and that each voting member submit a signed statement stating whether the member believes that the FSOC is taking all reasonable actions to mitigate systemic risk.

The success of the FSOC in accomplishing its goals will depend on the diligence and seriousness about those goals on the part of the members. So far, the FDIC believes that the FSOC member agencies are committed to the success of the Council, and we have been impressed with the quality of staff work in preparation for the meetings as well as the rigor and candor of the discussions. We also believe that the FSOC has provided an efficient means for agencies to jointly write rules required by the Dodd-Frank Act and to seek input from other agencies on independent rules. The FDIC strongly supports the FSOC's collective approach to identifying and responding to risks. Conducting multidisciplinary discussion and review of issues that cut across markets and regulatory jurisdictions is a highly effective way of identifying and mitigating risks, even before they become systemic.

In response to the Committee's request for additional information on potential risks to the financial stability of the United States, I would like to offer some observations on two specific topics: problems in mortgage servicing documentation and interest rate risk at financial institutions in light of rapid growth in U.S. Government debt.

Problems in Mortgage Servicing Documentation Mortgage servicing is a serious area of concern and one which the FDIC identified years ago. As early as the Spring of 2007, we were speaking to the need for mortgage servicers to build programs and resources to restructure troubled mortgages on a broad scale. When, over a year ago, we proposed a new safe harbor for bank-sponsored securitizations, we included requirements for effective loss mitigation and compensation incentives that reflect the increased costs associated with servicing troubled loans. In my testimony at the end of last year, in the wake of mounting problems with mortgage servicing and foreclosure documentation at some of the nation's largest servicing companies, I emphasized the need for specific changes to address the most glaring deficiencies in servicing practices, including a single point of contact for distressed borrowers, appropriate write-downs of second liens, and servicer compensation structures that are aligned with effective loss mitigation.

The FDIC believes that mortgage servicing documentation problems are yet another example of the implications of lax underwriting standards and misaligned incentives in the mortgage process. In particular, the traditional fixed level of compensation for loan servicing proved wholly inadequate to cover expenses required to implement the high-touch and specialized servicing on the scale needed to deal with the huge increase in problem mortgage loans caused by risky lending practices.

We now know that the housing bust and the financial crisis arose from a historic breakdown in U.S. mortgage markets. While emergency policies enacted at the height of the crisis have helped to stabilize the financial system and plant the seeds for recovery, mortgage markets remain deeply mired in credit distress and private securitization markets remain largely frozen. Serious weaknesses identified with mortgage servicing and foreclosure documentation have introduced further uncertainty into an already fragile market.

The FDIC is especially concerned about a number of related problems with servicing and foreclosure documentation. "Robo-signing" is the use of highly automated processes by some large servicers to generate affidavits in the foreclosure process without the affiant having thoroughly reviewed facts contained in the affidavit or having the affiant's signature witnessed in accordance with State laws. The other problem involves some servicers' inability to establish their legal standing to foreclose, since under current industry practices, they may not be in possession of the necessary documentation required under State law. These are not really separate issues; they are simply the most visible of a host of related problems that we continue to see, and that have been discussed in testimony to this Committee over the past several years.[6]

As you know, even though the FDIC is not the primary Federal regulator for the largest loan servicers, our examiners participated with other regulators in horizontal reviews of these servicers, as well as two companies that facilitate the loan securitization process. In these reviews, Federal regulators cited "pervasive" misconduct in foreclosures and significant weaknesses in mortgage servicing processes.

Unfortunately, the horizontal review only looked at processing issues. Since the focus was so narrow, we do not yet really know the full extent of the problem. The Consent Order, discussed further below, requires these servicers to retain independent, third parties to review residential mortgage foreclosure actions and report the results of those reviews back to the regulators. However, we have heard concerns regarding the thoroughness and transparency of these reviews, and we continue to press for a comprehensive approach to this "look back."

I want to underscore that the housing market cannot heal and begin to recover until this problem is tackled in a forthright manner and resolved. As the insurer of the deposits at these banks, we will not know the full extent of the problems and potential litigation exposure they face until we have a thorough review of foreclosed loan files.

These servicing problems continue to present significant operational risks to mortgage servicers. Servicers have already encountered challenges to their legal standing to foreclose on individual mortgages. More broadly, investors in securitizations have raised concerns about whether loan documentation for transferred mortgages fully conforms to applicable laws and the pooling and servicing agreements governing the securitizations. If investor challenges to documentation prove meritorious, they could result in "putbacks" of large volumes of defaulted mortgages to originating institutions.

There have been some settlements regarding loan buyback claims with the GSEs and some institutions have reserved for some of this exposure; however, a significant amount of this exposure has yet to be quantified. Given the weaknesses in the processes that have been uncovered during the review, there appears to be the potential for further losses. Litigation risk is not limited to just securitizations. Flawed mortgage banking processes have potentially infected millions of foreclosures, and the damages to be assessed against these operations could be significant and take years to materialize. The extent of the loss cannot be determined until there is a comprehensive review of the loan files and documentation of the process dealing with problem loans. This is one reason that I have urged the servicers and the State Attorneys General to reach a global settlement. We believe that the FSOC needs to consider the full range of potential exposure and the related impact on the industry and the real economy. FSOC members have a range of relevant expertise in regulating the various participants and processes associated with the foreclosure problem. We need to fully understand the potential risks and develop appropriate solutions to address these deficiencies.

In April 2011, the Federal banking agencies ordered fourteen large mortgage servicers to overhaul their mortgage-servicing processes and controls, and to compensate borrowers harmed financially by wrongdoing or negligence. The enforcement orders were only a first step in setting out a framework for these large institu-

---

[6] Hearings before the U.S. Senate Committee on Banking, Housing, and Urban Affairs: July 16, 2009; November 16, 2010; December 1, 2010.

tions to remedy deficiencies and to identify homeowners harmed as a result of servicer errors. The enforcement orders do not preclude additional supervisory actions or the imposition of civil money penalties. Also, a collaborative settlement effort continues between the State Attorneys General and Federal regulators led by the U.S. Department of Justice. It is critically important that lenders fix these problems soon to remedy the foreclosure backlog, which has become the single largest impediment to the recovery of U.S. housing markets.

Interest Rate Risk At the end of 2010, the U.S. domestic financial and nonfinancial sectors owed credit market debt totaling just over $50 trillion, a figure that is some 92 percent higher in nominal terms than it was just a decade ago. Much of this debt was issued during the recent period of historically low interest rates. Not only did the Federal Open Market Committee lower the Federal funds target rate to a 49-year low of 1 percent for a 12-month period in 2003 and 2004, but it has continuously held the fed funds target rate at an all-time low of 0 to 0.25 percent since December 2008. Long-term rates have also been at historic lows during this period. The average yield on 10-year Treasury bonds over the past decade was the lowest for any 10-year period since the mid-1960s. It is clear that the most likely direction of interest rates from today's historic lows is upward. The question is how far and how fast interest rates will rise, and how ready lenders and borrowers will be to cope with higher rates of interest.

In theory, rising interest rates will represent a zero-sum game in which the higher interest payments demanded of borrowers will be perfectly offset by the higher interest income of savers in the economy. In practice, however, rising interest rates can impose considerable distress on borrowers or lenders depending on how debts are structured. Floating-rate or short-term borrowers will see their interest costs rise over time with the level of nominal interest rates. Not only will this have an effect on their bottom line, but higher borrowing costs could lead them to demand a lower volume of credit that they did at lower rates. However, in the case of long-term, fixed-rate debt, it is often the lender that suffers a capital loss, a decline in operating income, or both as interest rates rise. Depository institutions are traditionally vulnerable to losses of this type in times of rising interest rates because their liabilities are typically of shorter duration than their assets.

Given the prospect for higher interest rates going forward, effective management of interest rate risk will be an essential priority for financial institution risk managers in coming years. Unfortunately, there is a tendency during periods of high credit losses, such as the past few years, for risk managers to focus their attention mostly on credit risk, and to divert their attention away from interest rate risk at just the time that their portfolio is becoming more vulnerable to rising rates. It was just this type of inattention to the implication of rising interest rates that contributed to growth in structured notes in the early to mid-1990s, when a number of banks took on complex and interest-rate-sensitive investments that they did not understand in search of higher yields.

The FDIC has been actively addressing the need for heightened measures to manage interest rate risk at this critical stage of the interest rate cycle. In January 2010 we issued a Financial Institution Letter (FIL) clarifying our expectations that FDIC-supervised institutions will manage interest rate risk using policies and procedures commensurate with their complexity, business model, risk profile, and scope of operations.[7] That same month, the FDIC hosted a Symposium on Interest Rate Risk Management that brought together leading practitioners in the field to discuss the challenges facing the industry in this area.[8]

Effective management of interest rate risk assumes a heightened importance in light of the recent high rates of growth in U.S. Government debt, the yield on which represents the benchmark for determining private interest rates all along the yield curve. Total U.S. Federal debt has doubled in the past 7 years to over $14 trillion, or more than $100,000 for every American household. This growth in Federal borrowing is the result of both the temporary effects of the recession on Federal revenues and outlays and a long-term structural deficit related to Federal entitlement programs. In 2010, combined expenditures on Social Security, Medicare and Medicaid accounted for 44 percent of primary Federal spending, up from 27 percent in 1975. The Congressional Budget Office (CBO) projects that annual entitlement spending could triple in real terms by 2035, to $4.5 trillion in 2010 dollars. According to CBO projections, Federal debt held by the public could rise from a level equal to 62 percent of gross domestic product in 2010 to an unsustainable 185 percent in 2035.

---

[7] See *http://www.fdic.gov/news/news/financial/2010/fil10002.html.*
[8] See *http://www.fdic.gov/news/conferences/symposium_irr_meeting.html.*

The U.S. has long enjoyed a unique status among sovereign issuers by virtue of its economic strength, its political stability, and the size and liquidity of its capital markets. Accordingly, international investors have long viewed U.S. Treasury securities as a haven, particularly during times of financial market uncertainty. However, as the amount of publicly held U.S. debt continues to rise, and as a rising portion of that debt comes to be held by the foreign sector (about half as of September 2010), there is a risk that investor sentiment could at some point turn away from dollar assets in general and U.S. Treasury obligations in particular.

With more than 70 percent of U.S. Treasury obligations held by private investors scheduled to mature in the next 5 years, an erosion of investor confidence would likely lead to sharp increases in Government and private borrowing costs. As recent events in Greece and Ireland have shown, such a reversal in investor sentiment could occur suddenly and with little warning. If investors were to similarly lose confidence in U.S. public debt, the result could be higher and more volatile long-term interest rates, capital losses for holders of Treasury instruments, and higher funding costs for depository institutions. Household and business borrowers of all types would pay more for credit, resulting in a slowdown in the rate of economic growth if not outright recession.

Over the past year, the U.S. fiscal outlook has assumed a much larger importance in policy discussions and the political process. Members of Congress, the Administration, and the Presidential Commission on Fiscal Responsibility and Reform have all offered proposals for addressing the long-term fiscal situation, but political consensus on a solution appears elusive at this time. It is likely that the capital markets themselves will continue to apply increasing pressure until a credible solution is reached. Already, the cost for bond investors and others to purchase insurance against a default by the U.S. Government has risen from just 2 basis points in January 2007 to a current level of 42 basis points.

Financial stability critically depends on public and investor confidence. Developing policies that will clearly demonstrate the sustainability of the U.S. fiscal situation will be of utmost importance in ensuring a smooth transition from today's historically low interest rates to the higher levels of interest rates that are inevitable in coming years. Government policies to slow the growth in U.S. Government debt will be essential to lessening the impact of this shock and reducing the likelihood that it will result in a costly new round of financial instability.

Conclusion

The inherent instability of financial markets cannot be regulated out of existence. Nevertheless, many of the Dodd-Frank Act reforms, if properly implemented, can make the core of our financial system more resilient to shocks by restoring market discipline, limiting financial leverage, and making our regulatory process more proactive in identifying and addressing emerging risks to financial stability.

Working together on these reforms, regulators and the financial services industry can improve financial stability and minimize the severity of future crises. With this in mind, the FDIC will continue to carefully and seriously perform its duties as a voting member of FSOC, expeditiously complete rulemakings, and actively exercise its new authorities related to orderly liquidation authority and resolution plans.

The stakes are extremely high. To continue the pre-crisis status quo would be to sanction a new and dangerous form of state capitalism, where the market assumes that large, complex, and powerful financial companies are in line to receive generous Government subsidies in times of financial distress. The result could be a continuation of the market distortions that led to the recent crisis, with all of the attendant implications for risk-taking, competitive structures, and financial instability. In order to avoid this outcome, we must follow through to fully implement the authorities under the Dodd-Frank Act and thereby restore market discipline to our financial system.

Finally, I would like to emphasize that many of the problems and challenges confronting the financial sector are beyond the control of the regulatory community. Obviously, restoration of fiscal discipline is the province of the executive and legislative branches. Similarly, tax code changes that could reduce or eliminate incentives for leverage by financial institutions and borrowers must be acted upon by Congress. So it is my hope that Senate Banking Committee members can play a leadership role in making sure that the ongoing budget and tax discussions include consideration of the ramifications of different policy options for the stability of the financial system going forward.

Thank you again for the opportunity to testify about these critically important issues. I would be pleased to answer any questions.

PREPARED STATEMENT OF JOHN WALSH
Acting Comptroller of the Currency
Office of The Comptroller of the Currency

May 12, 2011

I. Introduction

Chairman Johnson, Ranking Member Shelby, and Members of the Committee, I appreciate the opportunity to provide an update on the Office of the Comptroller of the Currency's (OCC) implementation of the Dodd-Frank Act, and in particular, those provisions related to monitoring systemic risk and promoting financial stability, and on the operations and activities of the Financial Stability Oversight Council (FSOC).*

As I described before this Committee in February, the OCC is actively working on approximately 85 Dodd-Frank Act projects. Broadly speaking, these projects fall into three major categories: our extensive efforts to prepare to integrate the OTS's staff and supervisory responsibilities into the OCC, and to facilitate the transfer of specific functions to the CFPB; our consultative role in a variety of rulemakings being undertaken by other agencies; and our own rule-writing responsibilities for implementing key provisions of the Act.

There are numerous provisions within the Dodd-Frank Act that address systemic issues that contributed to, or that accentuated and amplified the effects of, the recent financial crisis. These provisions include those that address flawed incentive structures and are designed to constrain excessive risk-taking activities; those that strengthen the resiliency of individual firms to financial shocks through stronger capital requirements and more robust stress-testing requirements; and those that address previous regulatory gaps, including the supervision of systemically important non-bank financial companies, and the orderly resolution of large banking organizations and non-bank financial companies in the event of failure. The OCC, along with other financial regulators, has rule-writing authority for many of these provisions, and I am pleased to report that we are making good progress on our rulemaking efforts on these critical provisions. Since I last appeared before the Committee, the OCC and other agencies have issued notices of proposed rulemaking on the following provisions:

- Section 956, that prohibits incentive-based compensation arrangements that encourage inappropriate risk taking by covered financial institutions and are deemed to be excessive, or that may lead to material losses;

- Section 941, that addresses adverse market incentive structures by requiring a securitizer to retain a portion of the credit risk on assets it securitizes, unless those assets are originated in accordance with conservative underwriting standards established by the agencies in their implementing regulations;

- Sections 731 and 764, that establish, for security-based swap dealers and major swap participants, capital requirements and margin requirements on swaps that are not cleared.

In my role as a director of the Federal Deposit Insurance Corporation, I also have approved the issuance of the FDIC's recent rulemakings under Title II of the Dodd-Frank Act related to its orderly liquidation authority.

Certainly one of the key provisions of the Dodd-Frank Act as it relates to systemic risk and financial stability, and the focus of my testimony today, is the creation of the Financial Stability Oversight Council. The FSOC brings together the views, perspectives, and expertise of Treasury and all of the financial regulatory agencies to identify, monitor, and respond to systemic risk. As my testimony will detail, Congress has set forth very specific mandates regarding the role and function of FSOC in a number of areas, but certainly the overarching mission that Congress assigned to the Council is to identify risks to the financial stability of the United States, to promote market discipline, and to respond to emerging threats to the stability of the U.S. financial system.[1]

I believe FSOC enhances the agencies' collective ability to fulfill this critical mission by establishing a formal, structured process to exchange information and to probe and discuss the implications of emerging market, industry, and regulatory developments for the stability of the financial system. Through the work of its committees and staff, FSOC also is providing a structured framework and metrics for track-

---

*Statement Required by 12 U.S.C. § 250: The views expressed herein are those of the Office of the Comptroller of the Currency and do not necessarily represent the views of the President.
[1] See Section 112(a)(1).

ing and assessing key trends and potential systemic risks. I would note that FSOC's activities and mandates complement the separate roles, responsibilities, and authorities that the OCC and other financial regulators have with respect to implementing specific provisions of the Dodd-Frank Act and more broadly in monitoring risks and conditions within the financial industry. For example, the OCC will continue to use our National Risk Committee and the insights we gain through our on- and offsite supervisory activities to identify, monitor, and respond to emerging risks to the banking system. We will, of course, also continue to share our insights and expertise with the FSOC in its deliberations.

While the process and systems that FSOC has created are positive steps forward, I would offer two cautionary notes.

First, FSOC's success ultimately will depend not on its structure, processes, or metrics, but on the willingness and ability of FSOC members and staff to engage in frank and candid discussions about emerging risks, issues, and institutions. These discussions are not always pleasant as they can challenge one's longstanding views or ways of approaching a problem. But being able to voice dissenting views or assessments will be critical in ensuring that we are seeing and considering the full scope of issues. In addition, these discussions often will involve information or findings that will need further verification; that are extremely sensitive either to the operation of a given firm or market segment; or if misconstrued, that could undermine public and investor confidence and thereby create or exacerbate a potentially systemic problem. As a result, the OCC believes that it is critical that these types of deliberations—both at the Council and staff level—be conducted in a manner that assures their confidential nature.

Second, even with fullest deliberations and best data, it is inevitable that there will still be unforeseen events that may result in substantial risks to the system, markets, or groups of institutions. Business and credit cycles will continue. It is not realistic to expect that FSOC will be able to prevent such occurrences. However, FSOC will provide a mechanism to communicate, coordinate, and respond to such events so as to help contain and limit their impact, including, where applicable, the resolution of systemically important firms.

The remainder of my testimony focuses on FSOC, with a discussion of the specific mandates Congress has given to the FSOC; its structure and operations; and finally its achievements to date.

II. FSOC's Statutory Mandates

FSOC's primary mission, as set forth in section 112 of the Dodd-Frank Act is to:

1) Identify risks to the financial stability of the United States that could arise from the material financial distress or failure, or ongoing activities, of large, interconnected bank holding companies or non-bank financial companies, or that could arise outside the financial services marketplace;

2) Promote market discipline by eliminating expectations on the part of shareholders, creditors, and counterparties of such companies that the Government will shield them from losses in the event of failure; and

3) Respond to emerging threats to the stability of the U.S. financial system. The Dodd-Frank Act assigns FSOC a variety of roles and responsibilities to carry out its core mission[2] that are described in greater detail throughout the Act. In some cases, the Council has direct and ultimate responsibility to make decisions and take actions. Most notable of these is the authority given to FSOC to determine that certain non-bank financial companies shall be supervised by the Federal Reserve Board and subject to heightened prudential standards, after an assessment as to whether material financial distress at such companies would pose a threat to the financial stability of the United States.[3] Similarly, the Council is charged with the responsibility to identify systemically important financial market utilities and payment, clearing, and settlement activities.

In addition, affirmation by two-thirds of the Council is required in those cases where the Federal Reserve determines that a large, systemically important financial institution poses a grave threat to the financial stability of the United States such that limitations on the company's ability to merge, offer certain products, or engage in certain activities are warranted, or if those actions are insufficient to mitigate

---

[2] See section 112.
[3] See section 113(a)(1).

risks, the company should be required to sell or otherwise transfer assets or off-balance items to unaffiliated entities.[4]

The FSOC is also empowered to collect information from member agencies and other Federal and State financial regulatory agencies as necessary in order to monitor risks to the financial system, and to direct the Office of Financial Research under the Treasury Department to collect information directly from bank holding companies and non-bank financial companies.[5]

The Dodd-Frank Act also identified specific areas where the Council is to provide additional studies, including recommendations, to inform future regulatory actions. These include studies of the financial sector concentration limit applicable to large financial firms imposed by the Act;[6] proprietary trading and hedge fund activities;[7] the treatment of secured creditors in the resolution process;[8] and contingent capital for nonbank financial companies.[9]

In other areas, the Council's role is more of an advisory body to the primary financial regulators. For example, the Dodd-Frank Act requires the Council to make recommendations to the Federal Reserve concerning the establishment of heightened prudential standards for risk-based capital, liquidity, and a variety of other risk management and disclosure matters for non-bank financial companies and large, interconnected bank holding companies supervised by the Board.[10] The Federal Reserve, however, retains the authority to supervise and set standards for these firms.[11] The Council is also given authority to review, and as appropriate, may submit comments to the Securities and Exchange Commission and any standard-setting body with respect to an existing or proposed accounting principle, standard, or procedure.[12] Similarly, FSOC is assigned a consultative role in several rulemakings by member agencies, including for all of the rules that the FDIC writes pursuant to Title II of the Dodd-Frank Act regarding the orderly liquidation of failing financial companies that pose a significant risk to the financial stability of the United States. The Council may also recommend to member agencies general supervisory priorities and principles [13] and issue nonbinding recommendations for resolving jurisdictional disputes among member agencies.[14]

The varied roles and responsibilities that Congress assigned to the Council appropriately balance and reflect the desire to enhance regulatory coordination for systemically important firms and activities while preserving and respecting the independent authorities and accountability of primary supervisors. For example, under section 120, FSOC has the authority to recommend to the primary financial agencies that they apply new or heightened standards and safeguards for a financial activity or practice conducted by firms under their respective jurisdictions should the Council determine that the conduct of such an activity or practice could create or increase the risk of significant liquidity, credit, or other problems spreading among financial institutions, the U.S. financial markets, or low-income, minority, or underserved communities. Each agency retains the authority to not follow such recommendations if circumstances warrant and the agency explains its reasons in writing to the Council.

III. FSOC Structure and Operations

The FSOC has established committees and subcommittees comprised of staff from the member agencies to help carry out its responsibilities and authorities. These groups report up through a Deputies Committee of senior staff from each agency. The Deputies Committee generally meets on a bi-weekly basis to monitor work progress, review pending items requiring consultative input, discuss emerging systemic issues, and help establish priorities and agendas for the Council. A Systemic Risk Committee and subcommittees on institutions and markets provide structure for the FSOC's analysis of emerging threats to financial stability. Five standing functional committees support the FSOC's work on the following specific provisions assigned to the Council: designations of systemically important non-bank financial companies and of financial market utilities and payment, clearing, and settlement activities; heightened prudential standards; orderly liquidation authority and resolu-

---

[4] See section 121.
[5] See section 112.
[6] See section 622.
[7] See section 619.
[8] See section 215.
[9] See section 115.
[10] See section 112.
[11] See section 165.
[12] See section 112.
[13] See section 112.
[14] See section 119.

tion plans; and data collection and analysis. OCC staff are active participants and contributors to each of these committees. In addition to these groups, the FSOC also has an informal interagency legal staff working group that assists with various legal issues concerning the Council's operations and proceedings. Each of these committees and work groups is supported by staff from Treasury.

IV. Accomplishments To Date

Since its creation with the enactment of the Dodd-Frank Act, the Council has met four times, with meetings occurring approximately every 6 weeks. As with any newly formed body, a large proportion of the Council's early work was focused on the necessary administrative rules and procedures that will govern the Council's operations. In addition to the creation and staffing of the aforementioned committees, this work has included the adoption of a transparency policy for Council meetings; rules of organization that describe the Council's authorities, organizational structure, and the rules by which the Council takes action; establishment of a framework for coordinating regulations or actions required by the Dodd-Frank Act to be completed in consultation with the Council; approval of an initial operating budget for the Council; and the publication of a proposed rulemaking to implement the Freedom of Information Act requirements as it pertains to Council activities.

The Council has also taken action on a number of substantive items directly related to its core mission and mandates. These include the following:

- *Study and Recommendations Regarding Concentration Limits on Large Financial Companies* [15]—Section 622 of the Dodd-Frank Act establishes a financial sector concentration limit that generally prohibits a financial company from merging, consolidating with, or acquiring another company if the resulting company's consolidated liabilities would exceed 10 percent of the aggregate consolidated liabilities of all financial companies. Pursuant to the mandate in section 622, on January 18, 2011, the Council approved the publication of this study of the extent to which the concentration limit would affect financial stability, moral hazard in the financial system, the efficiency and competitiveness of U.S. financial firms and financial markets, and the cost and availability of credit and other financial services to households and businesses in the United States. The study concludes that the concentration limit will have a positive impact on U.S. financial stability. It also makes a number of technical recommendations to address practical difficulties likely to arise in its administration and enforcement, such as the definition of liabilities for certain companies that do not currently calculate or report risk-weighted assets.

- *Study and Recommendations on Prohibitions on Proprietary Trading and Certain Relationships with Hedge Funds and Private Equity Funds* [16]—As mandated by the Dodd-Frank Act, FSOC conducted a study on how best to implement section 619 of the Act (commonly known as the "Volcker Rule"), which is designed to improve the safety and soundness of our nation's banking system by prohibiting propriety trading activities and certain private fund investments. To help formulate its recommendations, the Council published a Notice and Request for Information in the *Federal Register* on October 6, 2010, and received more than 8,000 comments from the public, Congress, and financial services market participants. Key themes in those comments urged agencies to:

- Prohibit banking entities from engaging in speculative proprietary trading or sponsoring or investing in prohibited hedge funds or private equity funds;

- Define terms and eliminate potential loopholes;

- Provide clear guidance to banking entities as to the definition of permitted and prohibited activities; and

- Protect the ability of banking firms to manage their risks and provide critical financial intermediation services and preserve strong and liquid capital markets.

After careful consideration of these comments, on January 18, 2011, the Council approved publication of its study and recommendations that are intended to help inform the regulatory agencies as they move forward with this difficult and complex

---

[15] A copy of the study is available at: *http://www.treasury.gov/initiatives/Documents/Study%20on%20Concentration%20Limits%20on%20Large%20Firms%2001-17-11.pdf*.

[16] A copy of the study is available at: *http://www.treasury.gov/initiatives/Documents/Volcker%20sec%20%20619%20study%20final%201%2018%2011%20rg.pdf*.

rulemaking. The study endorses the robust implementation of the Volcker Rule and makes ten broad recommendations for the agencies' consideration.[17]

As I noted at the Council meeting at which this matter was considered, the OCC believes this study strikes a fair balance between identifying considerations and approaches for future rulemaking, and being overly prescriptive. As noted earlier, this is an area where Congress chose to make a careful and, in my view, judicious distinction in authorities—requiring the Council to conduct the study and make recommendations, but leaving responsibility for writing the implementing regulations to the relevant supervisory agencies. Recognizing this distinction is essential to the process because the rulewriting agencies are required by law to invite—and consider—public comments as they develop the implementing regulations. This means the agencies must conduct the rulemaking without prejudging its outcome. We and the other agencies are in the midst of developing the proposed implementing rule and will be soliciting comment on all aspects of it when it is published.

- *Proposed Rulemakings on Authority to Require Supervision and Regulation of Certain Non-bank Financial Companies*—As noted earlier, in contrast to the Volcker Rule where the Council's role is primarily one of an advisory body, the Council is directly given authority under the Dodd-Frank Act to designate systemically important non-bank financial firms for heightened supervision. On October 1, 2010, the Council approved for publication an advance notice of proposed rulemaking (ANPR) that sought public comment on the implementation of this provision of the Dodd-Frank Act. Approximately 50 comments were received on the ANPR. On January 18, 2011, the Council approved publication of a notice of proposed rulemaking (NPRM) that outlines the criteria that will inform the Council's designation of such firms and the procedures the FSOC will use in the designation process. The NPRM closely follows and adheres to the statutory factors established by Congress for such designations. The framework proposed in the NPRM for assessing systemic importance is organized around six broad categories, each of which reflects a different dimension of a firm's potential to experience material financial distress, as well as the nature, scope, size, scale, concentration, interconnectedness, and mix of the company's activities. The six categories are: size, interconnectedness, substitutability, leverage, liquidity, and regulatory oversight.

The comment period for this NPRM closed on February 25, 2011, and staffs are in the process of reviewing the comments received and assessing how we should move forward with implementing this important provision of the Dodd-Frank Act. In response to concerns raised by commenters, there appears to be general agreement among the agencies on the need to provide and seek comment on additional details regarding FSOC's standards for assessing systemic risk before issuing a final rule. I fully support this decision. It is critical that FSOC strikes the appropriate balance in providing sufficient clarity in our rules and transparency in our designation process, while at the same time avoiding overly simplistic approaches that fail to recognize and consider the facts and circumstances of individual firms and specific industries. Ensuring that firms have appropriate due process throughout the designation process will be critical in achieving this balance. In this regard, consistent with statutory provisions, the designation of a non-bank firm as systemically important will require consent by no fewer than two-thirds of the voting members of the Council, including the affirmative vote of the Chairperson of the Council. Before being designated, a firm will be given a written notice that the Council is considering making a proposed determination with an opportunity to submit materials applicable to such a determination. Firms also are provided the right to a hearing once they receive a written notice of proposed determination.

- *Proposed Rulemakings on Authority to Designate Financial Markets Utilities as Systemically Important*—Section 804 of the Dodd-Frank Act provides FSOC with the authority to identify and designate as systemically important a financial market utility (FMU) if FSOC determines that the failure of the FMU could create or increase the risk of significant liquidity or credit problems spreading among financial institutions or markets and thereby threaten the stability of the U.S. financial system. On December 21, 2010, the Council published an ANPR regarding the designation criteria in section 804. The Council received 12 comments in response to the ANPR. At its March 18, 2011, meeting, the Council approved the publication of a NPRM that describes the criteria, analyt-

---

[17] *See:* Financial Oversight Council, *Study & Recommendations on Prohibitions on Proprietary Trading & Certain Relationships with Hedge Funds & Private Equity Funds,* (January 2011) at 3.

ical framework, and process and procedures the Council proposes to use to designate an FMU as systemically important. The NPRM includes the statutory factors the Council is required to take into consideration and adds subcategories under each of the factors to provide examples of how those factors will be applied. The NPRM also outlines a two-stage process for evaluating and designating an FMU as systemically important. This process includes opportunities for a prospective FMU to submit materials in support of or opposition to a proposed designation. Consistent with statutory provisions, any designation of an FMU will require consent by the same supermajority and affirmative vote procedure described above for designation of non-bank firms. The Council must also engage in prior consultation with the Federal Reserve Board and the relevant Federal financial agency that has primary jurisdiction over the FMU.

- *Systemic Risk Monitoring*—The Council and its committees are also making strides in providing a more systematic framework for identifying, monitoring, and deliberating potential systemic risks to the financial stability of the U.S. Briefings and discussions on potential risks and the implications of current market developments—such as recent events in Japan, the Middle East, and Northern Africa—on financial stability are a key part of the closed deliberations of each Council meeting, allowing for a free exchange of information and insights. As part of these discussions, members assess the likelihood and magnitude of the risks, the need for additional data or analysis, and whether there is a current need to supplement or redirect current actions and supervisory oversight to mitigate these risks. In addition, the Council's Data Subcommittee has overseen the development and production of a standard set of analyses that FSOC members receive prior to each Council meeting that summarize current conditions and trends related to the macroeconomic and financial environment, financial institutions, financial markets, and the international economy.

- *Annual Systemic Risk Report*—Section 112 of the Dodd-Frank Act requires the FSOC to annually report to and testify before Congress on the activities of the Council; significant financial market and regulatory developments; potential emerging threats to the financial stability of the United States; all determinations regarding systemically important non-bank financial firms or financial market utilities or payment, clearing and settlement activities; any recommendations regarding supervisory jurisdictional disputes; and recommendations to enhance the integrity, efficiency, competitiveness, and stability of U.S. financial markets, to promote market discipline, and to maintain investor confidence. Work is under way in preparing the first of these reports and much of the aforementioned work on systemic risk monitoring will help shape its content. It is our understanding that Treasury plans to issue the report later this year.

- *Consultative and Regulatory Coordination*—FSOC and its committees have also facilitated consultation and coordination on a number of important Dodd-Frank Act rulemakings. For example, Treasury played a coordinating role in the recently released notice of proposed rulemaking that would implement section 941 on credit risk retention, and is engaged in a similar role with respect to the Volcker rulemaking activities. As part of each Deputies Committee meeting, Treasury circulates a bi-weekly consultation report that provides a snapshot of pending rules for consultation. In this regard, the Council's Resolution Authority/Resolution Plans Committee has provided input to the FDIC and FRB, and recommendations to the Council, on issues related to the various Title II rulemaking initiatives. These have included input on the FDIC's and FRB's recent joint rulemaking to implement resolution plan requirements for certain non-bank financial companies and bank holding companies pursuant to Section 165(d) and the FDIC's rulemakings on its orderly liquidation authority pursuant to Section 209.

V. Conclusion

The Dodd-Frank Act has assigned FSOC important duties and responsibilities to help promote the stability of the U.S. financial system. The issues that the Council will confront in carrying out these duties are, by their nature, complex and far-reaching in terms of their potential effects on our financial markets and economy. Developing appropriate and measured responses to these issues will require thoughtful deliberation and debate among the members. The OCC is committed to providing its expertise and perspectives and in helping the Council achieve its mission.

PREPARED STATEMENT OF MARY L. SCHAPIRO
CHAIRMAN, SECURITIES AND EXCHANGE COMMISSION

MAY 12, 2011

Chairman Johnson, Ranking Member Shelby, Members of the Committee:

Thank you for the opportunity to testify[1] regarding the Securities and Exchange Commission's efforts to monitor systemic risk and promote financial stability, two functions that are critical in fulfilling our mission to protect investors, maintain fair, orderly, and efficient markets, and facilitate capital formation. Over the past few years, all financial regulators have been faced with key issues of systemic risk and financial stability. At the SEC, our activities have included a broad-based appraisal of both the strengths and weaknesses of our current equity market structure, and our capacity to monitor trading across all trading venues and to enforce the securities laws and regulations and self-regulatory organization (SRO) rules.

With the passage of the Dodd-Frank Wall Street Reform and Consumer Protection Act ("Dodd-Frank Act"), Congress provided the SEC with important tools to better meet the challenges of today's financial marketplace. These provisions included a mandate for oversight of the over-the-counter derivatives marketplace, private fund adviser registration and reporting, and rulemakings related to nationally recognized statistical rating organizations ("NRSROs"). Additionally, Title I of the Dodd-Frank Act created the Financial Stability Oversight Council ("FSOC"), and with it, a formal structure for coordination amongst the various financial regulators to monitor systemic risk and to promote financial stability across our nation's financial system. Each of these developments has enhanced the Commission's ability to protect America's investors and oversee financial markets.

Strengthening Market Structure

Market structure encompasses all aspects of the organization of a market, including the number and types of venues that trade a financial product and the rules by which they operate. Although these issues can be complex and the rules technical, a fair, orderly and efficient market structure is the backbone of the equity markets and has significant implications for our financial system more broadly. The Commission has undertaken a broad-based appraisal of both the strengths and weaknesses of our current equity market structure. This review includes an evaluation of recent market structure performance and an assessment of whether rules have kept pace with recent significant changes in trading technology and practices. The goal of this evaluation is to effectively address any market structure weaknesses while preserving its strengths.

In addition, last year, the SEC published a concept release on equity market structure in (the "Concept Release"). The Concept Release described the current market structure and then broadly requested comment from the public on three categories of issues: (1) the quality of performance of the current market structure, (2) high frequency trading, and (3) undisplayed liquidity in all its forms.

To date, the Commission has received more than 200 comments in response to the Concept Release. A number of commenters identified benefits of the current market structure, in particular noting that it has fostered competition among trading venues and liquidity providers that has lowered spreads and brokerage commissions. These investors cautioned against regulatory changes that might lead to unintended consequences. Other commenters, however, raised concerns about the quality of price discovery and questioned whether the current market structure continues to offer a level playing field to investors in which all can participate meaningfully and fairly. These commenters suggested a variety of possible initiatives.

The Commission continues to evaluate these issues in a responsible, timely, and comprehensive fashion, with particular focus on obtaining the appropriate data and analysis to support our decisions to proceed with or to table any particular initiative.

Responses to May 6 Trading Disruption

Just over 1 year ago, the U.S. equity markets experienced one of the most significant price declines and reversals since 1929. In September, the staffs of the SEC and the Commodity Futures Trading Commission (CFTC) published their second joint report on their inquiry into the day's events. Producing the report required an extraordinary amount of staff resources. On the securities side in particular, much

---

[1] The views expressed in this testimony are those of the Chairman of the Securities and Exchange Commission, a member of FSOC, and do not necessarily represent the views of the full Commission.

of the time and effort was devoted to collecting and then painstakingly sifting through the data necessary to reconstruct trading. These efforts highlighted the pressing need for enhanced data functionalities in the securities markets.

The joint report lays out the multiple factors that in our view significantly contributed to the liquidity failure and disruptive trading on that day, outlining the complex interplay of multiple factors across the securities and futures markets. This interplay is significant because it demonstrates the need for a multi-faceted regulatory response that addresses the full scope of the risks in a comprehensive and responsible way.

It is vital that the rules that govern market structure and market participant behavior support equity markets that warrant the full confidence of investors and listed companies. The Commission recently has adopted a number of important initiatives to further this goal:

- Less than 2 weeks after May 6, the Commission posted for comment proposed exchange rules that would halt trading for certain individual stocks if their price moved 10 percent in a 5-minute period. Barely more than 6 weeks after the event, exchanges began putting in place a pilot uniform circuit breaker program for S&P 500 stocks. In September, the program was extended to stocks in the Russell 1000 Index and specified exchange-traded products. The aim of this program is to halt trading under disorderly market conditions, which in turn should help restore investor confidence by ensuring that markets operate only when they can effectively carry out their critical price-discovery functions.

- In September, the Commission approved pilot exchange rules designed to bring order and transparency to the process of breaking "clearly erroneous" trades. On May 6, nearly 20,000 trades were invalidated for stocks that traded 60 percent or more away from their price at 2:40 PM. That 60 percent benchmark, however, was set after the fact. We now have consistent rules in place governing clearly erroneous trades that will apply to a future disruption.

- In November, the Commission approved exchange rules to enhance the quotation standards for market makers. In particular, the new rules eliminate "stub quotes"—a bid to buy or an offer to sell a stock at a price so far away from the prevailing market that it is not intended to be executed, such as a bid to buy at a penny or an offer to sell at $100,000. Executions against stub quotes represented a significant proportion of the trades that were executed at extreme prices on May 6 and were subsequently broken.

- Also in November, the Commission took an important step to promote market stability by adopting a new market access rule. Broker-dealers that access the markets themselves or offer market access to customers will be required to put in place appropriate pre-trade risk management controls and supervisory procedures. The rule effectively prohibits broker-dealers from providing customers with "unfiltered" access to an exchange or alternative trading system. By helping ensure that broker-dealers appropriately control the risks of market access, the rule should prevent broker-dealers or their customers from engaging in practices that threaten the financial condition of other market participants and clearing organizations, as well as the integrity of trading on the securities markets.

- In addition, the Commission recently proposed exchange and FINRA rules that provide for a limit up/limit down procedure that would directly prohibit trades outside specified parameters, while allowing trading to continue within those parameters. This procedure should prevent many anomalous trades from ever occurring, as well as limiting the disruptive effect of those that do occur.

In addition to these rules, the Commission has proposed large trader reporting requirements and a consolidated audit trail system to improve our ability to regulate the equity markets. These proposals would tremendously enhance regulators' ability to identify significant market participants, collect information on their activity, and analyze their trading behavior. Both of these initiatives seek to address significant shortcomings in the agency's present ability to collect and monitor data in an efficient and scalable manner and to address discrete market structure problems.

Today, there is not a standardized, automated system to collect data across the various trading venues, products and market participants. Some, but not all, markets have their own individual and often incomplete audit trails. As a result, regulators tracking suspicious activity or reconstructing an unusual event must obtain and merge a sometimes immense volume of disparate data from a number of different markets. And even then, the data does not always reveal who traded which security, and when. To obtain individual trader information the Commission must make a series of manual requests that can take days or even weeks to fulfill. In brief, the Commission's tools for collecting data and surveilling our markets do not incorporate the technology currently used by those we regulate. Further, they do not provide the Commission with adequate information to conduct timely reconstructions of market events.

If implemented, the consolidated audit trail would, for the first time, allow SROs and the Commission to track trade data across multiple markets, products and participants simultaneously. It would allow us to rapidly reconstruct trading activity and to more quickly analyze both suspicious trading and unusual market events. It is important to recognize, however, that implementation of the consolidated audit trail is a significant undertaking, and thus will need to be implemented in phases over time. In addition, in order to obtain the maximum benefit from this new infrastructure, the Commission's own technology and human resources will need to be expanded beyond their current levels.

Finally, a principal lesson of the financial crisis is that, because today's financial markets and their participants are dynamic, fast-moving, and innovative, the regulators who oversee them must continuously improve their knowledge and skills to regulate effectively. In response to the ever-changing nature of our financial system, the SEC's Office of Compliance, Investigations and Examinations and our Division of Enforcement have adopted new approaches to promote fair, orderly and efficient operation of the markets.

New Tools Provided by the Dodd-Frank Act

The Dodd-Frank Act includes over 100 rulemaking provisions applicable to the SEC. Several of those provisions will play an important role in enhancing the Commission's ability to mitigate systemic risk and promote financial stability.

Over-The-Counter Derivatives. The Dodd-Frank Act mandates oversight of the OTC derivatives marketplace. Title VII of the Act provides that the Commission will regulate security-based swaps and the CFTC will regulate other swaps. To implement the security based swap provisions, the SEC is writing rules that address, among other things, mandatory clearing, the operation of security-based swap execution facilities and data repositories, capital and margin requirements and business conduct standards for security-based swap dealers and major security-based swap participants, and regulatory access to and public transparency for information regarding security-based swap transactions. This series of rulemakings should improve transparency and facilitate the centralized clearing of security-based swaps, helping, among other things, to reduce counterparty risk. It should also enhance investor protection by increasing disclosure regarding security-based swap transactions and helping to mitigate conflicts of interest involving security-based swaps. In addition, these rulemakings should establish a regulatory framework that allows OTC derivatives markets to continue to develop in a more transparent, efficient, accessible, and competitive manner.

Private Fund Adviser Registration and Reporting. Under Title IV of the Dodd-Frank Act, hedge fund advisers and private equity fund advisers will be required to register with the Commission, which is expected to occur in the first quarter of 2012. Under the Act, venture capital fund advisers and private fund advisers with less than $150 million in assets under management in the United States will be exempt from the new registration requirements. In addition, family offices will not be subject to registration. To implement these provisions, the Commission has proposed:

- Amendments to Form ADV, the investment adviser registration form, to facilitate the registration of advisers to hedge funds and other private funds and to gather information about these private funds, including identification of the private funds' auditors, custodians and other "gatekeepers;"[2]

- To implement the Act's mandate to exempt from registration advisers to private funds with less than $150 million in assets under management in the United States; [3]

- A definition of "venture capital fund" to distinguish these funds from other types of private funds;[4] and

- A rule to exempt "family offices" and a definition of "family office" that focuses on firms that provide investment advice to family members (as defined by the

---

[2] *See* Release No. IA–3110, *Rules Implementing Amendments to the Investment Advisers Act of 1940* (November 19, 2010), *http://www.sec.gov/rules/proposed/2010/ia-3110.pdf.*
[3] *See id.*
[4] *See* Release No. IA–3111, *Exemptions for Advisers to Venture Capital Funds, Private Fund Advisers with Less Than $150 Million in Assets Under Management and Foreign Private Advisers* (November 19, 2010), *http://www.sec.gov/rules/proposed/2010/ia-3111.pdf.*

rule), certain key employees, charities and trusts established by family members and entities wholly owned and controlled by family members.[5]

In addition, following consultation with staff of the member agencies of the Financial Stability Oversight Council (FSOC), the Commission and CFTC jointly proposed rules to implement the Act's mandate to require advisers to hedge funds and other private funds to report information for use by the FSOC in monitoring for systemic risk to the U.S. financial system.[6] The proposal, which builds on coordinated work on hedge fund reporting conducted with international regulators, would institute a "tiered" approach to gathering the systemic risk data, which would remain confidential. Thus, the largest private fund advisers—those with $1 billion or more in hedge fund, private equity fund, or "liquidity fund" assets—would provide more comprehensive and more frequent systemic risk information than other private fund advisers.

Financial Stability Oversight Council

FSOC was created by Title I of the Dodd-Frank Act and has 10 voting members: the senior officials at each of the nine Federal financial regulators[7] and an independent member with insurance expertise appointed by the President. FSOC's composition also includes five nonvoting advisory members: three from various State financial regulators[8] as well as the Directors of the new Federal Insurance Office and Office of Financial Research ("OFR").[9]

Under the Dodd-Frank Act, Congress has given FSOC the following primary responsibilities:

- identifying risks to the financial stability of the United States that could arise from the material financial distress or failure—or ongoing activities—of large, interconnected bank holding companies or nonbank financial holding companies, or that could arise outside the financial services marketplace;

- promoting market discipline by eliminating expectations on the part of shareholders, creditors, and counterparties of such companies that the Government will shield them from losses in the event of failure (*i.e.*, addressing the moral hazard problem of "too big to fail"); and

- identifying and responding to emerging threats to the stability of the United States financial system.[10]

In fulfilling its responsibilities, FSOC is charged with identifying and designating certain nonbank financial companies as systemically important financial institutions ("SIFIs") for heightened prudential supervision by the Board of Governors of the Federal Reserve System ("Federal Reserve Board").[11] In addition, FSOC may make recommendations to the Federal Reserve Board concerning the establishment and refinement of heightened prudential standards for firms designated under the SIFI process and large, interconnected bank holding companies already supervised by the Federal Reserve Board.[12] Such recommendations may address, among other things, risk-based capital, leverage, liquidity, contingent capital, resolution plans and credit exposure reports, concentration limits, enhanced public disclosures and overall risk management.[13] In addition, FSOC must identify and designate financial market

---

[5] *See* Release No. IA–3098, Family Offices (October 12, 2010); *http://www.sec.gov/rules/proposed/2010/ia-3098.pdf.*

[6] See Release No. IA–3145, Reporting by Investment Advisers to Private Funds and Certain Commodity Pool Operators and Commodity Trading Advisors on Form PF (January 26, 2011), *http://www.sec.gov/rules/proposed/2011/ia-3145.pdf.*

[7] The senior officials are the Secretary of the Treasury (Chairperson); Chairman of the Board of Governors of the Federal Reserve; Comptroller of the Currency; Director of the Consumer Financial Protection Bureau; Chairman of the Securities and Exchange Commission; Chairperson of the Federal Deposit Insurance Corporation; Chairperson of the Commodity Futures Trading Commission; Director of the Federal Housing Finance Agency; and Chairman of the National Credit Union Administration. *See* Dodd-Frank Act § 111(b)(1).

[8] The State financial regulators include a State insurance commissioner designated by the State insurance commissioners; a State banking supervisor designated by the State banking regulators; and a State securities commissioner designated by the State securities commissioners. *See* Dodd-Frank Act § 111(b)(2).

[9] *See* Dodd-Frank Act § 111(b)(2).

[10] *See* Dodd-Frank Act § 112(a)(1).

[11] *See* Dodd-Frank Act §§ 112(a)(2)(H) and 113.

[12] *See* Dodd-Frank Act § 112(a)(2)(I).

[13] *See id.*

utilities ("FMUs") and payment, clearing, and settlement activities that are, or are likely to become, systemically important.[14]

The recent financial crisis demonstrated the potential for risks to quickly spread across the financial sector and undermine general confidence in the financial system. To address issues of "siloed" information and the potential for regulatory arbitrage, another key responsibility of FSOC is to monitor the financial markets and regulatory framework to identify gaps, weaknesses and risks and make recommendations to address those issues to its member agencies and to Congress.[15] In addition, by combining the information resources of its member agencies and working with the OFR, FSOC is responsible for facilitating the collection and sharing of information about risks across the financial system.[16]

FSOC Activities Update

Since passage of the Dodd-Frank Act, FSOC has taken steps to create an organizational structure, coordinate interagency efforts, and build the foundation for meeting its statutory responsibilities. In the weeks leading up to the inaugural October 1, 2010 meeting of the principals of the FSOC agencies, staff from the Treasury Department coordinated interagency staff work to establish by-laws and develop a transparency policy. During that period, FSOC also formed several interagency committees to address specific statutory requirements.

Designation of Systemically Important Financial Institutions

To begin defining and implementing the process to identify and designate SIFIs for heightened supervision by the Federal Reserve Board, FSOC established a SIFI designations committee and several staff subcommittees to tackle specific tasks.

On October 6, 2010, FSOC issued an advanced notice of proposed rulemaking soliciting public comment on the specific criteria and analytical framework for the SIFI designation process, with a focus on how to apply the statutory considerations for such designations. FSOC received over 50 comment letters from trade associations, financial firms, individuals, and others. These comment letters included views on the designation process itself, as well as suggestions on the specific criteria and metrics to be used and the frameworks for their application.

On January 26, 2011, FSOC issued a notice of proposed rulemaking regarding the SIFI designation process. The proposed rule describes the criteria that will inform— and the processes and procedures established under the Dodd-Frank Act for—designations by FSOC. Such criteria would be rooted in the eleven statutory considerations set forth in the Dodd-Frank Act for such designations, and would include, among other considerations, a firm's size, leverage, liquidity risk, maturity mismatch, and interconnectedness with other financial firms. The proposed rule also implements certain other provisions of the designation process, including: (1) the anti-evasion authority of FSOC; (2) procedures for notice of, and the opportunity for a hearing on, a proposed determination; and (3) procedures regarding consultation, coordination, and judicial review in connection with a determination. We plan to provide additional guidance regarding the Council's approach to designations and will seek public comment on it.

Designation of Systemically Important Financial Market Utilities

Financial Market Untilities (FMUs) are essential to the proper functioning of the nation's financial markets.[17] These utilities form critical links among marketplaces and intermediaries that can strengthen the financial system by reducing counterparty credit risk among market participants, creating significant efficiencies in trading activities, and promoting transparency in financial markets. However, FMUs by their nature create and concentrate new risks that could affect the stability of the broader financial system. To address these risks, Title VIII of the Dodd-Frank Act provides important new enhancements to the regulation and supervision of FMUs designated as systemically important by FSOC ("DFMUs") and of payment, clearance and settlement activities. This enhanced authority in Title VIII should provide consistency, promote robust risk management and safety and soundness, reduce systemic risks, and support the stability of the broader financial system.[18] Importantly, the enhanced authority in Title VIII is designed to be in addition to the

---

[14] See Dodd-Frank Act §§ 112(a)(2)(J) and 804(a).

[15] See Dodd-Frank Act § 112(a)(2)(C)–(G).

[16] See Dodd-Frank Act § 112(a)(2)(A)–(B).

[17] Section 803(6) of the Dodd-Frank Act defines a financial market utility as "any person that manages or operates a multilateral system for the purpose of transferring, clearing, or settling payments, securities, or other financial transactions among financial institutions or between financial institutions and the person."

[18] See Dodd-Frank Act § 802.

authority and requirements of the Securities Exchange Act and Commodity Exchange Act that may apply to FMUs and financial institutions that conduct designated activities.[19]

FSOC established an interagency DFMU committee to develop a framework for the designation of systemically important FMUs, in which staff from the SEC has actively participated. On December 21, 2010, FSOC published an advanced notice of proposed rulemaking seeking public comment on the designation process for FMUs. In response, FSOC received twelve comment letters from industry groups, advocacy and public interest groups, individual FMUs and financial institutions. Among other things, commenters generally encouraged the development of metrics and an analytical framework to further define the statutory considerations for designation contained in Title VIII, and also emphasized the need for FSOC to apply consistent standards for all FMUs under consideration for designation that incorporate both qualitative and quantitative factors.

On March 28, 2011, FSOC published a notice of proposed rulemaking to provide further information on the process it proposed to follow when reviewing the systemic importance of FMUs. FSOC is considering using a two-stage process for evaluating FMUs prior to a vote on a proposed designation by the Council. The first stage would consist of a largely data-driven process to identify a preliminary set of FMUs whose failure or disruption could potentially threaten the stability of the U.S. financial system. In the second stage, FMUs so identified would be subject to a more in-depth review, with a greater focus on qualitative factors and FMU- and market-specific considerations. Under the proposal, the Council expects to use the statutory considerations as a base for assessing the systemic importance of FMUs.[20] Application of this framework, however, would be adapted for the risks presented by a particular type of FMU and business model.

Systemic Risk Assessment

In addition to initiating work on the identification of SIFIs and DFMUs, FSOC has established a Systemic Risk Committee that seeks to identify, highlight and review possible risks that could develop across the financial system. The Dodd-Frank Act also requires FSOC to report annually to Congress regarding these risks,[21] and we expect the work of this committee will inform that report.

Other Activities

In addition to seeking to identify possible risks in the financial system, FSOC was required under Section 619(b) of the Dodd Frank Act to study and make recommendations on implementing the Act's restrictions on proprietary trading, commonly referred to as the "Volcker rule," to achieve certain goals enumerated in the statute, including:

- to promote and enhance the safety and soundness of banking entities;
- protect taxpayers and consumers; and
- enhance financial stability by minimizing the risk that insured depository institutions and their affiliates will engage in unsafe and unsound activities.

On January 18, 2011, FSOC released its study and recommendations on implementation of the Volcker rule. The study recommends the creation of rules and a supervisory framework that effectively prohibit proprietary trading activities throughout "banking entities"—as defined by the Dodd-Frank Act—and appropriately distinguish prohibited proprietary trading from statutorily described permitted activities. The recommended supervisory framework consists of a programmatic compliance regime, metrics, supervisory review and oversight, and enforcement procedures for violations for the respective regulatory agencies conducting supervisory review and oversight. In addition, the study identified potential challenges in delineating prohibited proprietary trading activities from permitted activities, including potential difficulties in determining whether a position was taken in anticipation of near term customer demand or for non-permissible prop trading purposes.

---

[19] *See* Dodd-Frank Act § 805.

[20] Section 804(a)(2) of the Dodd Frank Act provides that these considerations are: (1) the aggregate monetary value of transactions processed by the FMU or carried out through the PCS activity; (2) the aggregate exposure of the FMU or a financial institution engaged in PCS activities to its counterparties; (3) the relationship, interdependencies, or other interactions of the FMU or PCS activity with other FMUs or PCS activities; (4) the effect that the failure of or a disruption to the FMU or PCS activity would have on critical markets, financial institutions, or the broader financial system; and (5) any other factors that FSOC deems appropriate.

[21] *See* Dodd-Frank Act § 112(a)(2)(N).

The study also recognizes that effective oversight by the agencies will require specialized skills and be resource intensive. For example, the study notes agencies will need additional resources to develop appropriate data points, build infrastructure to obtain and review information, and hire and train additional staff with quantitative and market expertise to identify and investigate outliers and questionable trading activity.

Money Market Fund Roundtable

Earlier this week, the SEC hosted a Money Market Fund Roundtable, which included representatives of each of the voting members of FSOC. The roundtable featured an in-depth discussion of various policy options to address the risk that a run on money market funds could have on the broader financial markets. Participants at the roundtable included money market fund sponsors, investors, academics, industry observers and representatives from entities that issue the commercial paper in which many money market funds invest. The roundtable enabled SEC Commissioners, FSOC principals and their representatives to discuss first-hand—and in a public forum—a significant issue related to the ongoing monitoring of systemic risk. I look forward to continued work on coordination with FSOC with respect to money market funds.

Next Steps

While FSOC has made substantial progress in taking up its new responsibilities, its efforts are ongoing, and much remains to be done. Some of the most challenging issues regarding the potential designation of systemically important financial institutions and FMUs lie ahead, and public input both generally on this process—and specifically with respect to the notices of proposed rulemaking—will be critically important. In addition, as Dodd-Frank implementation proceeds, the coordination of the FSOC agencies will continue to be a vital consideration.

Conclusion

In sum, the Commission recognizes the importance of monitoring systemic risk and promoting financial stability, and has responded to the challenges presented by recent market developments. As the Commission moves forward, we will look comprehensively at the issues, and take appropriate steps, both within the Commission and with our regulatory partners in the FSOC, to address any threats to our nation's financial system in a balanced manner that preserves the strengths of the system and protects investors. As we move ahead, we look forward to working closely with Congress to continue addressing these critical issues. Thank you for inviting me to testify today. I would be happy to answer any questions you may have.

————

PREPARED STATEMENT OF GARY GENSLER
CHAIRMAN, COMMODITY FUTURES TRADING COMMISSION

MAY 12, 2011

Good morning Chairman Johnson, Ranking Member Shelby and Members of the Committee. I thank you for inviting me to today's hearing on monitoring systemic risk and promoting financial stability. I am pleased to testify alongside my fellow regulators.

This morning I will provide an update on the status of the Commodity Futures Trading Commission's (CFTC's) process to implement the derivatives titles of the Dodd-Frank Wall Street Reform and Consumer Protection Act and discuss the how the CFTC has contributed to the Financial Stability Oversight Council (FSOC). Before I begin, I'd like to thank my fellow Commissioners the hardworking staff of the CFTC for their continued efforts to implement the Dodd-Frank Act.

Dodd-Frank Implementation Status

The CFTC is working deliberatively, efficiently and transparently to implement the Dodd-Frank Act. At this point, we have substantially completed the proposal phase of our rule-writing to implement the Dodd-Frank Act. Since the President signed the Dodd-Frank Act last July, the Commission has promulgated rules covering all of the areas set out by the Act for swaps regulation, with the exception of the Volcker Rule, for which the Act set a different timeline.

With the substantial completion of the proposal phase of rule-writing, the public now has the opportunity to review the whole mosaic of rules. This will allow market participants to evaluate the entire regulatory scheme as a whole.

To further facilitate this process, last month the Commission approved reopening or extending the comment periods for most of our Dodd-Frank proposed rules for an additional 30 days.

This time will allow the public to submit any comments they might have after seeing the entire mosaic at once. As part of this, I am hopeful that market participants will continue to comment about potential compliance costs as well as phasing of implementation dates to help the agency as we go forward with finalizing rules.

We will begin considering final rules only after staff can analyze, summarize and consider comments, after the Commissioners are able to discuss the comments and provide feedback to staff, and after the Commission consults with fellow regulators on the rules.

One component that we have asked the public about is phasing of rule implementation. Earlier this month, CFTC staff worked with SEC staff to host a roundtable to hear directly from the public about the timing of implementation dates of Dodd-Frank rulemakings. Prior to the roundtable, CFTC staff released a document that set forth concepts that the Commission may consider with regard to the effective dates of final rules for swaps under the Dodd-Frank Act. We also opened a public comment file last month to hear specifically on this issue. The roundtable and public comments help inform the Commission as to what requirements can be met sooner and which ones will take a bit more time.

Though we have substantially completed the proposal phase of rule-writing, the public will not be adequately protected until the agency completes final rules.

Rules Relating to Systemic Risk

The CFTC has proposed rules in three primary areas that are intended, in part, to lower systemic risk: regulating swap dealers, promoting transparency in the swap markets and requiring clearing of standardized swaps.

Regulating Swap Dealers

The financial crisis demonstrated the risk to the public of ineffectively regulated swap dealers. The Dodd-Frank Act addresses this by requiring comprehensive oversight of swap dealers. The CFTC has proposed rules to fulfill the Dodd-Frank Act's mandate that dealers meet minimum capital requirements to prevent a dealer's failure. We also have proposed rules mandated by the Dodd-Frank Act to require margin—or collateral—requirements to help prevent one financial entity's failure from spreading through the financial system to other entities and the broader economy. Congress recognized the different levels of risk posed by transactions between financial entities and those that involve non-financial entities, as reflected in the non-financial end-user exception to clearing. Consistent with this, the CFTC's proposed margin rules focus only on transactions between financial entities rather than those transactions that involve non-financial end-users. Further, we have proposed business conduct standards, including documentation, confirmation and portfolio reconciliation requirements. Each of these is an important tool to lower risk that the swap markets pose to the economy.

We also have proposed rules under the Dodd-Frank Act that set business conduct rules and set position limits to promote market integrity and protect against fraud, manipulation and other abuses. This helps ensure that the users of derivatives get the benefit of transparent, open and competitive markets.

Promoting Transparency

The Dodd-Frank Act includes essential reforms to bring sunshine to the opaque swaps markets. Economists and policymakers for decades have recognized that market transparency benefits the public. Transparency also helps lower systemic risk. The more transparent a marketplace is, the more liquid it is for standardized instruments, the more competitive it is and the lower the costs for hedgers, borrowers and, ultimately, their customers.

The CFTC has proposed rules to implement the Dodd-Frank Act's mandate to bring transparency to the swaps market in each of the three phases of a transaction. First, we have proposed rules to bring transparency to the time immediately before the transactions are completed, so-called pre-trade transparency. This will be required for those standardized swaps—those that are cleared, made available for trading and not blocks—that the Dodd-Frank Act mandates be traded on exchanges or swap execution facilities (SEFs).

Exchanges and SEFs will allow investors, hedgers and speculators to meet in a transparent, open and competitive central market. This will benefit end-users by providing better pricing on derivatives transactions.

Second, as required by the Dodd-Frank Act, the CFTC has written rules to bring real-time transparency to the pricing immediately after a swap transaction takes place. This post-trade transparency provides all end-users and market participants with important pricing information as they consider whether to lower their risk through a similar transaction.

Third, the CFTC has proposed rules as mandated by the Dodd-Frank Act to bring transparency to swaps over the lifetime of the contracts. End-users and the public will benefit from knowing the valuations of outstanding swaps on a daily basis. If the contract is cleared, proposed rules would require the clearinghouse to publicly disclose the daily settlement price for each swap cleared by the clearinghouse. If the contract is bilateral, proposed rules would require swap dealers to share mid-market pricing with their counterparties every day and agree on valuation methodologies in their swap documentation. This daily valuation will help prevent similar scenarios to 2008 when we were unable to price "toxic assets."

Additionally, we have proposed rules to make the swaps markets transparent to regulators through swap data repositories. The Dodd-Frank Act Act includes robust recordkeeping and reporting requirements for all swaps transactions so that regulators can have a window into the risks posed in the system and can police the markets for fraud, manipulation and other abuses.

Lowering Risk through Central Clearing

The Dodd-Frank Act also requires that standardized swap transactions between financial entities be brought to clearinghouses. Central clearing has been a feature of the U.S. futures markets since the late-19th century. Clearinghouses act as middlemen between two parties to a derivatives transaction after the trade is arranged. They protect the financial system and the broader economy from the failure of a swap dealer. They require dealers to post collateral so that if one party fails, its failure does not harm its counterparties and reverberate throughout the financial system. They have functioned both in clear skies and during stormy times—through the Great Depression, numerous bank failures, two world wars and the 2008 financial crisis—to lower risk to the economy.

Currently, swap transactions stay on the books of the dealers that arrange them, often for many years after they are executed. Like AIG did, these dealers engage in many other businesses, such as lending, underwriting, asset management, securities trading and deposit-taking. These dealers often are interconnected with other financial entities. This interconnectedness heightens the risk that a dealer's failure will reverberate throughout the economy as a whole. Uncleared swaps allow the failure of one institution to potentially cascade, like dominoes, throughout the financial system and ultimately crash down on the public.

The CFTC has proposed rules to implement the Dodd-Frank Act's clearing mandate and its requirement for enhanced oversight of clearinghouses. In close consultation with our fellow domestic and international regulators, and particularly with the Federal Reserve and the Securities and Exchange Commission (SEC), the CFTC proposed rulemakings on risk management for clearinghouses. These rulemakings take account of relevant international standards, particularly those developed by the Committee on Payment and Settlement Systems and the International Organization of Securities Commissions.

The Financial Stability Oversight Council

The Dodd-Frank Act established the FSOC to ensure protections for the American public. The Council is an opportunity for regulators—now and in the future—to ensure that the financial system works better for all Americans. The financial system should be a place where investors and savers can get a return on their money. It should provide transparent and efficient markets where borrowers and people with good ideas and business plans can raise needed capital.

The financial system also should allow people who want to hedge their risk to do so without concentrating risk in the hands of only a few financial firms. One of the challenges for the Council and for the American public is that the financial industry has gotten very concentrated around a small number of very large firms. As it is unlikely that we could ever ensure that no financial institution will fail—because surely, some will in the future—we must do our utmost to ensure that when those challenges arise, the taxpayers are not forced to stand behind those institutions and that these institutions are free to fail.

There are important decisions that the Council will make, such as determinations about systemically important nonbank financial companies and systemically important financial market utilities, such as clearinghouses, resolving disputes between agencies and completing important studies as dictated by the Dodd-Frank Act. Though these specific decisions are important, to me it is essential that the Council make sure that the American public doesn't bear the risk of the financial system and that the system works for the American public, for investors, for small businesses, for retirees and for homeowners.

The Council's eight current voting members have coordinated closely. Treasury's leadership has been invaluable. To support the FSOC, the CFTC is providing both data and expertise relating to a variety of systemic risks, how those risks can spread through the financial system and the economy and potential ways to mitigate those risks. We also have had the opportunity to coordinate with Treasury and the Council on each of the studies and proposed rules issued by the FSOC.

I will focus this portion of my testimony discussing a number of matters that have been on the FSOC's agenda.

Clearinghouses

Title VIII of the Dodd-Frank Act gives the FSOC important roles in clearinghouse oversight by authorizing the Council to designate certain clearinghouses as systemically important. Title VIII also permits the Federal Reserve to join in the examination of such clearinghouses and to recommend heightened prudential standards in certain circumstances.

The FSOC's notice of proposed rulemaking on designating systemically important financial market utilities complements the CFTC's rulemaking efforts that I described above. Public input will be valuable in determining how the Council should apply statutory criteria to determine which clearinghouses qualify for designation as systemically important.

Volcker Rule Study

Section 619 of the Dodd-Frank Act provides that, other than certain permitted activities, "a banking entity shall not engage in proprietary trading, including trading in futures, options on futures and swaps." The CFTC is directed to adopt rules to carry out this requirement with respect to any entity "for which the CFTC is the primary financial regulatory agency."

As part of the Volcker rule's coordinated rulemaking requirement, CFTC staff has been meeting frequently with other agencies, including the Federal Deposit Insurance Corporation (FDIC), Federal Reserve, Office of the Comptroller of the Currency (OCC), SEC and Treasury Department. The goal of these meetings is to ensure, to the extent possible, that our rules on section 619 are comparable and provide for consistent application.

The FSOC's Study & Recommendations on Prohibitions on Proprietary Trading & Certain Relationships with Hedge Funds & Private Equity Funds, also known as the Volcker Rule study, provides thoughtful recommendations to carry out Congress's intent to separate proprietary trading from otherwise permitted activities of banking entities. The study also provides a basis upon which each of our agencies can move forward with the required rule-writing to carry out Congress's mandate.

In particular, the study covers financial instruments both in the cash market and in the derivatives and swaps markets. This is significant, as any risk that a banking entity could take on in the cash markets also could be expressed through swaps and derivatives. The inclusion of both prevents regulatory arbitrage. In addition, the study indicates that the books of banking entities, including swap dealers, would not be precluded from the definition of a trading account regardless of whether those accounts held illiquid financial instruments, such as swaps, and regardless of whether those positions are short-term or long-term.

Supervision of Certain Nonbank Financial Companies and Concentration Limits

Title I of the Dodd-Frank Act authorizes the FSOC to determine whether certain activities of nonbank financial companies could pose a threat to the financial stability of the United States. Those companies would be supervised by the Federal Reserve and subject to specific prudential standards. In January, the FSOC issued a proposed rulemaking concerning its Authority to Require Supervision of Certain Nonbank Financial Companies. Effective regulation of systemically important nonbank financial entities is essential to preventing the next AIG from threatening the financial system.

The Dodd-Frank Act also includes a provision that no financial company be permitted to grow through either merger or acquisition if the resulting companies' consolidated liabilities would exceed 10 percent of all the aggregate consolidated liabilities of all financial companies. The FSOC's Study & Recommendations Regarding Concentration Limits on Large Financial Companies is an important step in implementing Congress's direction. These limits are designed to promote financial stability by preventing the liabilities of the financial sector from becoming too concentrated in any given financial entity. The 2008 financial crisis demonstrated the potential repercussions to the American public of concentration within our financial sector.

Annual FSOC Report to Congress

Under section 112 of the Dodd-Frank Act, the FSOC is to report annually to Congress. Staff of the CFTC, including in our Chief Economist's office, Division of Market Oversight, and Division of Clearing and Intermediary Oversight, have been contributing to that effort. I believe this annual report can serve as an important means for the Council to communicate to Congress on the stability of the financial system and make recommendations to enhance the U.S. financial markets and protect the public.

Coordination with FSOC Member Agencies

The CFTC is consulting heavily with the member agencies of the FSOC to implement the Dodd-Frank Act. We are working very closely with the SEC, Federal Reserve, FDIC, OCC and other prudential regulators, which includes sharing many of our memos, term sheets and draft work product. We also are working closely with the Treasury Department and the new Office of Financial Research. CFTC staff has had more than 600 meetings with other regulators on implementation of the Act. This close coordination has benefited the rulemaking process and will strengthen the markets. The CFTC will consider final rules only after we have the opportunity to consult with our fellow regulators.

Conclusion

Thank you for the opportunity to testify. I'd be happy to take questions.

RESPONSE TO WRITTEN QUESTIONS OF SENATOR SHELBY
FROM NEAL S. WOLIN

Q.1. Currently one of the voting seats of the FSOC is empty; no insurance expert has been nominated for the Council. Will any decisions with respect to the designation of insurance companies be made before an insurance expert has been named?

A.1. On June 27, the President nominated Roy Woodall as the FSOC's independent member having insurance expertise. Mr. Woodall is a former Commissioner of Insurance for the Commonwealth of Kentucky. He has also served as a Senior Insurance Policy Analyst at the Department of the Treasury, an Insurance Consultant for the Congressional Research Service, and as President of the National Association of Life Companies (NALC). Expeditious Senate confirmation of Mr. Woodall to this position will allow him to begin offering his considerable expertise to the FSOC.

In the meantime, as the FSOC works carefully and deliberately to satisfy its responsibilities under the Dodd-Frank Act, two of its non-voting members have substantial insurance expertise: Federal Insurance Office Director Michael McRaith, who most recently served as the Director of the Illinois Department of Insurance, provides relevant expertise that helps inform the FSOC's work, and John Huff, the Director of the Missouri Department of Insurance, Financial Institutions and Professional Registration, offers the important perspective of the primary functional insurance regulators.

Q.2 The SEC and CFTC are regulating an overlapping set of market participants engaging in transactions in similar products. They are taking two different approaches to the regulatory mandates they have been given. Is the Council considering whether the fact that two regulators are regulating in the same space will dilute accountability and lead to regulatory arbitrage that could endanger the financial system?

A.2. One of the duties of the FSOC, which the Secretary of the Treasury chairs, is to facilitate information-sharing and coordination among the member agencies regarding rulemaking, examinations, reporting requirements, and enforcement actions. However, while the Dodd-Frank Act establishes the FSOC as a forum for collaboration and consultation, it also preserves the independence of regulators such as the SEC and CFTC. The FSOC has worked to develop an approach that recognizes that independence while acting as a coordinator to facilitate a consistent and integrated approach to implementation. The SEC and CFTC, as independent regulators, are working together on their derivatives rulemakings to develop a consistent approach that reduces regulatory arbitrage. Treasury, as Chair of the FSOC, has and will continue to prioritize coordination among the regulators, including the SEC and CFTC on their derivatives rulemakings, to promote financial stability and market discipline.

Q.3. In your testimony you mentioned how valuable a recent executive order by President Obama was in "seeking to ensure cost-effective, evidence-based regulations that are compatible with economic growth, job creation, and competitiveness." What are you doing to encourage the agencies charged with Dodd-Frank rulemaking to undertake cost-effective, evidence-based regulations that are compatible with economic growth, job creation, and competitiveness? Will the FSOC's rulemaking be subject to the executive order?

A.3. The Treasury Secretary has encouraged FSOC members to adopt the principles and guidelines set forth in the President's Executive Order 13563 of January 18, 2011 "Improving Regulation and Regulatory Review." Although the Executive Order does not apply to independent regulatory agencies, the Secretary encouraged all FSOC members agencies to adopt the principles and guidelines it sets forth. In addition, earlier this month, the President signed Executive Order 13579, asking the independent regulatory agencies to follow the cost-saving, burden-reducing principles in Executive Order 13563. These priorities and guidelines can help strike the right regulatory balance: ensuring that regulations improve the performance of our economy and protect consumers and investors, without imposing unreasonable costs on society.

The FSOC strives to perform its duties efficiently and effectively in achieving its mandate under the Dodd-Frank Act while avoiding undue burdens on the private sector. In addition, the FSOC works to fulfill its statutory mandate under the Dodd-Frank Act to coordinate across member agencies and, where practicable, ensure consistent regulation.

Q.4. Your testimony mentions that the Council has begun monitoring for potential risks to U.S. financial stability. Please provide more detail about who is conducting the monitoring, how it is being done, and how the monitoring differs from monitoring that individual Council members undertook prior to the establishment of the FSOC.

A.4. The Dodd-Frank Act established the FSOC as a forum for regulators to work together on a permanent basis to identify issues that could affect financial stability and impact the economy. The FSOC members—nine Federal regulators, an independent member with insurance expertise, the Office of Financial Research (OFR) Director, the Federal Insurance Office (FIO) Director, and State banking, insurance, and securities supervisors—contribute their expertise about sectors and institutions to develop a broader view of trends, risks, and challenges in the financial system. The FSOC has collective accountability for identifying, monitoring and responding to threats to U.S. financial stability.

The FSOC has designed a collaborative structure to promote the appropriate coordination, cooperation, information-sharing and transparency necessary for FSOC members to identify, analyze and respond to vulnerabilities in the system and emerging threats to U.S. financial stability. The FSOC has instituted a three-pronged committee structure: the Deputies Committee, the Systemic Risk Committee and the standing functional committees. These committees, which are composed of staff of FSOC member agencies with supervisory, examination, data, surveillance, and policy expertise, share information to assess risks that affect financial markets and institutions. The Systemic Risk Committee, with its subcommittees on financial institutions and markets, is accountable for interagency coordination and information-sharing regarding issues that could impact financial stability. The OFR is also working closely with the FSOC and member agencies to support this work, including through the development of tools for risk measurement and monitoring.

Q.5. The FSOC has an ambitious mandate. It is not clear how this mandate will work in practice. Has the FSOC developed a strategic plan for achieving its goals? If so, please provide the plan.

A.5. The FSOC has identified goals that it is working diligently to achieve. These goals include building an effective forum for collaboration and coordination between its members; carrying out the statutory requirements of the Dodd-Frank Act; identifying, monitoring, and responding to potential risks to U.S. financial stability; and laying the groundwork for designations of nonbank financial companies and financial market utilities.

To meet these goals, the FSOC has met six times since inception, exceeding the statutory requirement. Each of the FSOC member agencies has also designated a senior official to serve on the Deputies Committee, which meets every 2 weeks to discuss and make decisions that advance the FSOC's work. In addition to the Deputies Committee, the FSOC has established a Systemic Risk Committee and various standing functional committees focused on policy areas including heightened prudential standards, resolution, and data. These committees, which are composed of member agency officials and staff who have relevant supervisory, examination, data, surveillance, and policy expertise, communicate and meet regularly to support the FSOC's ongoing work. The FSOC's statutorily required annual report, which the FSOC expects to release later this month, will reflect the extensive discussions and analysis that have occurred through this collaborative interagency process.

Q.6. The FSOC's transparency policy states that the FSOC will close meetings, *inter alia,* under circumstances that "necessarily and significantly compromise the mission or purposes of the FSOC, as determined by the Chairman with the concurrence of a majority of the voting member agencies or by a majority of the voting member agencies." What types of circumstances would call for holding closed meetings under this provision of the transparency policy?

A.6. The FSOC's transparency policy states that a central mission of the FSOC is to monitor risk and emerging threats to U.S. financial stability. To fulfill this mission, the FSOC will discuss confidential supervisory information and market-sensitive data during Council meetings. This information may concern individual firms, as well as specific transactions and markets. Protection of this information is necessary to prevent destabilizing market speculation that could occur if the information were to be disclosed publicly. The FSOC is committed to holding open meetings and will hold closed meetings only when appropriate. It is important to note that the FSOC has held four public meetings since its inception.

Q.7. In January, the Council issued a Notice of Proposed Rule-making Regarding Authority to Require Supervision and Regulation of Certain Nonbank Financial Companies. There have been questions about whether the Dodd-Frank Act gives the Council the authority to adopt such a rule. Does the Council have the authority to adopt this rule?

A.7. The FSOC has the authority to issue its proposed regulations on the process for determining that a nonbank financial company will be supervised by the Federal Reserve, and to re-propose those rules for further public comment. The FSOC has already exercised its rulemaking authority to issue a notice of proposed rulemaking and plans to issue for further public comment additional guidance regarding its approach to designations of nonbank financial companies. The FSOC plans to release a final rule and guidance that will reflect the input received on its proposals.

Q.8. The Council has established a Deputies Committee and six other standing committees. Please identify the members of the Deputies Committee, the six committees, and their subcommittees. Please also identify the permanent staff and detailees on the FSOC staff and provide a synopsis of their qualifications.

A.8. Each of the FSOC member agencies has designated a senior official to serve on the Deputies Committee. Treasury has designated Jeffrey Goldstein, the Under Secretary for Domestic Finance. In addition to the Deputies Committee, the FSOC also has established a Systemic Risk Committee and various standing functional committees focused on policy areas including heightened prudential standards, resolution, and data. These committees are composed of member agency officials and staff who have relevant supervisory, examination, surveillance, and policy expertise. Moreover, the FSOC itself is supported by a Treasury Deputy Assistant Secretary and a small number of permanent career Government employees, all of whom have the necessary experience and expertise to help coordinate and implement the policies set by the FSOC members' agencies. Finally, the FSOC member agencies have made various personnel available through short-term detail arrangements to offer the FSOC additional support and subject-matter expertise.

Q.9. Under Dodd-Frank, swap data repositories, before sharing any information with a regulator other than their primary regulator, must obtain an indemnification agreement with that other regulator. Will this requirement adversely affect regulators' ability to obtain a comprehensive view of the swaps markets?

A.9. The Dodd-Frank Act requires swap data repositories (SDRs) and security-based swap data repositories (SB–SDRs) to make data available, on a confidential basis, to certain domestic and foreign regulators. The Dodd-Frank Act further requires regulators (other than the primary regulator) that request data to execute a written confidentiality and indemnification agreement with the SDR or SB–SDR prior to receiving any data. The CFTC and the SEC have proposed rules for SDRs and SB–SDRs, respectively, that require such confidentiality and indemnification agreements (see 75 FR 80808 (December 23, 2010) and 75 FR 77306 (December 10, 2010), respectively).

Both agencies acknowledged in their proposed rules that the indemnification requirement could affect other regulators' access to the information maintained by SDRs and SB–SDRs. However, both agencies also highlighted the importance of ensuring that other regulators have access to swap data to carry out their regulatory mandates and responsibilities. The CFTC and SEC have requested comment on the required confidentiality and indemnification agreements and are evaluating feedback.

Q.10. One of the Council's purposes is to monitor systemic risk and alert Congress and regulators of any systemic risks it discovers. What are the most serious systemic risks presently facing the U.S. economy?

A.10. The Dodd-Frank Act charges the Council with the responsibility for identifying risks to the financial stability of the United States, promoting market discipline, and responding to emerging threats to the stability of the U.S. financial system. To help satisfy its mandate, the FSOC established a Systemic Risk Committee which identifies, analyzes, and monitors vulnerabilities in the financial system and emerging threats to maintaining stability. As part of its ongoing efforts, the Council and its members monitor emerging issues such as the state of mortgage foreclosures in the United States, sovereign fiscal developments in Europe and the United States, and natural disasters such as the earthquake and tsunami in Japan. The Council will continue to think broadly about threats to stability from external shocks as well as structural vulnerabilities within the system. Later this month, the Council will address a number of these issues in its statutorily required annual report.

————

RESPONSE TO WRITTEN QUESTIONS OF SENATOR REED FROM NEAL S. WOLIN

Q.1. In early January, I was assured by Secretary Geithner that Treasury is committed to working with the other FSOC member agencies to mobilize all tools available to fix that nation's system of mortgage servicing and foreclosure processing. What tools have been mobilized? Do these consent orders represent a full mobilization of all the tools available to FSOC member agencies? Why or why not? What additional tools do you believe are necessary?

A.1. The consent decrees issued in April 2011 by the OCC, OTS, and Federal Reserve to certain financial institutions represent just one of the tools available to address mortgage servicer misconduct. Other tools follow from the work that Federal agencies, including Treasury and other FSOC member agencies, and their State partners are doing to coordinate a law enforcement effort that addresses mortgage servicer misconduct and improper foreclosure processing. Among other things, members of this group have been conducting onsite reviews of major mortgage servicers and vendors. These reviews revealed critical deficiencies in foreclosure processing and mortgage servicing, including the failure to follow State and Federal law. Servicers that engaged in improper foreclosure processing in violation of the law must be held fully accountable for their actions, and any deficiencies must be corrected.

In addition, Treasury is working with the OCC, the Federal Reserve, the Federal Housing Finance Agency (FHFA), and the Federal Deposit Insurance Corporation (FDIC) to develop national mortgage servicing standards. Work underway includes a study of measures that would improve borrower protections and provide clarity and consistency to borrowers and investors regarding their treatment by servicers, especially in the event of delinquency. The working group is building on modification standards Treasury developed for its Making Home Affordable Program (MHA). The MHA standards have improved mortgage modifications, including short sales and deeds-in-lieu of foreclosure, across the industry and have made key changes in the way mortgage servicers assist struggling homeowners. Treasury also supports the FHFA's review of servicing compensation structures and possible alternatives, which could help improve incentives for servicers to invest the time and effort to work with borrowers to avoid foreclosure.

Treasury believes continued coordination among Federal and State partners will be important for developing additional tools for addressing issues related to foreclosure processing and mortgage servicing.

Q.2. The GAO also recommended that the Federal Reserve, OCC, OTS, and FDIC "assess the risks of potential litigation or repurchases due to improper mortgage loan transfer documentation" and "require that the institutions act to mitigate the risks, if warranted" Has this been done? What are the estimated costs of potential litigation? Has this issue been discussed or considered by FSOC? What is Treasury doing, as Chair of the FSOC, to ensure that these recommendations are considered?

A.2. Treasury cannot speak on behalf of the independent regulators regarding analysis, potential litigation, or the specific regulatory actions they may undertake. However, the Dodd-Frank Act charges the FSOC with the responsibility for identifying risks to the financial stability of the United States, promoting market discipline, and responding to emerging threats to the stability of the U.S. financial system. Working groups addressing mortgage servicing and foreclosure processing have briefed the FSOC, which the Treasury Secretary chairs, on these issues, and the FSOC will continue to monitor developments.

Q.3. On April 29th, the Department of the Treasury announced its intention to exempt foreign exchange swaps and forwards from the scope of Dodd-Frank. Why should the foreign exchange swaps and forwards not be subject to the same transparency provisions as the rest of the derivatives marketplace? Please explain in detail.

A.3. Recognizing that the unique characteristics and existing oversight of the foreign exchange swaps and forwards market already incorporate many of Dodd-Frank's objectives for reform—including high levels of transparency, effective risk management, and financial stability—Congress provided the Secretary of the Treasury with the authority to determine whether central clearing and exchange trading requirements should apply to foreign exchange (FX) swaps and forwards. On May 5, 2011, Treasury requested public comment on a Notice of Proposed Determination to exempt FX swaps, FX forwards, or both, from the definition of a "swap" under the Commodity Exchange Act (CEA). As explained in the notice, FX swaps and forwards trade in a highly transparent market with well-developed settlement protections. Market participants already have access to readily available pricing information through multiple sources, and the prevalence of electronic trading platforms in these markets—approximately 41 percent and 72 percent of FX swaps and forwards, respectively, already trade on these platforms—also provides a high level of pre-and post-trade transparency. The Dodd-Frank Act will further heighten this transparency by subjecting all derivatives, including FX swaps and forwards, to mandatory reporting to swap data repositories.

RESPONSE TO WRITTEN QUESTIONS OF SENATOR CRAPO FROM NEAL S. WOLIN

Q.1. According to the American Banker, Annette L. Nazareth, a former SEC Commissioner, called the timetables imposed by the Dodd-Frank Act "wildly aggressive." "These agencies were dealt a very bad hand," she said. "These deadlines could actually be systemic-risk raising." Given the importance of rigorous cost-benefit and economic impact analyses and the need for due consideration of public comments, would additional time for adoption of the Dodd-Frank Act rules improve your rulemaking process and the substance of your final rules?

A.1. A guiding principle for implementation of the Dodd-Frank Act has been to move quickly and carefully. Regulators are working to meet statutory deadlines and to quickly provide clarity to the public and the markets. At the same time, rulewriters understand the importance of getting the rules right and are taking additional time where necessary to improve the process and substance of their final rules.

The Dodd-Frank Act does not require the FSOC to issue substantive regulations. Nonetheless, the FSOC has chosen to conduct rulemakings on the designations of nonbank financial companies and financial market utilities to promote transparency regarding the FSOC's decisionmaking process, to solicit public input, and to provide clarity on the criteria and process for designations.

Q.2. Chairman Bair's testimony was unclear regarding whether the FSOC has the authority to issue a revised rule on the designation of nonbank financial institutions. She and others indicated some type of guidance might be issued instead. Is it in fact the case, in general, that the FSOC does not have authority to issue rules under Title I that have the force and effect of law? If the FSOC has the authority in general to issue such rules on designation, why specifically would the FSOC be precluded from re-proposing a rule that is currently pending? Is there additional authority the FSOC would need from Congress to issue such rules or to proceed with re-proposing its NPR on designation? If yes, what specific authority would the FSOC need from Congress for the FSOC to have the ability to proceed?

The FSOC has the authority to issue its proposed regulations on the process for determining that a nonbank financial company will be supervised by the Federal Reserve, and to re-propose those rules for further public comment. The FSOC has already exercised its rulemaking authority to issue a notice of proposed rulemaking and plans to issue for further public comment additional guidance regarding its approach to designations of nonbank financial companies. The FSOC plans to release a final rule and guidance that will reflect the input received on its proposals.

Q.3. In an August speech at NYU's Stern School of Business, Treasury Secretary Geithner outlined six principles that he said would guide implementation, and then he added, "You should hold us accountable for honoring them." His final principle was bringing more order and integration to the regulatory process. He said the agencies responsible for reforms will have to work "together, not against each other. This requires us to look carefully at the overall interaction of regulations designed by different regulators and assess the overall burden they present relative to the benefits they offer." Do you intend to follow through with this commitment with some form of status report that provides a quantitative and qualitative review of the overall interaction of all the hundreds of proposed rules by the different regulators and assess the overall burden they present relative to the benefits they offer?

A.3. One of the duties of the FSOC, which the Secretary of the Treasury chairs, is to facilitate information-sharing and coordination among the member agencies and other Federal and State agencies regarding financial services policy development, rulemakings, examinations, reporting requirements, and enforcement actions. In this capacity, the Secretary recently sent FSOC members a letter encouraging them to review their regulations in accordance with the principles and guidelines identified in the President's Executive Order 13563 "Improving Regulation and Regulatory Review." The Treasury Department, after conducting its own review, published a preliminary plan under which it will periodically review its existing significant regulations in order to identify rules that may be outmoded, ineffective, insufficient, or excessively burdensome. The principles and guidelines set forth in the Executive Order can help ensure that regulations protect our citizens and improve the performance of our economy without imposing unreasonable costs on society.

In addition, the FSOC has worked to develop an approach to coordination that recognizes the independence of the regulators while bringing consistency and integration to the regulatory process. For example, soon after Dodd-Frank's passage, the FSOC worked with member agencies to release an "Integrated Implementation Roadmap" that sets forth a coordinated timeline of statutory and nonstatutory goals for implementation. The FSOC is also coordinating implementation of rulemakings, including the Volcker Rule, so that the regulations issued by the various agencies will be comparable and consistent.

_____

RESPONSE TO WRITTEN QUESTIONS OF SENATOR CORKER FROM NEAL S. WOLIN

Q.1. Your institutions have been assigned the task of macro prudential risk oversight. Specifically, the Dodd-Frank Act tasked the FSOC with "identifying risks to the financial stability that could arise from the material financial distress or failure of large inter-

connected bank holding companies or nonbank financial companies." As you know nearly all banks carry U.S. Treasury bills,
notes, and bonds on their balance sheet with no capital against
them. They are deemed, both implicitly and explicitly, as risk free.
But with a $14 trillion debt, no one can guarantee that the bond
market will continue to finance U.S. securities at affordable rates.
What steps have you taken to ensure that systemically important
financial institutions could withstand a material disruption in the
U.S. Treasury market from an event such as a major tail at an auc-
tion, the liquidation of securities by a major investor such as a foreign central bank, concerns that the United States will attempt to
inflate its way out of its debt obligations, an outright debt down-
grade by a major rating agency, or market concern over the pros-
pects for a technical default? What impact would an event such as
the loss of market confidence in U.S. debt and subsequent increase
in U.S. borrowing rates have on the institutions in your purview?
And what steps can you take to ensure that the balance sheets of
systemically important institutions could withstand such an event
and that such an event would not lead to a systemic crisis similar
to or worse than that experienced in 2008?

A.1. The Treasury Department does not believe the potential disruptions to Treasury markets that you mention are likely to occur
because we believe that Congress will raise the debt limit in a
timely fashion. Demand for Treasuries remains extremely strong.
Rates are at historically low levels, and auctions are showing high
levels of coverage. This reflects the confidence that markets currently have in the creditworthiness of the United States.

The Financial Stability Oversight Council (FSOC) continues to
identify, monitor, and respond to vulnerabilities in the financial
system and emerging threats to financial stability, including the
risks you mention. More immediately, the threat posed by the failure to raise the debt limit grows every day that we fail to address
it, and FSOC members remain focused on this issue. If the debt
limit is not raised on a timely basis, the United States would be
forced to default on the existing legal obligations made by past
Congresses and Presidents of both parties.

The Administration is committed to addressing the serious fiscal
challenges our country faces and working with you and other Members of Congress to do so. The ongoing discussions convened by the
President with leaders from both parties and both houses of Congress have been constructive and all participants are working to
reach agreement as soon as possible. However, regardless of the
path we choose to bring down our deficits, Congress must raise the
statutory debt limit.

Q.2. What other major systemic risks are you currently most concerned about? What steps are you taking to address these?

A.2. The Dodd-Frank Wall Street Reform and Consumer Protection
Act (Dodd-Frank Act) charges the FSOC with the responsibility to
identify and monitor risks to the financial stability of the United
States to promote market discipline, and to respond to emerging
threats to the stability of the U.S. financial system. To help satisfy
this mandate, the FSOC established a Systemic Risk Committee
which identifies, analyzes, and monitors vulnerabilities in the fi-

nancial system and emerging threats to financial stability. As part of its ongoing efforts, the FSOC and its members monitor emerging issues such as the state of mortgage foreclosures in the United States, sovereign fiscal developments in Europe, and natural disasters such as the earthquake and tsunami in Japan. The FSOC will continue to monitor and assess the threats to financial stability from external shocks as well as structural vulnerabilities within the system. Later this month, the FSOC will address a number of these issues in its statutorily required annual report.

RESPONSE TO WRITTEN QUESTIONS OF SENATOR VITTER FROM NEAL S. WOLIN

Q.1. Dodd-Frank set forth a comprehensive list of factors that FSOC must consider when determining whether a company posed a systemic risk and deserves Fed oversight. The council, in its advanced notice of proposed rulemaking, sets forth 15 categories of questions for the industry to comment on and address. However, the proposed rules give no indication of the specific criteria or framework that the council intends to use in making SIFI designations-other than what is already set forth in Dodd-Frank. As a result, potential SIFIs have no idea where they may stand in the designation process. Will the council provide additional information about the quantitative metrics it will use when making an SIFI designation?

A.1. The Council will seek comment on additional guidance regarding its approach to these designations. The Council is working to strike the right balance between the use of quantitative metrics and for the exercise of judgment when assessing the unique risks that a particular firm may present to the financial system.

Q.2. Would the council agree that leverage is likely to be the one factor that is most likely to create conditions that result in systemic risk? If so, how will the council go about identifying which entities use leverage?

A.2. The Dodd-Frank Act requires the Council to consider a variety of factors, including leverage, when evaluating what firms will be designated. No one factor will form the basis of a designation. Every designation will be firm-specific, taking into account each firm's comprehensive risk profile. The FSOC intends to obtain relevant data from its members, the OFR, and publicly available information. The Council continues to work toward an approach that will allow firms to assess whether they are likely candidates for designation while maintaining flexibility as the nature of institutions and markets changes.

Q.3. One of the first steps in the systemic designation process, as outlined in the proposed rule, is that after identifying a nonbank financial company for possible designation the FSOC will provide the company with a written preliminary notice that the council is considering making proposed determination that the company is systemically significant. Is receipt of such a notice a material event that might affect the financial situation or the value of a company's shares in the mind of the investors? If so, wouldn't it need to be disclosed to investors under securities laws?

A.3. The SEC is charged with determining the disclosure requirements applicable to public companies, and I respectfully defer to the SEC's judgment on this question.

RESPONSE TO WRITTEN QUESTIONS OF SENATOR TOOMEY FROM NEAL S. WOLIN

Q.1. As FSOC considers how to determine the systemic relevance of the investment fund asset management industry, wouldn't it be more appropriate for FSOC to look at the various individual funds themselves, of which there may be several under one advisor, rather than focus on the advisor entity?

  a. Isn't it true that each of those funds may operate with separate and distinct investment strategies, each with its own unique risks?

  b. Isn't it the case that the vast majority of the assets are located at the funds and not at the adviser entity?

A.1. Individual investment funds may operate with their own strategies and unique risk profiles, and for many asset management firms, most of the assets are not held on the balance sheet of the advisor entity. The FSOC recognizes that there are differences between the advisor entity and the individual funds, and both the funds and advisor may present different sets of risks. In accordance with the Dodd-Frank Act, in making determinations of nonbank financial companies to be supervised by the Federal Reserve, the FSOC will consider the extent to which assets are managed, rather than owned, by investment advisors.

Q.2. What additional protection/supervision could the Fed provide for mutual funds that the SEC isn't already providing? Do we really need to subject this industry to an additional layer of regulation, especially a "systemic risk" regulation?

A.2. Section 113 of the Dodd-Frank Act gives the FSOC authority to designate U.S. nonbank financial companies "if the Council determines that material financial distress at the U.S. nonbank financial company, or the nature, scope, size, scale, concentration, interconnectedness, or mix of the activities of the U.S. nonbank financial company, could pose a threat to the financial stability of the United States." Additionally, one of the 10 considerations the Dodd-Frank Act requires the FSOC to take into account during the designation process is "the degree to which the company is already regulated by one or more primary financial regulatory agencies."

Categorical exclusion of mutual funds, or any other type of nonbank financial company, from the possibility of designation without evaluating all of the considerations the FSOC is statutorily required to take into account would be premature.

Q.3. Can you share with us what the FSOC, OFR, FDIC and Fed are contemplating by way of fees that they may assess on SIFIs?

A.3. The Dodd-Frank Act created the Financial Research Fund to support the operations of the OFR and the FSOC. The Federal Reserve Board is required by statute to provide interim funding for the first 2 years after enactment of the Dodd-Frank Act. After this period, the Treasury Secretary, with the Council's approval, must establish by rule an assessment schedule for Federal Reserve-supervised bank holding companies and designated nonbank financial companies to cover these expenses.

The FSOC and the OFR have not finalized their budget estimates beyond FY 2012; however, funding estimates for the Financial Research Fund for FY 2011 and FY 2012 were made public in the President's budget request earlier this year.

International Competitiveness

Q.4.a. It is critical for the continued competitiveness of the U.S. markets that a regulatory arbitrage does not develop among markets that favors markets in Europe and Asia over U.S. markets. Will the FSOC commit to ensuring that the timing of the finalization and implementation of rulemaking under Dodd Frank does not impair the competitiveness of U.S. markets?

Q.4.b. How will FSOC ensure that U.S. firms will have equal access to European markets as European firms will have to U.S. markets?

Q.4.c. How will FSOC ensure that Basel III will be implemented in the United States in a manner that is not more stringent than in Europe, making U.S. firms less competitive globally?

A.4.a.–c. The Council understands that major financial centers in Europe and Asia need to adopt strong measures similar to the Dodd-Frank Act to help maintain a level playing field for U.S. firms and reduce the opportunity for regulatory arbitrage. The United States has taken a leading role in laying the groundwork to set an international effort in motion, and the Council's members are playing an important part in coordinating this effort so that implementation across national authorities is consistent and timely.

The Council's members are working through international forums like the G–20 and Financial Stability Board to build a global regulatory framework, including areas like capital standards and derivatives regulation, so that markets remain competitive and accessible. The Council's members are also engaging with their counterparts around the globe, including through bilateral financial dialogues with the European Commission, Japan, China, India, Singapore, and Canada, to develop consistent approaches of regulating major financial jurisdictions.

Q.5. Is a broker/dealer that is not self-clearing less likely to pose systemic risk because it receives the financial backing and risk management attention of its clearing firm which already performs extensive monitoring of risk for the broker-dealers and which in all likelihood will itself be a SIFI?

A.5. As reflected in Title VII of the Dodd-Frank Act, central clearing is an important means of addressing the threats to the financial system posed by counterparty defaults in the context of certain derivatives transactions. However, these threats can also spread through other transmission mechanisms, including asset fire sales, withdrawals of funding or demands for additional collateral. As a result, broker-dealer clearing arrangements, including clearing

83

through a clearing firm, may reduce, but do not eliminate these risks.

Q.6. Titles I and II of Dodd-Frank references an entity's "asset threshold" or "total consolidated assets" several times. Are such calculations to be made in accordance with generally accepted accounting principles (GAAP)?

A.6. When establishing capital measures, many U.S. regulators require an entity to adjust its GAAP-based results and apply regulatory accounting principles. This adjustment is made to ensure that the regulators' objectives are met.

For purposes of calculating "asset threshold" and "total consolidated assets," we expect that regulators would adopt a similar approach. They would use the principles established under U.S. GAAP, but would require adjustments to these calculations to meet their objectives.

————

RESPONSE TO WRITTEN QUESTIONS OF SENATOR MORAN FROM NEAL S. WOLIN

Q.1. One of the first steps in the designation process is that after identifying a nonbank financial company for possible designation, the FSOC will provide the firm with a written notice that the Council is considering them for possible designation. Can you walk us through this step and describe possible scenarios in which there is some question as to a firm's systemic significance? Who decides to whom the notice will be sent if no vote is taken?

A.1. The FSOC issued a notice of proposed rulemaking regarding the criteria and procedures for the designation of nonbank financial companies. The FSOC requested public comment on various parts of the proposed rule, including on the provisions governing notice of a proposed determination. The FSOC is continuing to work through the details of this process, and expects to release for public comment additional guidance on the proposed procedures.

Q.2. You are aware of my concerns with the structure established in Dodd-Frank. In fact, I favor the approach first sent to the Hill by your Administration almost 2 years ago; a 5-member Board. That being said, can you please tell us why it has taken more than 10 months to secure a suitable candidate for this position? Back in November of 2010, Congressman Bachus asked Secretary Geithner when we might expect the President to nominate someone to head the CFPB and the Secretary responded "soon." When will we see a nomination? Would it have been more appropriate for the first Director of this Bureau to be the individual hiring several hundred employees, establishing the agenda, setting a budget?

A.2. Earlier this week, the President nominated Richard Cordray, who is currently the Chief of Enforcement at the CFPB, to serve as its Director. Mr. Cordray is a former Attorney General and State Treasurer of Ohio. Earlier in his career, Mr. Cordray was an adjunct professor at the Ohio State University College of Law, served as a Ohio State Representative, and was the first Solicitor General in Ohio's history. In the Dodd-Frank Act, Congress granted the Secretary of the Treasury interim authority to stand up the CFPB before a Director is confirmed. To ensure an orderly stand-up of the agency and a responsible transfer of functions from seven Federal agencies, this process has necessitated extensive research, planning, budgeting, and hiring.

Q.3. My initial research tells me that over the past 100-years or more of U.S. history, there is not a single instance in which an agency of this size and status was filled with a recess appointed head in its inception. Can you commit to us that your Administration will not break this long-established precedent and make an end-run around the Senate?

A.3. Filling existing vacancies, including the CFPB Director position, is a priority for this Administration. I cannot, however, speak for the President with respect to any particular nominations.

———

RESPONSE TO WRITTEN QUESTIONS OF SENATOR CORKER FROM BEN S. BERNANKE

Q.1. Your institutions have been assigned the task of macro prudential risk oversight. Specifically, the Dodd-Frank Act tasked the FSOC with "identifying risks to the financial stability that could arise from the material financial distress or failure of large interconnected bank holding companies or nonbank financial companies." As you know nearly all banks carry U.S. Treasury bills, notes, and bonds on their balance sheet with no capital against them. They are deemed, both implicitly and explicitly, as risk free. But with a $14 trillion debt, no one can guarantee that the bond market will continue to finance U.S. securities at affordable rates. What steps have you taken to ensure that systemically important financial institutions could withstand a material disruption in the U.S. Treasury market from an event such as a major tail at an auction, the liquidation of securities by a major investor such as a foreign central bank, concerns that the United States will attempt to inflate its way out of its debt obligations, an outright debt downgrade by a major rating agency, or market concern over the prospects for a technical default?

What impact would an event such as the loss of market confidence in U.S. debt and subsequent increase in U.S. borrowing rates have on the institutions in your purview? And what steps can you take to ensure that the balance sheets of systemically important institutions could withstand such an event and that such an event would not lead to a systemic crisis similar to or worse than that experienced in 2008?

A.1. I agree that the fiscal situation is a serious problem that must be addressed. Currently, the Federal debt-to-income ratio is at levels not seen since World War II in part because the budgetary position of the Federal Government has deteriorated substantially during the past two fiscal years. The recent deterioration was largely the result of a sharp decline in tax revenues brought about by the recession and the subsequent slow recovery, as well as by increases in Federal spending needed to alleviate the recession and stabilize the financial system. Looking out a few years, under current policy settings, the Federal budget will be on an unsustainable path, with the debt-to-income ratio of the United States rising at an increasing pace.

That said, financial market participants evidently expect the Congress and the Administration to come to a solution that puts the United States on a sustainable fiscal path. Yields on 10-year Treasury bonds are currently at extremely low levels, consistent with investors requiring little compensation for the risk of lending the U.S. Government for an extended horizon. If investors were to seriously doubt the United States' willingness to meet its obligations, the result could be widespread financial disruptions that could derail the recovery and that would almost certainly raise the long-term cost of borrowing for the Government, further complicating our fiscal problem.

As a regulator, we have conducted extensive analyses of the impact that an abrupt rise in interest rates would have on the institutions we supervise and will continue to monitor any impact that interest rates increases have on these institutions. However, we recognize that a material disruption in the U.S. Treasury market from investor concerns about a sustainable fiscal path would not just affect these institutions but, as noted, would have more widespread consequences.

Q.2. What other major systemic risks are you currently most concerned about? What steps are you taking to address these?

A.2. There are a number of risks that we are monitoring and assessing in our role as a member of the FSOC, as well as in meeting the Federal Reserve's independent responsibility to promote financial stability. The FSOC Annual Report, submitted to Congress in July, identifies a number of potential systemic risks and makes recommendations to mitigate these risks and promote financial stability. Among those identified are structural risks, including features of money market funds that make them susceptible to runs, fragilities in the tri-party repo market, inadequate mortgage servicing practices, and weaknesses in capital and liquidity risk management practices at some of the largest financial institutions. The Federal Reserve, as well as the FSOC, has publicly urged the SEC to take additional steps to mitigate the risk of runs in money market funds, including pursuing reform alternatives such as mandatory floating net asset value (NAV), capital buffers to absorb fund losses, or deterrents to redemptions. In addition, the Fed is an active participant in the Task Force on Tri-Party Repo Infrastructure, which is taking steps to reduce intraday credit exposures and strengthen collateral management practices to increase the stability of this market. As a banking supervisor, we are working to establish improved national mortgage servicing practices. We also conducted the Comprehensive Capital Analysis and Review exercise earlier this year, and have been working with institutions to further improve their capital planning processes, including contingencies for resolution that would facilitate resolvability without Government assistance. In addition, the Fed is working on proposed enhanced prudential standards for certain large and complex financial firms, which need to be implemented in a consistent manner across the global financial system, and is working with FSOC to designate systemically important nonbank financial institutions. There also are a number of emerging risks that the FSOC identified, including unexpected increases in interest rates, declining discipline in underwriting standards for some financial assets, and more generally new and developing emerging financial products and practices, and the Federal Reserve is closely monitoring these developments. Going forward, the Federal Reserve will continue to work with the FSOC and its other member agencies to identify risks and structural vulnerabilities in the financial system, and to take steps to increase its resilience.

RESPONSE TO WRITTEN QUESTION OF SENATOR MORAN
FROM BEN S. BERNANKE

Q.1. In a recent speech, Governor Tarullo stated that the list of "systemically significant" institutions will be short, and that the standard for designation set by Congress "should be quite high." There has been conflicting reports that there are some on the FSOC which would like a more inclusive group of firms, in effect casting a wider net. Do you agree with Governor Tarullo that the list is likely to be limited to a small group of truly interconnected institutions?

A.1. I believe that the Financial Stability Oversight Council (FSOC) should designate any nonbank financial company if the FSOC determines that material financial distress at the nonbank financial company, or the nature, scope, size, scale, concentration, interconnectedness, or mix of the activities of the nonbank financial company, could pose a threat to the financial stability of the United States. Whether a firm meets this standard inevitably involves a judgment on the combined effect of all potential transmission channels from the firm to the broader financial system and economy. At this time, I expect that a relative handful of firms likely meet this standard. Because the FSOC is still developing its analytic framework and is still working on a final rule for the designation process, it is too soon to know how many firms the FSOC will designate.

RESPONSE TO WRITTEN QUESTIONS OF SENATOR SHELBY
FROM SHEILA C. BAIR

Q.1. In your testimony, you note—and I agree—that allowing continuation of the pre-crisis status quo would be to sanction a new and "dangerous form of state capitalism." However, you also state that "the FDIC should have a continuous presence at all designated SIFIs" and the FDIC and the Federal Reserve should "actively" use their authority to require organizational changes at SIFIs. Does such an active Government-financial institution partnership run the risk of laying the groundwork for, as you described it, a dangerous form of state capitalism in which a few large financial entities operate under the shadow and protection of the Government?

A.1. It is important at the outset to clarify that being designated as a SIFI will in no way confer a competitive advantage or suggest that it operates under the protection of the Government by anointing an institution as "too big to fail." SIFIs will be subject to heightened supervision and higher capital requirements. They also will be required to maintain resolution plans and could be required to restructure their operations if they cannot demonstrate that they

are resolvable. In light of these significant regulatory requirements, the FDIC has detected absolutely no interest on the part of
any financial institution in being named a SIFI. Indeed, many institutions are vigorously lobbying against such a designation.

As shown by the recent crisis, the larger, more complex, and
more interconnected a financial company is, the longer it takes to
assemble a full and accurate picture of its operations and develop
a resolution strategy. By requiring detailed resolution plans in advance, and authorizing an onsite FDIC team to conduct pre-resolution planning, the SIFI resolution framework regains the ability to
gather information that was lacking in the crisis of 2008. The FDIC
should have a continuous presence at all designated SIFIs under
the new resolution framework, working with the firms and reviewing their resolution plans as part of their normal course of business. Thus, our presence should in no way be seen as a sign of Government protection or a signal of distress. Instead, it is much more
likely to provide a stabilizing influence that encourages management to more fully consider the downside consequences of its actions, to the benefit of the institution and the stability of the system as a whole.

Q.2. Your testimony calls into question claims that higher capital
requirements will adversely affect economic growth. If higher capital requirements had been in effect before the crisis, what effect
do you think that would have had on the number of institutions
that failed?

A.2. At the height of the crisis, the large financial companies that
make up the core of our financial system proved to have too little
capital to maintain market confidence in their solvency. Thin levels
of capital exacerbated the limited tools policymakers had to deal
with several large, complex U.S. financial companies at the center
of the 2008 crisis when they became nonviable.

With respect to banks that failed during the crisis, failures were
highest in certain areas of the country that were hardest hit by the
collapse of the real estate market, such as the southern States of
Florida and Georgia, the Great Lakes Region, and along the Pacific
Coast. Many of these banks had other risk factors, such as high
concentrations in construction loans and other higher-risk types of
real estate loans, heavy reliance on noncore funding dependence,
and poor underwriting and risk management practices, among others. However, even when operating in difficult markets, many
banks survived because they took steps to mitigate risks, for example, by not engaging in lax underwriting or credit practices and by
maintaining sufficient capital to absorb losses or successfully re-
capitalizing when market conditions changed.

Q.3. One of the Council's purposes is to monitor systemic risk and
alert Congress and regulators of any systemic risks it discovers.
What are the most serious systemic risks presently facing the U.S.
economy?

A.3. From the FDIC's perspective, the most important systemic
risks and emerging threats to our financial system at the present
time involve excessive reliance on debt and financial leverage, continued lack of market discipline due to perceptions of "too big to
fail," lingering problems in mortgage servicing, and interest rate

risk. My written statement to the Committee describes these areas more fully, along with the steps being taken to address them.

RESPONSE TO WRITTEN QUESTIONS OF SENATOR REED FROM SHEILA C. BAIR

Q.1. At your speech at the Chicago FRB conference, you offered some interesting ways forward on the designation of nonbank financial institutions (SIFI). In that speech, you noted that the resolvability of the non-bank financial firm should be the ultimate deciding factor in the designation process. That approach seems logical—can you elaborate on how it would work?

A.1. SIFIs will be subject to heightened supervision and higher capital requirements. They also will be required to maintain resolution plans and could be required to restructure their operations if they cannot demonstrate that they are resolvable. We believe that the ability of an institution to be resolved in a bankruptcy process without systemic impact should be a key consideration in designating a firm as a SIFI. Further, we believe that the concept of resolvability is consistent with several of the statutory factors that the FSOC is required to consider in designating a firm as systemic, those being size, interconnectedness, lack of substitutes, and leverage. If an institution can reliably be deemed resolvable in bankruptcy by the regulators, and operates within the confines of the leverage requirements established by bank regulators, then it should not be designated as a SIFI.

The approach of using resolvability as the deciding factor in the SIFI designation process seems relatively straightforward. However, we are concerned with the lack of information we might have about *potential* SIFIs that may impede our ability to make an accurate determination of resolvability before the fact. This potential blind spot in the designation process raises the specter of a "death-bed designation" of a SIFI, whereby the FDIC would be required to resolve the firm under a Title II resolution without the benefit of a resolution plan or the ability to conduct advance planning, both of which are critical to an orderly resolution. This situation, which would put the resolution authority in the worst possible position, should be avoided at all costs.

Thus, we need to be able to collect detailed information on a limited number of potential SIFIs as part of the designation process. We should provide the industry with some clarity about which firms will be expected to provide the FSOC with this additional information, using simple and transparent metrics such as firm size, similar to the approach used for bank holding companies under the Dodd-Frank Act. This should reduce some of the mystery surrounding the process and should eliminate any market concern about which firms the FSOC has under its review. In addition, no one should jump to the conclusion that by asking for additional information, the FSOC has preordained a firm to be "systemic." It is likely that after we gather additional information and learn more about these firms, relatively few of them will be viewed as systemic, especially if the firms can demonstrate their resolvability in bankruptcy at this stage of the process.

Q.2. The interaction of global capital requirements (Basel III) and U.S. requirements (FSOC) could result in different criteria being applied to the same financial institution. For example, an institution could be deemed systemically important to the global financial system but not to the financial system in the United States. How is this being addressed? Does this pose any unique risks?

A.2. Per the Dodd-Frank Act, all bank holding companies operating in the United States with $50 billion or more in assets have been deemed systemically important and thus subject to enhanced supervision and prudential supervision, including risk-based capital requirements. The asset threshold for globally systemically important banks (G–SIBs) set by the Basel Committee will likely be many times higher than that set by the Dodd-Frank Act. Therefore, it is unlikely that a U.S. bank holding company designated as G–SIB by the Basel Committee would not also be systemically important in the United States.

As members of the Basel Committee, the U.S. banking agencies are actively participating in the Committee's designation of G–SIBs and determining the capital surcharge that will be imposed. At the same time, in the United States, the FDIC and our fellow FSOC members are addressing any issues and potential risks as they arise to ensure both approaches are complementary. Finally, the implementation of both the Basel proposals for G–SIBs and the U.S. approach for systemically important bank holding companies will be subject to the U.S. notice and comment rulemaking process.

Q.3. A number of commentators and academics have asserted that Basel III capital requirements are too low. For example, a recent Stanford University study (Admati *et al*, published in March 2011) stated that "equity capital ratios significantly higher than 10 percent of un-weighted assets should be seriously considered." It also noted that "bank equity is not socially expensive" and "better capitalized banks suffer from fewer distortions in lending decisions and would perform better." In addition, Switzerland has adopted capital ratios for its banks in excess of Basel III. What are the strengths and weaknesses of capital adequacy ratios in excess of those considered under Basel III? (Adinanti, DeMarzo, Hellwig, Pfleiderer, "Fallacies, Irrelevant Facts, and Myths in the Discussion of Capital Regulation: Why Bank Equity is not Expensive." Stanford Graduate School of Business Research Paper No. 2065, March 2011.)

A.3. The FDIC agrees that strong, uniform capital requirements are an essential element of a stable banking system. The first and most obvious reason is that banking and financial crises have devastating effects on economic growth and job creation. Maintaining strong capital levels consistent with a safe-and-sound banking system both promotes long-term economic growth and makes bank lending less procyclical.

The rapid depletion of capital in the early stages of the crisis contributed to a massive deleveraging in banks and other financial intermediaries. Loans and leases held by FDIC-insured institutions have declined by nearly $750 billion from peak levels, while unused loan commitments have declined by $2.5 trillion. Trillions more in capital flows were lost with the collapse of the securitization market and other "shadow" providers of credit. A similar pattern has been observed following previous financial crises around the world.

Some observers, especially those representing banks, have expressed concern that higher capital requirements will curtail credit availability and hurt economic growth. However, the consensus of recent academic literature, including the March 2011 studies by Admati *et al*, is that increases in capital requirements, within the ranges currently being discussed, have a net positive effect on long-term economic growth. The reason for this conclusion is that the costs of banking crises for economic growth are severe, as outlined in my written testimony, so that reducing their frequency and severity is highly beneficial. On the other hand, the literature suggests the cost of higher capital requirements in terms of lost economic output is modest.

Arguments that balance sheet constraints associated with higher capital requirements reduce banks' ability to lend typically assume, explicitly or implicitly, that banks simply cannot raise new capital. Thus, according to this argument, the industry's fixed dollar amount of capital can support less lending the higher the capital requirement. But it is the FDIC's experience that most banks can and do raise capital when needed, often even banks in extreme financial difficulties.

As I have testified previously, I was disappointed the Basel Committee did not propose somewhat higher capital requirements than were contained in the Basel III paper published in December 2010. I had hoped for a total common equity requirement across all banks of 8 percent, but the Committee agreed on 7 percent—a 4.5 percent minimum plus a 2.5 percent capital conservation buffer, all comprised of common equity. Nonetheless, that is a significant improvement over the pre-crisis requirement of what was effectively 2 percent common equity.

Now the Basel Committee is working on an additional capital surcharge for globally systemically important banking organizations (G–SIBs). Switzerland has adopted an additional capital surcharge for their largest banks additional common equity and a requirement for contingent capital in addition to the additional common equity. The additional common equity Switzerland is requiring for its largest banks may prove to be in line with the Basel requirements for G–SIBs.

Finally, although the focus has been on the risk-based capital ratios, the Basel Committee has taken the important step of proposing an international leverage ratio as a backstop for the risk-based capital ratios. A major shortcoming of the Basel II regime (the advanced approaches) is that it allowed large banks to use their own models to steadily reduce their capital requirements, while their leverage increased. The leverage ratio is an essential part of a strong regulatory capital framework.

Q.4. In March, Bloomberg noted that 77 percent of the banking assets are held by the nation's ten largest banks—with 35 banks holding assets of $50 billion or more. In February, Moody's granted higher ratings to eight large U.S. banks because of an expectation of future Government support—implicitly suggesting that risky behavior by large banks would be more tolerated, and they would be insulated from failure. Has systemic risk increased after the financial crisis? Why or why not? How is this being addressed?

A.4. While banks and other financial companies continue to address elevated levels of problem assets and cope with refining their business plans during what has been a sluggish recovery, overall, bank balance sheets and the financial system as a whole are healing slowly. In the wake of the recent crisis, the FDIC and other regulators are working to implement an updated statutory mandate under the Dodd-Frank Act to reduce systemic risk by improving the resilience of our financial system.

As described more fully in my written statement, several large, complex U.S. financial companies at the center of the 2008 crisis could not be wound down in an orderly manner when they became nonviable, which resulted in a terrible dilemma for policymakers: bail out these firms or expose the financial system to destabilizing liquidations through the normal bankruptcy process. While necessary, there is genuine alarm about the immense scale and seemingly indiscriminate nature of the Government assistance provided to large banks and nonbank financial companies during the crisis, and what effects these actions will have on the competitive landscape in banking.

Nevertheless, the "uplift" in ratings for large financial institutions suggests that despite having recently seen the nation's largest financial institutions receive hundreds of billions of dollars in taxpayer assistance, the market appears to believe that they are "too big to fail," although rating agencies have recently indicated a reassessment of the likelihood of Federal support. Under a regime of "too big to fail," the largest U.S. banks and other financial companies have every incentive to render themselves so large, so complex, and so opaque that no policymaker would dare risk letting them fail in a crisis. With the benefit of this implicit safety net, these institutions have been insulated from the normal discipline of the marketplace that applies to smaller banks and practically every other private company.

A major improvement in reducing systemic risk and restoring market discipline for large financial companies, and one that, in my opinion, has been somewhat underestimated by the skeptics, is the requirement for SIFI resolution plans. When a large, complex financial institution gets into trouble, time is the enemy. The larger, more complex, and more interconnected a financial company is, the longer it takes to assemble a full and accurate picture of its operations and to develop a resolution strategy. By requiring detailed resolution plans in advance, and authorizing an onsite FDIC team to conduct pre-resolution planning, the SIFI resolution framework regains the ability to gather information that was lacking in the crisis of 2008.

The large financial companies that collapsed during the crisis (and many other companies today) maintained thousands of subsidiaries and managed their activities within business lines that cross many different organizational structures and regulatory jurisdictions. This can make it very difficult to implement an orderly resolution of one part of the company without triggering a costly collapse of the entire company. To solve this problem, the FDIC and the Federal Reserve must define high informational standards for resolution plans and be willing to insist on organizational changes where necessary in order to ensure that large financial companies meet the standard of resolvability well before a crisis occurs. Unless these structures are rationalized and simplified in advance, there is a real danger that their complexity could make a large financial company resolution far more costly and more difficult than it needs to be.

RESPONSE TO WRITTEN QUESTION OF SENATOR HAGAN FROM SHEILA C. BAIR

Q.1. Chairwoman Bair, inherent in any discussion of capital levels is a tradeoff between economic growth and the possibility of disruptive bank failures. With high unemployment, sluggish output, and extraordinary monetary policy in many developed countries, the economic impact of higher capital levels requires special attention. It is my understanding that the Basel Committee on Banking Supervision and the Financial Stability Board are considering a further increase in capital requirements for Systemically Important Financial Institutions, including the possibility of as much as 300 basis points on firms deemed to be systemically important on a global basis.

One of the costs traditionally associated with a bank failure is the loss of proprietary information and knowledge at the institution. This is one argument for higher capital requirements. With the robust resolution mechanisms in place in the United States, should domestic banks face equal capital charges as institutions in jurisdictions with less robust resolution frameworks?

A.1. A robust resolution framework, combined with resolution plans for large bank holding companies and SIFIs, can mitigate the impact on the financial system of the failure of a large, complex, and interconnected financial company. Even more importantly, we need a robust cross-border resolution framework internationally that harmonizes national resolution laws and processes. While there is much to be done internationally, we are making progress—there are new statutory regimes in Germany, the United Kingdom, and of course in the United States.

To spur the development of robust resolution frameworks internationally, the Basel Committee's consultative paper on the capital surcharge on systemically important banks includes the understanding that a country can add an additional 1 percent common equity requirement if the banking organization does not have an acceptable resolution and recovery plan This additional 1 percent would be on top of the 2.5 percent capital surcharge for globally systemically important banks, all of which will be filled with common equity. The Basel Committee and the Governors and Heads of Supervision agreed that there was too much uncertainty about contingent capital and bail-in debt to consider these hybrid capital instruments as loss absorbing capital for the capital surcharge. (The consultative paper on the capital surcharge for systemically important banks should be published in mid-July 2011.)

RESPONSE TO WRITTEN QUESTIONS OF SENATOR CRAPO
FROM SHEILA C. BAIR

Q.1. According to the American Banker, Annette L. Nazareth, a former SEC Commissioner, called the timetables imposed by the Dodd-Frank Act "wildly aggressive." "These agencies were dealt a very bad hand," she said. "These deadlines could actually be systemic-risk raising." Given the importance of rigorous cost-benefit and economic impact analyses and the need for the consideration of public comments, would additional time or adoption of the Dodd-Frank Act rules improve your rulemaking process and the substance of your final rules?

Chairman Bair's testimony was unclear regarding whether the FSOC has the Authority to issue a revised rule on the designation of nonbank financial institutions. She and others indicated some type of guidance might be issued instead. Is it in fact the case, in general, that the FSOC does not have authority to issue rules under Title I that have the force and effect of law? If the FSOC has the authority in general to issue such rules on designation, why specifically would the FSOC be precluded from re-proposing a rule that is currently pending? Is there additional authority the FSOC would need from Congress to issue such rules or to proceed with reproposing its NPR on designation? If yes, what specific authority would the FSOC need from Congress for the FSOC to have the ability to proceed?

In an August speech at NYU's Stern School of Business, Treasury Secretary Geithner outlined six principles that he said would guide implementation, and then he added, "You should hold us accountable for honoring them." His final principle was bringing more order and integration to the regulatory process. He said the agencies responsible for reforms will have to work "together, not against each other. "This requires us to look carefully at the overall interaction of regulations designed by different regulators and assess the overall burden they present relative to the benefits they offer." Do you intend to follow through with this commitment with some form of status report that provides a quantitative and qualitative review of the overall interaction of all the hundreds of proposed rules by the different regulators and assess the overall burden they present relative to the benefits they offer?

A.1. The FDIC is actively engaged in striving to meet the mandated timeframes for the interagency rulemakings set forth in the Dodd-Frank Act. With respect to questions about the FSOC's authority to issue regulations, the FDIC defers to the Treasury Secretary's legal counsel. The FSOC issued an ANPR and NPR describing the processes and procedures that will inform the FSOC's designation of SIFIs. Concerns have been raised about the lack of detail and clarity regarding the designation process, and the FDIC agrees that it is important that the FSOC seek further comment on its plans for designating firms and provide additional specificity, both qualitative and quantitative, that the Council expects to employ when making SIFI designations.

One of the purposes of the FSOC is to facilitate regulatory coordination and information sharing regarding policy development, rulemaking, supervisory information, and reporting requirements. The FDIC and other financial regulators have had a longstanding practice of information sharing, but the FDIC believes that the FSOC has provided more order and integration to that process.

The FDIC assesses the costs or burden versus the benefits of its rulemakings in the normal course of our business. Many of our regulations are required by statute and/or are aimed at protecting the Deposit Insurance Fund. That being said, the FDIC has had a long-standing policy to ensure that the rules it adopts are the least burdensome to achieve those goals. The FDIC's policy recognizes our commitment to minimizing regulatory burdens on the public and the banking industry and the need to ensure that our regulations and policies achieve legislative and safety and soundness goals effectively.

The FDIC also follows express statutory requirements that mandate consideration of the economic and other effects of proposed rules, such as the Regulatory Flexibility Act (effect on small entities), the Paperwork Reduction Act, the Congressional Review Act, and the Federal Deposit Insurance Act (for example, in connection with assessments). The FDIC is fully prepared to cooperate with the Treasury Secretary, in the capacity as FSOC Chairman, if he decides to prepare an integrated status report of rulemaking cost benefit analyses across the FSOC agencies.

As you know, the FDIC's Office of Inspector General recently provided a review, at the request of you and some of your colleagues on the Senate Banking Committee, on the FDIC's economic analysis performed in three specific rulemakings. The FDIC OIG reported that, in all three cases, the FDIC performed quantitative analysis of relevant data, considered alternative approaches to the extent allowed by the legislation, requested comments from the public on numerous facets of the rules, and included information about the analysis that was conducted and the assumptions that were used in the text of he proposed rule. In addition, the report notes that the FDIC is also considering the cumulative burden of all Dodd-Frank Act rulemakings.

Q.2. On April 12, 2011, the Federal Reserve Board, the Federal Deposit Insurance Corporation, the Federal Housing Finance Agency, the Farm Credit Administration, and the Office of the Comptroller of the currency published proposed rules governing margin and capital requirements applicable to covered swap entities that are banks. The proposed rules appear (i) to require those covered swap entities to collect margin from nonfinancial end-users that exceed margin thresholds, and (ii) to specify that such margin be in the form of cash or cash equivalents only. Is this proposal consistent with section 731 of the Dodd-Frank Act which specifically provides that prudential regulators "shall permit the use of noncash collateral, as the regulator . . . determines to be consistent with . . . preserving the financial integrity of markets trading swaps; and . . . preserving the stability of the United States financial system"?

A.2. For swap dealers, major swap participants, and financial end-users, the Agencies were cautious in the proposed rule with respect to the allowable types of noncash collateral; limiting such collateral to only certain types of highly liquid, high-quality debt securities. The Agencies' are concerned about the procyclicality associated with other forms of collateral. That is, during a period of financial stress, the value of non-cash collateral pledged as margin is more likely also to come under stress just as counterparties default and the noncash collateral is required to offset the cost of replacing defaulted swap positions. However, the Agencies are mindful of the need to fully consider other forms of noncash collateral and have included in the NPR a request for comment on whether the Agencies should broaden the list of acceptable noncash collateral and, if so, what haircut should be applied to such collateral.

The Agencies noted in the NPR that even without expanding the list of acceptable collateral, counterparties that wish to rely on other noncash assets to meet margin requirements could pledge those assets with a bank or group of banks in a separate arrangement, such as a secured financing facility, and could draw cash from that arrangement to meet margin requirements. For non-financial end-users, who are the most likely type of counterparty to wish to post noncash collateral, the proposed rule provides credit exposure thresholds, under which a covered swap entity may determine the extent to which available noncash collateral appropriately reduces the covered swap entity'scredit risk, consistent with its credit underwriting expertise. As such, commercial end-users will likely find that they will be able to continue to post the same forms of noncash collateral as they currently post.

———

RESPONSE TO WRITTEN QUESTIONS OF SENATOR CORKER FROM SHEILA C. BAIR

Q.1. Your institutions have been assigned the task of macro prudential risk oversight. Specifically, the Dodd-Frank Act tasked the FSOC with "identifying risks to the financial stability that could arise from the material financial distress or failure of large interconnected bank holding companies or nonbank financial companies." As you know nearly all banks carry U.S. Treasury bills, notes, and bonds on their balance sheet with no capital against them. They are deemed, both implicitly and explicitly, as risk free. But with a $14 trillion debt, no one can guarantee that the bond market will continue to finance U.S. securities at affordable rates. What steps have you taken to ensure that systemically important financial institutions could withstand a material disruption in the U.S. Treasury market from an event such as a major tail at an auction, the liquidation of securities by a major investor such as a foreign central bank, concerns that the United States will attempt to inflate its way out of its debt obligations, an outright debt downgrade by a major rating agency, or market concern over the prospects for a technical default? What impact would an event such as the loss of market confidence in U.S. debt and subsequent increase in U.S. borrowing rates have on the institutions in your purview? And what steps can you take to ensure that the balance sheets of systemically important institutions could withstand such an event and that such an event would not lead to a systemic crisis similar to or worse than that experienced in 2008?

A.1. Financial institutions as well as other investors have significant holdings in U.S. Government-related debt, so material events related to these investments could have a substantial credit impact on these firms. Moreover, as more fully described in response to question 2 below, the loss of confidence in U.S. debt could create sudden volatility in interest rates, which could prove challenging to bank and bank-holding company revenue streams. These firms are in a substantially better position with regard to capital and liquidity to withstand stress than they were in 2008; however, depending on the length and depth of an event such as described, this would have a significant adverse impact on their operations.

The largest banks and bank-holding companies are generally supervised by the Office of the Comptroller of the Currency and the Board of Governors of the Federal Reserve System (Federal Reserve). Nevertheless, in the normal course, the FDIC works with these agencies to evaluate the level of capital and liquidity they hold relative to specific asset classes and their overall risk structure and to evaluate these firms' ability to withstand stress events. Going forward, Section 165 of the *Dodd-Frank Wall Street Reform and Consumer Protection Act* (Dodd-Frank Act) requires stress testing by the regulators and the firms themselves, for large banking organizations and systemically important nonbank financial institutions (SIFIs) supervised by the Federal Reserve.

Additionally, just last week, Federal banking regulators issued supervisory guidance for comment to outline broad principles for a satisfactory stress testing framework and how stress testing can be employed as an important component of risk management.

Q.2. What other major systemic risks are you currently most concerned about? What steps are you taking to address these?

A.2. The primary purpose of the Financial Stability Oversight Council (FSOC) is to identify risks to financial stability, respond to emerging threats in the system, and promote market discipline. From the FDIC's perspective, the most important systemic risks and emerging threats to our financial system at the present time involve excessive reliance on debt and financial leverage, continued lack of market discipline due to perceptions of "too big to fail," lingering problems in mortgage servicing, and interest rate risk. My written statement to the Committee describes these areas more fully, along with the steps being taken to address them.

RESPONSE TO WRITTEN QUESTIONS OF SENATOR VITTER FROM SHEILA C. BAIR

Q.1. Dodd-Frank set forth a comprehensive list of factors that FSOC must consider when determining whether a company posed a systemic risk and deserves Fed oversight. The council, in its advanced notice of proposed rulemaking, sets forth 15 categories of questions for the industry to comment on and address. However, the proposed rules give no indication of the specific criteria or framework that the council intends to use in making SIFI designations—other than what is already set forth in Dodd-Frank. As a result, potential SIFIs have no idea where they may stand in the designation process. Will the council provide additional information about the quantitative metrics it will use when making a SIFI designation?

A.1. The FSOC issued an ANPR and NPR describing the processes and procedures that will inform the FSOC's designation of SIFIs under the Dodd-Frank Act. Concerns have been raised about the lack of detail and clarity regarding the designation process in the ANPR and NPR. The FDIC agrees that it is important that the FSOC move forward and develop some hard metrics to guide the SIFI designation process. The FSOC is in the process of developing further clarification of the metrics for comment that will provide more specificity as to the measures and approaches being considered.

Q.2. Would the council agree that leverage is likely to be the one factor that is most likely to create conditions that result in systemic risk? If so, how will the council go about identifying which entities use leverage?

A.2. The FDIC does not speak for the FSOC as a whole, but from the FDIC's perspective, excessive reliance on debt and financial leverage is currently one of the most important systemic risks and emerging threats to our financial system, along with continued lack of market discipline due to perceptions of "too big to fail," lingering problems in mortgage servicing, and interest rate risk. My written statement to the Committee describes these areas more fully, along with the steps being taken to address them.

The Federal banking agencies that are members of FSOC closely monitor leverage in the banking system through the normal supervision process. Also, under the Dodd-Frank Act, the largest, most interconnected financial institutions—banks and nonbank financial companies—will be subject to enhanced prudential standards. Core elements of these enhanced standards will be strengthened capital and liquidity requirements.

The FDIC believes that recent efforts to strengthen the capital base of our largest financial institutions are an important element to restraining financial leverage and enhancing the stability of our system. Going forward, the FSOC and its member agencies will need to continue to monitor and look for ways to reduce excess leverage throughout the system.

Q.3. One of the first steps in the systemic designation process, as outlined in the proposed rule, is that after identifying a nonbank financial company for possible designation the FSOC will provide the company with a written preliminary notice that the council is considering making proposed determination that the company is systemically significant. Is receipt of such a notice a material event that might affect the financial situation or the value of a company's shares in the mind of the investors? If so, wouldn't it need to be disclosed to investors under securities laws?

A.3. The FSOC is responsible for designating nonbank SIFIs. A company designated as a SIFI will continue to be required to comply with other applicable laws, such as the securities laws, which require certain public disclosures. The FDIC does not administer securities laws and thus defers to the Securities and Exchange Commission on questions regarding a public company's disclosure requirements under U.S. securities laws.

While a preliminary notice from the FSOC could be significant for a company, in many cases the market may already have anticipated such a designation with respect to the value of a company's shares.

RESPONSE TO WRITTEN QUESTIONS OF SENATOR TOOMEY
FROM SHEILA C. BAIR

Q.1. Last week, Chairman Bernanke indicated that bank holding companies larger than $50 billion, designated as systemically significant by the Dodd-Frank Act, will be treated on a tiered scale when you establish enhanced supervisory standards. These institutions range from relatively basic commercial banks not much larger than the $50 billion to more complex and interdependent global financial firms that are up to 40 times the threshold. Do you expect the tiered standards to be based on a firm's asset size or on factors more directly related to financial system risk, such as complexity of a firm's businesses, its funding sources and liquidity, its importance to the daily functioning of the capital markets and its interconnectedness to other financial firms?

A.1. The tiered standards mentioned in the question relate to the way the Federal Reserve will apply heightened prudential standards to bank holding companies as the primary Federal regulator of these companies. The FDIC will be dealing with these firms from a resolution perspective, and their resolution plans will reflect the complexity of their operations. While there will not be any formal tiering of plan review and monitoring at this point, there are some natural breaks in the size and complexity of the firms. The larger more complex and interdependent global financial firms' resolution plans will be very large and will require substantial resources to analyze and monitor. They are expected to cover every aspect of a firm's operations so the larger the firm the more extensive the plan. Smaller firms will be expected to have the same comprehensive coverage of their operations; however, because of the smaller size and less complex nature of their operations, the firm's plans will be significantly smaller and therefore take less time to analyze and monitor.

Q.2. As FSOC considers how to determine the systemic relevance of the investment fund asset management industry, wouldn't it be more appropriate for FSOC to look at the various individual funds themselves, of which there may be several under one advisor, rather than focus on the advisor entity?

- Isn't it true that each of those funds may operate with separate and distinct investment strategies, each with its own unique risks?
- Isn't it the case that the vast majority of the assets are located at the funds and not at the adviser (sic) entity?

A.2. In March, the FSOC reviewed broad risks in the structure of a particular type of mutual fund, money market mutual funds (MMMFs), SEC regulatory actions to address these risks, and the additional risk-constraining options presented in the President's Working Group on Financial Markets' (PWG) report on MMMFs. As described in the PWG report, MMMFs can be a risk transmission mechanism for the financial system. For example, the September 2008 run on money market funds, which began after the failure of Lehman Brothers, caused significant capital losses at a large MMMF. Amid broad concerns about the safety of MMMFs and other financial institutions, investors rapidly redeemed MMMF shares, and the cash needs of MMMFs exacerbated strains in short-term funding markets.

These strains, in turn, threatened the broader economy, as firms and institutions dependent upon those markets for short-term financing found credit increasingly difficult to obtain. Forceful Government action was taken to stop the run, restore investor confidence, and prevent the development of an even more severe recession. Even so, short-term funding markets remained disrupted for some time. Last month, the FDIC participated with other FSOC members in an SEC-sponsored roundtable with interested stakeholders to discuss reform options further.

While the FSOC has considered broad systemic risks related to MMMFs, the thrust of the question above appears to relate to whether and how the FSOC would designate mutual funds and/or their advisors as SIFIs. The SEC is the primary regulator of mutual funds, and we cannot dispute the statements above about the operations of mutual funds. Nevertheless, the process of designating which SIFIs will be subject to heightened supervision by the Federal Reserve under Title I of the Dodd-Frank Act is not yet complete. Therefore, it is still uncertain which entities will receive a SIFI designation.

In determining the appropriate way to designate SIFIs, the FDIC is focused on getting the metrics right rather than identifying specific types of entities for designation. Importantly, and as described more fully above, the FDIC believes that the ability of an entity to be resolved in bankruptcy without systemic impact should be a key consideration in the SIFI designation process.

Q.3. What additional protection/supervision could the Fed provide for mutual funds that the SEC isn't already providing? Do we really need to subject this industry to an additional layer of regulation, especially a "systemic risk" regulation?

A.3. The SEC is the primary regulator for mutual funds. As described above, the SIFI designation process is not yet complete. Therefore, no heighted prudential standards or capital requirements have been imposed by the Federal Reserve on any SIFI, nor have any additional regulations on a particular industry been proposed incident to the SIFI designation process.

Q.4. Can you share with us what the FSOC, OFR, FDIC and Fed are contemplating by way of fees that they may assess on SIFIs?

A.4. Section 155(d) of the Dodd-Frank Act requires the Treasury Secretary, beginning 2 years after enactment, to establish, by regulation, an assessment schedule applicable to bank holding companies with total consolidated assets of $50 billion or greater and nonbank financial holding companies supervised by the Federal Reserve to collect assessments equal to the total expenses of the Office of Financial Research (OFR). The FDIC is not aware of any proposed rule by the Treasury Secretary in this regard. The FDIC is not contemplating assessing fees on SIFIs and is not aware of any plans by FSOC to assess such fees.

International Competitiveness

Q.5. It is critical for the continued competitiveness of the U.S. markets that a regulatory arbitrage does not develop among markets that favors markets in Europe and Asia over U.S. markets. Will the FSOC commit to ensuring that the timing of the finalization and implementation of rulemaking under Dodd Frank does not impair the competitiveness of U.S. markets?

How will FSOC ensure that U.S. firms will have equal access to European markets as European firms will have to U.S. markets?

A.5. The FSOC's statutory duties under section 112(a)(2) of the Dodd-Frank Act include monitoring domestic and international regulatory proposals and developments and advising Congress and making recommendations in such areas that will enhance the competitiveness of U.S. financial markets as well as the integrity, efficiency, and stability of such markets. Also, under section 752 of the Dodd-Frank Act, the CFTC, the SEC, and the prudential regulators are required to consult and coordinate with foreign regulatory authorities on establishing consistent international standards with respect to the regulation of covered derivatives.

Consistent standards will ensure equal access to all markets. The FDIC, however, would not support weak standards in order to be consistent with lower standards adopted by a foreign jurisdiction.

With respect to timing, the prudential regulators, the CFTC, and the SEC have primary authority to address the effective date of derivatives reform regulations and are able to take international coordination into account.

Q.6. How will FSOC ensure that Basel III will be implemented in the United States in a manner that is not more stringent than in Europe, making U.S. firms less competitive globally?

A.6. International consistency in capital requirements is a worthy goal. We must, however, guard against pursuing the competitiveness of U.S. firms in a way that compromises their safety-and-soundness and the stability of our banking system. The cost of financial crises for the real economy is severe, and we need to pursue the changes in capital regulation needed to prevent a recurrence.

The Federal banking agencies will have primary responsibility for implementing the Basel III capital and liquidity standards. Within the Basel Committee we have worked to ensure as level a playing field as possible for U.S. banking organizations, not only in Europe but across the rest of the global financial system. In seeking to restore the resilience of the international financial system, we have allied ourselves with those Basel Committee members seeking strong capital and liquidity standards. However, as always in the international arena, certain countries believe the Basel III capital and liquidity standards are too stringent. Of necessity, Basel III is a compromise. Even so, Basel III goes a long way toward addressing the weaknesses in the regulatory capital framework exposed by the financial crisis.

The Basel capital standards always have been stated minimums and, in the United States, we consistently have had higher standards than Basel required (and many other Basel member countries are in the same situation). For example, the Basel I and Basel II minimum capital requirements were 4 percent tier 1 and 8 percent total risk-based capital ratios. However, in the United States, to be well capitalized a bank must have 6 percent tier 1 and 10 percent total risk-based capital ratios. When Basel II was introduced in the United States, we set higher floors over a longer period to ensure that regulatory capital at the largest internationally active U.S. banks would not decline precipitously. Currently, we also are one of the few countries to have a leverage ratio that complements our risk-based capital requirements. We believe our higher capital requirements strengthen our banks and support their international competitiveness. However, we are aware that implementation of capital requirements across a number of Basel member countries is not as rigorous as in the United States, and we continually monitor this as part of our normal supervisory process and through the Basel Committee.

RESPONSE TO WRITTEN QUESTION OF SENATOR KIRK FROM SHEILA C. BAIR

Q.1. Much about SIFI designation focuses on "too big to fail" institutions. What about financial management practices that can weaken a number of smaller players in an industry? What can FSOC do to encourage best practices of asset/liability management, or assure the proper allocation of capital that reflects the risk underlying assets held?

A.1. The primary purpose of the FSOC is to identify risks to financial stability, respond to emerging threats in the system, and promote market discipline. The statutory language of the Dodd-Frank Act in Section 112 addresses these responsibilities largely in terms of large interconnected bank holding companies and SIFIs because they can pose significant risks to the financial stability of the United States, as demonstrated in the recent crisis.

However, as the primary Federal supervisor for most community banks in the United States, the FDIC is keenly aware of their importance in our financial system. Community banks provide credit, depository, and other financial services to consumers and businesses on main street, and are playing a vital economic role as cities and towns recover from the recession. As the FSOC discusses and issues recommendations regarding broad issues and best practices, including those described above, they should consider effects on all players in the financial system, large and small. In my capacity as an FSOC voting member and in the FDIC's role as a community bank supervisor, I am particularly focused on ensuring that the Council considers community banks and the communities they serve in its deliberations.

RESPONSE TO WRITTEN QUESTION OF SENATOR SHELBY FROM JOHN WALSH

Q.1. One of the Council's purposes is to monitor systemic risk and alert Congress and regulators of any systemic risks it discovers. What are the most serious systemic risks presently facing the U.S. economy?

A.1. The potential loss of investor confidence in U.S. debt and the impact such a loss would have on interest rates and the overall economy, is a serious concern that we are monitoring closely. While current Treasury yields and implied volatilities remain relatively low, suggesting continued market confidence, I share the views of many others that over the long term our nation's current fiscal imbalance is not sustainable and must be addressed. More generally, we are concerned that the prolonged low interest rate environment has created incentives for banks and other investors to take on significant levels of interest rate risk. In response, the OCC and other U.S. banking agencies have been emphasizing the need for bankers to improve their interest rate risk management systems.

As the economy begins to recover, we are seeing some signs of weakening underwriting standards, especially in the leveraged loan markets. While our recent annual underwriting survey did not indicate that standards have weakened systematically across lending products, we are concerned that banks not return to the lax underwriting practices that became widespread prior to the crisis. When we released our survey results, we cautioned national banks on the need to maintain prudent underwriting standards. The agencies' Shared National Credit review, currently underway, will be another key window in helping us to evaluate the current quality of banks' large credit portfolios and whether additional action is needed.

The housing sector continues to be an area that poses substantial risk to the overall economy and many banks' credit portfolios. While there are many factors affecting this market, the overhang of distressed properties that need to be resolved is certainly one of them. The action taken against the mortgage servicers under our jurisdiction to fix their servicing and mortgage foreclosure processing problems should help unblock the system. More broadly, we continue to closely monitor trends in mortgage loan portfolios, including mortgage modifications, through our comprehensive Mortgage Metrics database and reports.

Through the FSOC's systemic risk committee, we continue to monitor a number of other potential risk areas including the European debt situation, continued vulnerabilities in short-term funding markets, and concentrations within the financial sector.

Finally, as noted in recent remarks before the Housing Policy Council of The Financial Services Roundtable, I agree with others that the sheer volume and magnitude of regulatory changes forthcoming under the Dodd-Frank Act and Basel III reforms has created uncertainty as supervisors and market participants attempt to digest and assess the cumulative impact that these changes may have on markets and business models.

RESPONSE TO WRITTEN QUESTIONS OF SENATOR REED FROM JOHN WALSH

Q.1.a. The Interagency Review of Foreclosure Policies and Practices notes that about 2,800 borrower foreclosure files in various stages of foreclosure were reviewed.

The second footnote in The Interagency Review of Foreclosure Policies and Practices briefly explains how these files were selected, but please describe, with as much detail as possible, the sampling methodology and the population from which the samples were selected. What attributes were selected for testing? Please provide the deviations that were found. We would be particularly interested in what factors affected "examiner judgment" in the selection of these files.

A.1.a. The file review sample was judgmentally selected to include loans from all States where the servicer had foreclosure activity—both judicial as well as non-judicial States. In selecting file samples, examiners gave consideration to States with the highest foreclosure activity and those where internal self assessments noted issues or concerns. Examiners also considered complaints filed with the OCC.

Q.1.b. How is the OCC confident that these 2,800 borrower files constitute a statistically significant sample size?

A.1.b. The file review was not intended to make any statistical inferences with respect to foreclosure actions. Instead, it was intended to draw and support general conclusions about servicer processes, including the accuracy and compliance of legal filings. While this was not a statistical sample, it was an objective and unbiased reflection of each servicer's foreclosure activities.

Q.1.c. Of these 2,800 borrower foreclosure files, how many of these files reflected completed foreclosures?

A.1.c. Of the 1,697 files reviewed at the eight OCC banks, 623 were completed foreclosure sales.

Q.2.a. The OCC's Consent Order requires banks to hire an independent consultant to review foreclosures from 2009 and 2010 to ensure that everything was done in accordance with applicable laws and regulations.

What factors, if any, prevented the OCC from conducting such a review?

A.2.a. The extraordinary resource demands needed to conduct foreclosure reviews of the scope that the OCC will require, make it impossible for the OCC to perform that work within any reasonable timeframe. In addition, the Government procurement process for awarding contracts directly with third parties to conduct foreclosure reviews would be lengthy and significantly delay implementation of the foreclosure reviews and restitution to any affected customers. As described below, the OCC has applied a number of measures to assure that the consultants are independent and conduct their work independently.

Q.2.b. Please describe all criteria to be used by the OCC in determining that an independent consultant is acceptable to the OCC. Will an independent consultant be expected to have expertise in servicing issues? If so, how will the OCC determine that this independent consultant has sufficient expertise to qualify as an independent consultant?

A.2.b. The OCC considers various factors concerning a consultant's prior work in determining the independence of the consultant. We also determine if the proposed consultant has sufficient resources and expertise to successfully complete the review. And we have required that specific language be included in the engagement letters entered into between the servicer and the consultant that makes clear that the consultant takes direction from the OCC, not the servicer.

Q.2.c. Please describe the process for the OCC to review the selection of an independent consultant and, if necessary, object to the selection.

A.2.c. Per the Consent Orders, the OCC must approve the independent consultant and their engagement letter that sets forth: (a) the methodology for conducting the foreclosure review, including: (i) a description of the information systems and documents to be reviewed, including the selection of criteria for cases to be reviewed; (ii) the criteria for evaluating the reasonableness of fees and penalties; (iii) other procedures necessary to make the required determinations (such as through interviews of employees and third parties and a process for submission and review of borrower claims and complaints); and (iv) any proposed sampling techniques; and (b) expertise and resources to be dedicated to the foreclosure review. The independence, expertise and resources of each consultant will be reviewed by OCC examiners in consultation with OCC Enforcement and Compliance attorneys.

Q.2.d. What is the definition of an "independent consultant"? What is considered to be independent? Would an independent public accounting firm or contractor that has previously performed auditing services or other services for the bank be considered independent?

A.2.d. Consultants hired to undertake the foreclosure review must function as true "independent" parties, with no conflicting interests or priorities. For example, firms and/or counsel that currently, or have in the past represented the servicer in any manner concerning areas addressed in the Consent Orders may not meet the standards of independence. In addition, sample segments and sizes must be decided by the independent consultant and final results must be the product and opinion of the independent consultant, unaffected by the views of the institution or its directors or management.

The independent consultants may retain outside counsel to provide necessary legal expertise in completing the foreclosure review. However, any such outside counsel must be independent of the outside counsel retained by the institution to provide legal representation to the institution with respect to the Consent Orders or legal advice concerning matters covered by the Consent Orders. The independent consultant's work may not be subject to direction or influence from counsel for the institution.

Likewise, an independent public accounting firm that has previously performed auditing services or other services for the bank may be independent, but only if previous work performed does not conflict with foreclosure review and there is a clear separation of duties between auditors performing the foreclosure review and those performing other auditing services.

Q.2.e. Who at the Bank will be engaging the independent consultant? The Board of Directors, the CEO, the CFO, an independent committee, or someone else? Will the OCC be a party to the engagement letter or have any rights under the engagement letter?

A.2.e. The OCC requires the independent consultant to be retained by the bank, and the OCC will not be a party to the engagement letters. The Board of Directors is responsible for engagement of the independent consultant, but it may delegate authority to execute the engagement letter to senior management.

Q.2.f. Will the letters of engagement be made available to the relevant Congressional Committees? If the protection of proprietary information is a concern, will the OCC make the necessary arrangements to share these letters with the relevant Congressional Committees so that Congress may conduct its oversight role?

A.2.f. The engagement letters are confidential supervisory information.

Q.2.g. How will the OCC ensure that the consultant's procedures for the Foreclosure Review will be sufficient?

A.2.g. OCC onsite examiners will review action plans developed by independent consultants including methodology for conducting foreclosure reviews. In addition, the OCC will conduct a horizontal review of all engagement letters and action plans across banks to ensure consistency in foreclosure review methodology and identify and address common deficiencies. Per the Orders, the engagement letters will set forth: (a) the methodology for conducting the foreclosure review, including: (i) a description of the information systems and documents to be reviewed, including the selection of criteria for cases to be reviewed; (ii) the criteria for evaluating the reasonableness of fees and penalties; (iii) other procedures necessary to make the required determinations (such as through interviews of employees and third parties and a process for submission and review of borrower claims and complaints); and (iv) any proposed sampling techniques; and (b) expertise and resources to be dedicated to the foreclosure review. Onsite examiners will maintain ongoing contact with the independent consultants during the review process to ensure that the action plans are appropriately implemented.

Q.3.a. As part of this review, the consultants are supposed to determine if any errors, misrepresentations, or other deficiencies identified in the review resulted in financial injury to the borrower.

Will a consistent methodology be applied to ensure that the selection criteria provides for a representative sample? If not, why not? How will the sampling results be considered reliable absent a statistically valid sampling methodology?

A.3.a. On May 20, 2011, the OCC provided and discussed Foreclosure Review guidance with all institutions subject to Consent Orders. The Foreclosure Review guidance addressed supervisory expectations for the review, including the process for selecting a representative sample of customer cases. Certain segments of the population of foreclosure cases may be subject to a statistically valid sampling methodology to achieve the objective of the foreclosure review, while other segments may require more extensive or 100 percent review. The guidance is expected to be applied consistently across OCC-supervised institutions.

Q.3.b. If sampling is used, what methodology will OCC utilize to provide adequate compensation to all persons that were harmed?

A.3.b. The OCC has instructed all institutions subject to the Consent Orders that any sampling methodology must include procedures for extensive investigation of identified errors, including further "deep-dive" reviews as necessary, to ensure that as many similarly affected borrowers as possible are identified for appropriate remediation. The biggest factor in determining an appropriate remedy is to determine the actual financial harm suffered by homeowners as a result of an improper foreclosure action. The Consent Orders require the independent consultants to develop and submit for OCC approval a plan to remediate all financial injury to borrowers caused by any errors, misrepresentations, or other deficiencies identified in the Foreclosure Review Report. The identification of financial harm will be done through the foreclosure review by the independent consultant. Given that every case is different, the remedy must be specific to the details of the individual case. This could include reimbursing impermissible or excessive penalties, fees, or expenses, or other financial injury suffered that could include taking appropriate steps to remediate any improper foreclosure sale. Restitution will begin after the OCC has provided supervisory non-objection to the remediation plan.

Q.3.c. How will you ensure that this Foreclosure Review is comprehensive, fair, and reliable? What specifically, will you insist on regarding these points?

A.3.c. OCC actions taken and/or planned to ensure the foreclosure review is comprehensive, fair and reliable include:

1. On May 20, 2011, the OCC provided expectations for foreclosure reviews, including guidance on consultant independence, sampling methodology, scope of review, and the process for submission and review of customer complaints, to all of the banks and thrifts subject to Consent Orders.

2. The OCC will review all engagement letters to determine their acceptability prior to the consultants beginning their review. This supervisory review will include an assessment of each engagement letter with the requirements of the Consent Order as well as foreclosure review guidance. Shortcomings will need to be corrected prior to commencing the review.

3. The independent foreclosure review will achieve identification of harmed borrowers through two distinct means: 1) a public complaint process which will provide borrowers who believe they may have suffered financial harm as a result of the banks' foreclosure process with the opportunity to have their complaint reviewed by the independent consultant, and 2) a sampling of loans to uncover, for example, borrowers in high risk segments. We intend to require mortgage servicers to deliver notice letters to every borrower covered by the look-back period to inform them of their right to have their complaint reviewed by an independent consultant. Multiple attempts to reach borrowers will be required for any returned notices. Servicers will be required to undertake a broad range of efforts to reach borrowers that includes broadscale advertising, outreach to State attorneys general, Department of Justice, and other Federal regulatory agencies to solicit information about borrowers who may have filed foreclosure-related complaints with those authorities in the 2009–2010 time period. As well, the consultants are required to conduct a targeted review of high risk segments that includes a robust and tar-

geted sampling methodology to detect borrowers most at risk of harm. This might include a review of covered borrowers who were denied loan modifications, or those who submitted a foreclosure-related complaint to the servicer. Certain borrower segments will require a 100 per cent review such as borrowers protected by the Servicemembers Civil Relief Act and borrowers in bankruptcy whose mortgage was foreclosed upon and whose home was sold.

4. Any foreclosure-related complaints received by the OCC's Customer Assistance Group will be forwarded to the bank for review by the independent consultant.

5. OCC examiners will review foreclosure review findings and results on an ongoing basis and require independent consultants to take action to address any supervisory concerns.

6. Independent consultants must develop and submit for OCC approval a plan to remediate all financial injury to borrowers caused by any errors, misrepresentations, or other deficiencies identified in the Foreclosure Review Report.

7. OCC will review all remediation plans submitted by independent consultants. Restitution will begin after the OCC has provided supervisory non-objection to the remediation plans, and the bank is required to provide the OCC with a report detailing all payments and credits made under the plan.

Q.3.d. How will the OCC determine what qualifies as "financial injury" to the borrower or mortgagee? If an affiant, as part of a foreclosure affidavit, did not have personal knowledge of the assertions in the affidavit, would this qualify as "financial injury" according to the OCC?

A.3.d. For purposes of OCC Consent Orders, "financial injury to the borrower or mortgagee" means monetary harm to the borrower or the mortgagee or owner of the mortgage loan directly caused by errors, misrepresentations, or other deficiencies identified in the foreclosure review. Monetary harm does not include physical injury, pain and suffering, emotional distress or other non-financial harm. This definition of financial injury will be used by independent consultants to determine financial injury. Cases involving affidavits prepared by affiants without personal knowledge will need to be evaluated by the independent consultant for the existence of financial harm.

Q.3.e. If the independent consultant uncovers potentially illegal acts, how is the independent consultant expected to proceed? Will the consultant be required to report this to the Bank's Audit Committee? Other than the OCC, are there other regulators who will be informed about these discoveries? Will these potentially illegal acts be covered and disclosed in the consultant's written report?

A.3.e. Potentially illegal acts discovered should be included in the Foreclosure Review Report prepared by the independent consultant. Under the OCC's supervision, the findings from the Foreclosure Review Report will be submitted to the Board of Directors for review and action.

Q.3.f. Why have you limited the scope of this review just to 2009 and 2010? Is the OCC confident that prior to 2009, there were no

108

"significant problems in foreclosure processing" among the banks under the OCC's jurisdiction? As part of its normal examinations from year to year, did the OCC previously uncover the issues and problems cited in The Interagency Review of Foreclosure Policies and Practices? If so, how did the OCC address these issues and problems? If not, please explain why the OCC did not identify these issues earlier?

A.3.f. OCC/OTS Mortgage Metrics data shows that the majority of foreclosure actions occurred in the 2009 and 2010 timeframe. The OCC did not previously identify the type of unsafe and unsound practices that were noted in the Interagency Review of Foreclosure Policies and Practices because: (1) supervisory efforts were focused on loss mitigation activities; (2) examiners placed reliance on internal audit and compliance functions and other third party, external reviews which did not identify major concerns; and (3) foreclosure processing was historically considered a low-risk activity performed with the assistance of outside legal counsel.

Q.3.g. Once the consultant has completed the review, the consultant, per the OCC's consent order, will be required to submit a written report detailing the findings of the foreclosure review. Will this written report be publicly available? If not, why not? If the protection of proprietary information will be the reason for not making this report public, will the OCC, at the very least, make the necessary arrangements to share this report with the relevant Congressional Committees so that Congress may conduct its oversight role?

A.3.g. The Consent Orders require the independent consultants retained by the servicers to prepare a written report detailing the findings of the Foreclosure Review within 30 days of completion of the review, and to submit the report to the OCC. The reports constitute confidential supervisory information, subject to privilege and other legal restrictions on disclosure and, consequently, they will not be publicly available. However, we expect to provide a public interim report on the look-back process once the details of the look-back are finalized, and then to provide a public report on the results at the end of the process.

Q.4.a. Also as part of this review, the independent consultant will be reviewing the bank's loss mitigation activities.

Will the OCC be requiring the independent consultant to review all denied loan modification files as part of this review? If not, why not?

A.4.a. Foreclosures where the borrower was denied for a loan modification was discussed with the institutions as a distinct sampling segment that could be included in their foreclosure review. To the extent errors are found, we will extensively investigate identified errors, including further "deep-dive" reviews as necessary, to ensure that as many similarly affected borrowers as possible are identified for appropriate remediation.

Q.4.b. The Interagency Review of Foreclosure Policies and Practices notes that the review "did not focus on the loan-modification process." Why not, especially in light of the fact that you are asking the consultants to review loss mitigation activities as part of their review?

A.4.b. The primary scope of the review was centered on foreclosure documentation preparation, governance and vendor management because of documented and publicized cases of "robo signing." However, as part of this foreclosure review, examiners checked to determine if loss mitigation actions, including loan modifications, were offered to borrowers in the sample. If a borrower was denied a loan modification, examiners determined if there was a documented and sufficient reason for the denial.

Q.5. The interaction of global capital requirements (Basel III) and U.S. requirements (FSOC) could result in different criteria being applied to the same financial institution. For example, an institution could be deemed systemically important to the global financial system but not to the financial system in the United States. How is this being addressed? Does this pose any unique risks?

A.5. There are a number of areas where the Basel III capital requirements and the capital-related provisions of the Dodd-Frank Act intersect that the agencies will need to resolve and address as we move forward with our rulemakings. Sorting through and resolving these interactions is one reason why we have moved more slowly than originally anticipated on some of these initiatives. With respect the designation of systemically important financial institutions (SIFIs), we believe the $50 billion threshold established in Dodd-Frank will be more inclusive than the threshold that will be adopted for the so-called global SIFI provisions. Thus we do not believe it is likely that a U.S. bank would be deemed systemically important to the global financial system but not to the United States.

Q.6. A number of commentators and academics have asserted that Basel III capital requirements are too low. For example, a recent Stanford University study (Admati *et al*, published in March 2011) stated that "equity capital ratios significantly higher than 10 percent of un-weighted assets should be seriously considered." It also noted that "bank equity is *not* socially expensive" and "better capitalized banks suffer from fewer distortions in lending decisions and would perform better." In addition, Switzerland has adopted capital ratios for its banks in excess of Basel III. What are the strengths and weaknesses of capital adequacy ratios in excess of those considered under Basel III? (Admati, DeMarzo, Hellwig, Pfleiderer, "Fallacies, Irrelevant Facts, and Myths in the Discussion of Capital Regulation: Why Bank Equity is Not Expensive." Stanford Graduate School of Business Research Paper No. 2065, March 2011.)

A.6. While parts of the paper by Admati, DeMarzo, Hellwig, and Pfleiderer[1] (hereafter ADHP) are thoughtful and well argued, many of their arguments are too simplistic in important respects. The framework used by ADHP to analyze the case for higher capital standards is incomplete, because there is no clear mechanism in the paper to create *any* upper limit to the required capital ratio.

---

[1] Anat R. Admati, Peter M. DeMarzo, Martin F. Hellwig, and Paul Pfleiderer, "Fallacies, Irrelevant Facts, and Myths in the Discussion of Capital Regulation: Why Bank Equity is *Not* Expensive," unpublished manuscript, Graduate School of Business, Stanford University, March 23, 2011.

In their hypothetical world, there is little or no downside to higher capital, because there are unlimited amounts of liquid assets for banks to hold, and unlimited amounts of equity capital that can be raised:

> [H]igher equity capital requirements do not mechanically limit banks' activities, including lending, deposit taking and the issue of liquid, money-like, informationally insensitive securities. Banks can maintain all their existing assets and liabilities and reduce leverage through equity issuance and the expansion of their balance sheets. (ADHP, p.ii)

But the U.S. banking system is in fact fairly large relative to existing markets for equity and liquid securities, so the banking system cannot in practice adopt the approach suggested in the ADHP quote above. As a consequence, although ADHP use the reasoning above to dismiss suggestions that higher capital requirements might reduce the aggregate amount of banking activity, they conduct the discussion within a framework that is incapable of fully addressing the issue.

With regard to higher proposed capital standards in other countries, it is correct that Switzerland recently announced minimum capital requirements well above those under discussion by the Basel Committee as part of Basel III, and that the UK has announced similar measures. However, these other countries face situations markedly different from the United States. In particular, both Switzerland and the UK are home to banks that are far larger relative to their domestic financial systems than is the case in the United States. Each of the three largest UK-based banks has assets that exceed the size of the British economy. The largest Swiss banks are two to three times the size of the entire Swiss economy. In contrast, in the United States the situation is reversed; annual U.S. GDP is about seven times the asset size of even the largest U.S. bank-holding company.

As a result, countries such as Switzerland and the UK face a much different and more acute systemic challenge than the United States; failure or financial distress at firms of such sizes relative to the domestic economy would pose an almost insurmountable challenge for the sovereign. It should not be surprising that those governments feel compelled to take drastic measures to reduce the risks associated with large institutions, and might be willing to do so even at significant expected economic cost in the near-term. While it is important not to be complacent about the significant risks posed by large systemically important institutions in the United States, the nature and scale of the challenge is distinguishable from that in many other developed countries. The U.S. economy is much larger, as are the resources potentially available for addressing problems. This fact reduces the value of comparisons to other countries.

Capital requirements that prevent instability are valuable because unstable banks can be extremely costly to the economy, as is evident during financial crises. But at some level, higher capital also tends to raise the cost of providing banking services, and higher costs lead to those banking services being provided at higher prices (higher interest rates on loans, lower interest rates on deposits, and so on), or to a reduction in the quantity of banking services provided to the economy, or both.

Q.7. In March, Bloomberg noted that 77 percent of the banking assets are held by the nation's ten largest banks—with 35 banks holding assets of $50 billion or more. In February, Moody's granted higher ratings to eight large U.S. banks with higher ratings because of an expectation of future Government support—implicitly suggesting that risky behavior by large banks would be more tolerated, and they would be insulated from failure. Has systemic risk increased after the financial crisis? Why or why not? How is this being addressed?

A.7. The mergers and failures resulting from the financial crisis have left the banking sector more concentrated. Concentration within the financial sector is an issue that FSOC is discussing and addressing on a number of fronts. First and foremost are the efforts being led by the FDIC and Federal Reserve to implement the orderly liquidation authorities under Title II of the Dodd-Frank Act that will facilitate liquidation of large firms. An important corollary to this work will be heightened prudential capital, liquidity, and risk management standards that these firms will be required to meet. Pursuant to section 622 of the Dodd-Frank Act, the FSOC has also issued a study and made recommendations on the implementation of section 622 of the Dodd-Frank Act that establishes a financial-sector concentration limit generally prohibiting a financial company from merging, consolidating with, or acquiring another company if the resulting company's consolidated liabilities would exceed 10 percent of the aggregate consolidated liabilities of all financial companies. The study, published for comment, concluded that a concentration limit will have a positive impact on U.S. financial stability. It also made a number of technical recommendations to address practical difficulties likely to arise in its administration and enforcement, such as the definition of liabilities for certain companies that do not currently calculate or report risk-weighted assets. Final recommendations, following the notice and comment period, are expected later this year.

***

RESPONSE TO WRITTEN QUESTIONS OF SENATOR CRAPO FROM JOHN WALSH

Q.1.a. According to the American Banker, Annette L. Nazareth, a former SEC Commissioner, called the timetables imposed by the Dodd-Frank Act "wildly aggressive." "These agencies were dealt a very bad hand," she said. "These deadlines could actually be systemic-risk raising." Given the importance of rigorous cost-benefit and economic impact analyses and the need for due consideration of public comments, would additional time for adoption of the Dodd-Frank Act rules improve your rulemaking process and the substance of your final rules?

A.1.a. I share the view that the Dodd-Frank Act requires the agencies to issue a very large number of rules that will affect businesses and consumers profoundly. The OCC recognizes that we must balance the requirement that we meet applicable statutory deadlines with the need to carefully consider the impact of regulations, and to provide a comment period that allows the public sufficient time to contribute meaningful comments. While meeting all of our statutory deadlines will be a challenge, in my view, we should not favor speed over a robust process designed to ensure that we get a rule right.

Q.1.b. Chairman Bair's testimony was unclear regarding whether the FSOC has the authority to issue a revised rule on the designation of nonbank financial institutions. She and others indicated some type of guidance might be issued instead. Is it in fact the case, in general, that the FSOC does not have authority to issue rules under Title I that have the force and effect of law? If the FSOC has the authority in general to issue such rules on designation, why specifically would the FSOC be precluded from re-proposing a rule that is currently pending? Is there additional authority the FSOC would need from Congress to issue such rules or to proceed with re-proposing its NPR on designation? If yes, what specific authority would the FSOC need from Congress for the FSOC to have the ability to proceed?

A.1.b. The FSOC has the authority to issue rules setting forth its understanding and interpretation of the governing statute.

The process of making systemic risk determinations is a critical function of the FSOC. As I noted in my testimony, the FSOC must achieve the right balance between providing sufficient clarity in our rules and transparency in our designation process and avoiding overly simplistic approaches that fail to recognize and consider the facts and circumstances of individual firms and specific industries and fail to maintain the necessary flexibility to react to the evolving nature of firms and markets. In response to concerns raised by industry participants, the FSOC plans to seek comment on additional details regarding its standards for assessing systemic risk before issuing a final rule.

Q.1.c. In an August speech at NYU's Stern School of Business, Treasury Secretary Geithner outlined six principles that he said would guide implementation, and then he added, "You should hold us accountable for honoring them." His final principle was bringing more order and integration to the regulatory process. He said the agencies responsible for reforms will have to work "together, not against each other. This requires us to look carefully at the overall interaction of regulations designed by different regulators and assess the overall burden they present relative to the benefits they offer." Do you intend to follow through with this commitment with some form of status report that provides a quantitative and qualitative review of the overall interaction of all the hundreds of proposed rules by the different regulators and assess the overall burden they present relative to the benefits they offer?

A.1.c. I agree that the various rules required by the Dodd-Frank Act involve complex issues and, as I have noted, they will interact in ways that we cannot yet envision. I believe that an accurate assessment of the overall interaction of all of the hundreds of rules being proposed by different regulators cannot be made until the final rules have been issued and we begin to judge the effect they have on how institutions conduct business.

Q.2. On April 12, 2011 the Federal Reserve Board, the Federal Deposit Insurance Corporation, the Federal Housing Finance Agency, the Farm Credit Administration, and the Office of the Comptroller of the Currency published proposed rules governing margin and capital requirements applicable to covered swap entities that are banks. The proposed rules appear (i) to require those covered swap entities to collect margin from nonfinancial end-users that exceed margin thresholds, and (ii) to specify that such margin be in the form of cash or cash equivalents only. Is this proposal consistent with section 731 of the Dodd-Frank Act which specifically provides that prudential regulators "shall permit the use of noncash collateral, as the regulator . . .determines to be consistent with . . . preserving the financial integrity of markets trading swaps; and . . . preserving the stability of the United States financial system?

A.2. Currently, the customer relationship between a bank swap dealer and a commercial end-user generally is broader than swaps. In addition to acting as the commercial firm's swap dealer, the bank will typically also act as a lender to the commercial firm, extending working capital lines of credit and other types of loans.

Like a line of credit, a swap transaction exposes the bank to credit risk—the risk that the counterparty will not be able to make future payments due under the terms of the swap transaction. Accordingly, banking regulators require banks under their supervision to manage the credit risk of the swaps aspect of their customer relationships the same way they manage other credit relationships, and to manage the combined credit risks of each customer on an aggregate basis. This includes steps such as performing independent credit underwriting of new customers to set a combined credit exposure limit for the particular customer, monitoring their financial condition and creditworthiness on an ongoing basis, and reporting all credit exposures with each customer to management on a combined basis. If a customer's financial condition declines such that their existing credit limit is no longer justified, or if the customer's credit exposure to the bank is nearing the limit for other factors—such as unanticipated changes in the market factors underlying swap transactions—banking regulators expect management of the bank to be proactive in addressing the situation. Appropriate steps by the bank include enhanced monitoring, working with the customer to reduce the credit exposure, working with other credit institutions to see if they will take over portions of the bank's credit relationships with the customer, obtaining additional collateral, etc. This supervisory oversight is a core component of safety and soundness supervision, and the banking regulators have maintained published guidance requiring these measures for years.

The proposed rule makes something of a change, in that it would codify the central tenet of this guidance into a regulation. But importantly, it does not contemplate any fundamental change in current practice. It simply requires banks, in determining whether to enter into a swap with a nonfinancial customer, to evaluate the range of credit exposure that is expected to arise under the swap and, if it exceeds the bank's all-in credit exposure limit for that customer, decline the transaction or take other appropriate steps before proceeding, such as obtaining collateral, freeing up additional credit limit by reducing undrawn lines of credit, obtaining a guarantee, etc. If unexpected market factors cause the credit exposure to exceed the limit over the life of an executed swap transaction, the bank would be expected to manage it proactively, as per current standards. But if the bank intends to enter into swaps exceeding its internal credit exposure limit for the customer, it must obtain margin. Any other approach would be contrary to core safety and soundness principles.

On the topic of noncash collateral and commercial counterparties, the preamble of the proposed rule notes that banks may determine the extent to which available noncash collateral appropriately reduces the bank's credit risk in setting the commercial counterparty's credit limit, consistent with the bank's credit underwriting expertise. We believe this appropriately allows commercial end-users to obtain the benefit of their noncash collateral in swap transactions consistent with section 731. There would be profound practical difficulties incorporating most types of noncash collateral into the definition of eligible collateral under the regulations. In order to serve the purpose of having margin requirements in the first place, margin collateral must be highly liquid in times of crisis and susceptible to certainty in its valuation. While certain forms of noncash items can meet this standard, such as very high quality debt instruments subject to regulatory-specified "haircuts" to account for their interest rate price risk and liquidity risk as observed in periods of previous market stress, it is impractical to attempt to establish haircuts for all the different possible types of noncash collateral that commercial counterparties might want to offer. In addition, the haircuts, in order to be prudent, would of necessity be quite steep.

***

RESPONSE TO WRITTEN QUESTIONS OF SENATOR CORKER FROM JOHN WALSH

Q.1. Your institutions have been assigned the task of macro prudential risk oversight. Specifically, the Dodd-Frank Act tasked the FSOC with "identifying risks to the financial stability that could arise from the material financial distress or failure of large interconnected bank holding companies or nonbank financial companies." As you know nearly all banks carry U.S. Treasury bills, notes, and bonds on their balance sheet with no capital against them. They are deemed, both implicitly and explicitly, as risk free. But with a $14 trillion debt, no one can guarantee that the bond market will continue to finance U.S. securities at affordable rates. What steps have you taken to ensure that systemically important financial institutions could withstand a material disruption in the U.S. Treasury market from an event such as a major tail at an auction, the liquidation of securities by a major investor such as a foreign central bank, concerns that the United States will attempt to inflate its way out of its debt obligations, an outright debt downgrade by a major rating agency, or market concern over the prospects for a technical default? What impact would an event such as the loss of market confidence in U.S. debt and subsequent increase in U.S. borrowing rates have on the institutions in your purview? And what steps can you take to ensure that the balance sheets of systemically important institutions could withstand such an event and that such an event would not lead to a systemic crisis similar to or worse than that experienced in 2008?

A.1. The U.S. fiscal situation, and its potential impact on the market's confidence in U.S. debt securities and on the role of the dollar as the principal international reserve asset, has been and continues to be an issue that FSOC is closely monitoring. Treasury Department staff provides periodic briefings on their assessments of the U.S. Treasury debt markets and available short-term tools to provide continued funding of the U.S. Government under the current statutory debt limit. Although current Treasury yields and implied volatilities remain relatively low, suggesting continued market confidence, I share the views of many others that over the long term, our nation's current fiscal imbalance is not sustainable and must be addressed. And indeed there are some signs of increasing concerns by some market players. For example, the volume of trading on credit-default swaps insuring U.S. Treasuries is up sharply.

U.S. Treasury securities represent a fairly small proportion of national banks' total investment securities portfolios. As of March 31, 2011, U.S. Treasury securities in national banks' securities portfolios totaled approximately $137 billion, representing 8.4 percent of their total securities holdings and 1.6 percent of total assets. An additional $28 billion was held in national banks' trading portfolios (representing only 4 percent of trading assets and 0.3 percent of total national bank assets). While it is true that under the OCC's risk-based capital rules, U.S. Treasuries are assigned a zero credit risk-weight, these holdings are included in a bank's leverage capital ratio and in the market risk capital requirements for banks with significant trading portfolios.

Rather than direct losses on their Treasury holdings, the greater risk posed to national banks from the loss of investor confidence in U.S. debt is the potential impact such a loss would have on interest rates and banks' attendant interest rate risk exposures, and the secondary effects that higher interest rates would have on the overall economy, and hence banks' credit portfolios. The potential effect of higher interest rates on banks' capital and earnings is a risk that the OCC monitors and our examiners assess as part of our ongoing supervision of national banks. We have been particularly concerned that the prolonged low interest rate environment, coupled with a relatively steep yield curve and lackluster loan demand, has provided incentives for banks to take on additional interest rate risk. In January 2010, the OCC and other Federal banking agencies issued an advisory to all financial institutions on interest rate risk management. The advisory highlights the need for institutions to identify, monitor, and manage their interest rate risk exposures and to conduct periodic stress tests of their exposures beyond typical industry conventions, including changes in rates of greater magnitude (*e.g.,* up and down 300 and 400 basis points) across different tenors to reflect changing slopes and twists of the yield curve. Monitoring and assessing banks' interest rate risk continues to be an area of emphasis in our examinations. At large national banks that have significant trading operations, examiners likewise regularly evaluate the market, operational, liquidity, and credit risks arising from those activities. These assessments include evaluating the banks' contingency funding plans, and the use of U.S. Treasury securities as collateral in those operations.

Q.2. What other major systemic risks are you currently most concerned about? What steps are you taking to address these?

A.2. In addition to heightened interest rate risk, there are several other risk areas that we are closely monitoring. As the economy begins to recover, we are seeing some signs of weakening underwriting standards, especially in the leveraged loan markets. While our annual underwriting survey does not indicate that standards have weakened systematically across lending products, we are concerned that banks not return to the lax underwriting practices that became widespread prior to the crisis. When we released our survey results, we cautioned national banks on the need to maintain prudent underwriting standards. The agencies' Shared National Credit review, currently underway, will be another key window in helping us to evaluate the current quality of banks' large credit portfolios and whether additional action is needed.

The housing sector continues to be an area that poses substantial risk to the overall economy and many banks' credit portfolios. While there are many factors affecting this market, the overhang of distressed properties that need to be resolved is certainly one of them. The action taken against the mortgage servicers under our jurisdiction to fix their servicing and mortgage foreclosure processing problems should help unblock the system. More broadly, we continue to closely monitor trends in mortgage loan portfolios, including mortgage modifications, through our comprehensive Mortgage Metrics database and reports.

Through the FSOC's systemic risk committee, we continue to monitor a number of other potential risk areas including the European debt situation, continued vulnerabilities in short-term funding markets, and concentrations within the financial sector.

Finally, as noted in recent remarks before the Housing Policy Council of The Financial Services Roundtable, I agree with others that the sheer volume and magnitude of regulatory changes forthcoming under the Dodd-Frank Act and Basel III reforms has created uncertainty as supervisors and market participants attempt to digest and assess the cumulative impact that these changes may have on markets and business models.

RESPONSE TO WRITTEN QUESTIONS OF SENATOR VITTER FROM JOHN WALSH

Q.1. Dodd-Frank set forth a comprehensive list of factors that FSOC must consider when determining whether a company posed a systemic risk and deserves Fed oversight. The council, in its advanced notice of proposed rulemaking, sets forth 15 categories of questions for the industry to comment on and address. However, the proposed rules give no indication of the specific criteria or framework that the council intends to use in making SIFI designations—other than what is already set forth in Dodd-Frank. As a result, potential SIFIs have no idea where they may stand in the designation process. Will the council provide additional information about the quantitative metrics it will use when making an SIFI designation?

A.1. In response to concerns raised by commenters and others, FSOC has agreed to provide and seek comment on additional details regarding FSOC's standards for assessing systemic risk before issuing a final rule. While the details of such additional guidance is still being developed, I anticipate it will include more specific examples of some of the metrics and thresholds that FSOC will consider in making these determinations. As I noted in my written statement, it will be critical that FSOC strikes the appropriate balance in providing sufficient clarity in our rules and transparency in our designation process, while at the same time avoiding overly simplistic approaches that fail to recognize and consider the facts and circumstances of individual firms and specific industries. Ultimately, the decision to designate a company must be based on an assessment of the unique risks that a particular firm may present to the financial system.

Q.2. Would the council agree that leverage is likely to be the one factor that is most likely to create conditions that result in systemic risk? If so, how will the council go about identifying which entities use leverage?

A.2. Yes, consistent with the statutory provisions and lessons learned from the financial crisis, leverage is one of the six categories of risk factors that FSOC has proposed to consider in making SIFI designations. As commenters have suggested, FSOC will need to consider and distinguish between different types and sources of leverage when evaluating the effect that such leverage may have on a firm. To the extent possible, FSOC will use information from existing public and supervisory sources to make initial assessments about a firm's leverage and other risk factors. This information may be supplemented with requests for more specific information from the firm.

Q.3. One of the first steps in the systemic designation process, as outlined in the proposed rule, is that after identifying a nonbank financial company for possible designation the FSOC will provide the company with a written preliminary notice that the council is considering making proposed determination that the company is systemically significant. Is receipt of such a notice a material event that might affect the financial situation or the value of a company's shares in the mind of the investors? If so, wouldn't it need to be disclosed to investors under securities laws.

A.3. The FSOC has not taken up the issue of disclosure in this regard. The rulemaking is still pending and no designations have been made yet. As with other possible regulatory actions with respect to which institutions receive advance notice, an institution should consult counsel to determine whether receipt of the notice is a material event requiring disclosure under securities laws.

RESPONSE TO WRITTEN QUESTIONS OF SENATOR TOOMEY FROM JOHN WALSH

Q.1. Last week, Chairman Bernanke indicated that bank holding companies larger than $50 billion, designated as systemically significant by the Dodd-Frank Act, will be treated on a tiered scale when you establish enhanced supervisory standards. These institutions range from relatively basic commercial banks not much larger than the $50 billion to more complex and interdependent global financial firms that are up to 40 times the threshold. Do you expect the tiered standards to be based on a firm's asset size or on factors more directly related to financial system risk, such as complexity of a firm's businesses, its funding sources and liquidity, its importance to the daily functioning of the capital markets and its interconnectedness to other financial firms?

A.1. The Federal Reserve has primary rulemaking authority for this provision of the Dodd-Frank Act. We expect to be consulting with the Federal Reserve as it moves forward with its rulemaking.

Q.2. Can you share with us what the FSOC, OFR, FDIC and Fed are contemplating by way of fees that they may assess on SIFIs?

A.2. While we are aware of the FDIC's recent announced changes to its insurance assessment structure, the Federal Reserve and OFR have not yet disclosed their plans for assessing fees on systemically important institutions.

International Competitiveness

Q.3.a. It is critical for the continued competitiveness of the U.S. markets that a regulatory arbitrage does not develop among markets that favors markets in Europe and Asia over U.S. markets. Will the FSOC commit to ensuring that the timing of the finalization and implementation of rulemaking under Dodd Frank does not impair the competitiveness of U.S. markets?

A.3.a. The OCC recognizes that the Federal banking agencies must proceed carefully as we implement the Dodd-Frank provisions, so that we do not create unnecessary limitations that restrict the ability of U.S. banking institutions to manage risk efficiently, and to compete internationally. As we draft regulations to implement these provisions, we have attempted to address these concerns to the extent possible given the statutory framework. We also support Treasury's efforts to address any competitive inequalities caused by the Dodd-Frank Act through the G–20 process.

Q.3.b. How will FSOC ensure that U.S. firms will have equal access to European markets as European firms will have to U.S. markets?

A.3.b. Rules and regulations promulgated by the United States as well as foreign jurisdictions should be assessed periodically to ensure "equivalent/national treatment" across borders. The FSOC member agencies will have the ability to look across sectors and jurisdictions to identify areas where "equivalent/national treatment" is not afforded to U.S. firms. Where this is identified, U.S. agencies will work with their foreign counterparts to effect change, but also assess whether U.S. rules need to be changed. The FSOC may also seek legislative changes where needed.

Q.3.c. How will FSOC ensure that Basel III will be implemented in the United States in a manner that is not more stringent than in Europe, making U.S. firms less competitive globally?

A.3.c. To implement Basel III in the United States, a rule must first be drafted. Through the rulemaking process, areas of potential inconsistency with other jurisdictions may be identified and rectified to the extent possible. The U.S. agencies responsible for the supervision of Basel III implementation are currently responding to questions from firms about Basel III and reviewing capital plans to determine how the firms are factoring Basel III into their capital planning processes. The U.S. agencies will coordinate to ensure consistent implementation by U.S. firms.

On the international front, the Basel Committee on Banking Supervision (BCBS) has initiated an "evergreen" Basel III implementation questionnaire that will be completed periodically to gauge the progress of Basel III implementation by member jurisdictions. This process will also facilitate the identification of areas of inconsistency that may require clarification and/or more guidance from the BCBS regarding Basel III. The U.S. agencies are actively involved in the BCBS and will work with their global counterparts to address areas of inconsistency.

RESPONSE TO WRITTEN QUESTION OF SENATOR KIRK FROM JOHN WALSH

Q.1. Much about SIFI designation focuses on "too-big-to-fail" institutions. What about financial management practices that can weaken a number of smaller players in an industry? What can FSOC do to encourage best practices of asset/liability management, or assure the proper allocation of capital that reflects the risk underlying assets held?

A.1. The OCC and other Federal banking agencies have well-established mechanisms in place to coordinate efforts to promote and encourage sound risk management practices for financial institutions of all sizes, including smaller community banks. Much of this work is facilitated by the Federal Financial Institutions Examination Council. Because of heightened concerns about interest rate and liquidity risk, in 2010 the agencies issued an interagency policy statement on funding and liquidity risk management, and a joint advisory on interest rate risk management. These policy statements provide guidance to bankers on sound practices for asset/liability management. Similarly, virtually all of the Federal banking agencies' capital rules are developed and issued on a collaborative basis. As part of the implementation of the enhanced capital provisions set forth in Basel III, the agencies are considering and plan to propose revisions to the general risk-based capital rules that apply to small banking institutions. Such changes would only go into effect after a notice and comment process.

RESPONSE TO WRITTEN QUESTIONS OF SENATOR SHELBY FROM MARY L. SCHAPIRO

Q.1. If a public company is told by the Council that it is considering designating it as systemically significant, the company may believe that such information is material and must be disclosed to the public under the securities laws. What is your view on whether a company would have to publicly disclose the fact that it has been informed that it may be designated by the Council?

A.1. There are currently no specific "line item" requirements to disclose that a company has been notified that it is being considered for possible designation or if it has been notified and not designated. However, a company would need to review its description of its regulatory status and requirements to determine whether its disclosure requires updating. The company and its advisors would need to determine whether being notified that the company may be systemically important (and, once a determination has been made with regard to designation, the outcome of that determination) is material information that must be disclosed to investors. The test for materiality is whether there is a substantial likelihood that the disclosure of the omitted fact would have been viewed by the reasonable investor as having significantly altered the total mix of information made available. Whether a contingent or speculative event is material requires a balancing of both the indicated probability that the event will occur and the anticipated magnitude of the event in light of the totality of the company activity.

If material, the company would need to disclose the possible designation and/or the final determination as to designation, for example, in an annual or quarterly report. The possible designation and/or the final determination as to designation are more likely to be material if FSOC designations have had a material effect on other companies' stock prices. The materiality determination also would be affected by the consequences of being designated systemically important, such as capital requirements and limitations on business activities.

Q.2. You began your written testimony with a lengthy discussion of market structure issues. Do you believe these issues to be the biggest potential source of systemic risk on your regulatory agenda? If so, should the Council be paying more attention to market structure issues than it is now?

A.2. The SEC's regulatory agenda encompasses a broad range of complex financial activity and firms, including, among others, equity market structure, broker-dealers, clearing agencies, money market funds, hedge funds, and over-the-counter derivatives; and we have been working with the Council members on all of these. Clearly, however, maintaining the integrity of the U.S. equity market structure is a vitally important part of the SEC's regulatory agenda. Accordingly, as discussed in my testimony, the SEC has undertaken a series of steps to promote fair and orderly trading and to help prevent extraordinary volatility in the future.

Q.3. Under Dodd-Frank, swap data repositories, before sharing any information with a regulator other than their primary regulator, must obtain an indemnification agreement with that other regulator. Will this requirement adversely affect regulators' ability to obtain a comprehensive view of the swaps markets?

A.3. The Securities Exchange Act of 1934, as amended by the Dodd-Frank Act, requires a security-based swap data repository (SDR) to obtain a written agreement from certain domestic and foreign regulators whereby the regulator agrees to indemnify the SDR and the Commission for litigation expenses arising from the disclosure of data maintained by the SDR as a condition for the SDR to provide information directly to a regulator other than the Commission.

Some domestic and foreign regulators have expressed concern about their ability to comply with the requirement to enter into an indemnification agreement with an SDR in order to obtain information directly from the SDR. In a recent letter to Michel Barnier, European Commissioner for Internal Markets and Services, Chairman Gensler and I noted these potential difficulties, and set forth circumstances in which this requirement would not apply to foreign regulators, including when the SDR is also registered with a foreign regulator and that regulator, acting within the scope of its jurisdiction, seeks information from the SDR.

The Commission staff is still considering issues relating to the indemnification requirement, and is consulting and coordinating with CFTC staff regarding such issues. Because the Commission staff has not yet completed its recommendations for final rules in this area, the Commission has not had the opportunity to fully consider the application of the indemnification provision in all scenarios involving requests from regulators for information in SEC-registered trade repositories. I anticipate that the Commission will consider recommendations from our staff designed, consistent with the provisions of the Dodd-Frank Act and the statutes we administer, to facilitate the access to information at trade repositories that regulators need to carry out their responsibilities.

Q.4. One of the Council's purposes is to monitor systemic risk and alert Congress and regulators of any systemic risks it discovers. What are the most serious systemic risks presently facing the U.S. economy?

A.4. The FSOC is working to complete its annual report called for by the Dodd-Frank Act, which will describe the overall macroeconomic environment, significant trends and risks, including systemic risks, and recommendations for regulatory action.

RESPONSE TO WRITTEN QUESTION OF SENATOR HAGAN FROM MARY L. SCHAPIRO

Q.1. Chairwoman Schapiro and Chairwoman Bair, In March Federal financial regulators published a proposed rule that would implement Section 956 of the Dodd-Frank Act. Section 956 requires regulators to issue rules that prohibit "covered financial institutions" from entering into incentive-based compensation arrangements that encourage inappropriate risks.

"Covered financial institutions" are defined to include investment advisers that have $1 billion or more in total consolidated assets (as opposed to assets under management).

On what basis did the SEC choose to consider only consolidated assets on the balance sheet of the investment adviser and not take into account assets under management?

A.1. Paragraph (f) of Section 956 of the Dodd Frank Act exempts covered financial institutions with "assets of less than $1,000,000,000" from the requirements of Section 956. In carving out institutions with less than $1 billion in assets, Congress thus determined that the "covered financial institutions" listed in Section 956(e) with $1 billion or more in assets are covered by Section 956.

In drafting the proposed rules, the SEC and the six other agencies charged with rulemaking under Section 956 (together, the

"Agencies") considered that the statute uses the term "assets," which is predominantly understood to mean the total assets of a firm, and does not refer to "assets under management," which is predominantly understood to mean the assets that a firm manages on behalf of its clients. Additionally, the measurement of asset size for most firms generally is made with reference to the assets on the balance sheet of the firm. For example, we understand that the size of a bank generally would be described by reference to the total assets on the balance sheet of the bank, not by reference to the amount of customer assets the bank manages (for example, as the trustee of a customer's trust). Similarly, an investment adviser's assets under management generally do not appear as assets on the firm's balance sheet because the assets under management belong to another individual or entity. As a result, the Agencies did not propose to include customer assets, such as assets under management, in the calculation of the $1 billion threshold.

The other important factor to note is that Section 956 requires the Agencies to engage in joint rulemaking. The Agencies interpreted this statutory directive as requiring the Agencies to propose a rule that was substantially similar from agency to agency to the greatest extent practicable, and sought to maintain the general consistency of the rule from agency to agency, and between types of covered financial institutions regulated by the SEC (broker-dealers and investment advisers). Thus, the SEC proposed an asset test for investment advisers intended to mirror the way such asset tests are proposed to be calculated and applied to the other covered financial institutions, which are based on the total assets on the balance sheet of each firm, and which exclude in each case assets that are held for others.

Finally, all of the covered financial institutions, except investment advisers, report to their respective regulator the amount of their "assets." For example, banks regulated by the OCC, Federal Reserve, and FDIC report total assets on Call Reports, and broker-dealers regulated by the SEC file a year-end audited consolidated statement of their financial condition that includes "total consolidated assets." The proposed rule would rely on the total assets reported in these reports to determine the size of each firm's "assets" for purposes of section 956. Recently, the SEC proposed to require advisers to report on Form ADV whether they have $1 billion or more in total balance sheet assets. Requiring advisers to use the amount of total assets on their balance sheets, as proposed, would dovetail with this proposal and be consistent with the method for evaluating other intermediaries under the proposed rule.

The Agencies requested comment on whether all of the Agencies should use a uniform method to determine whether an institution has $1 billion or more in assets, and whether any of the Agencies should define total consolidated assets differently than the proposed calculations. The Agencies also specifically requested comment on the proposed method of determining asset size for investment advisers, including whether the determination of total assets should be further tailored for certain types of advisers. The Agencies will carefully review and consider public comments that have been received discussing this and any other issues. The interagency drafting committee will take all such comments into account when developing a final rule proposal for consideration by the Agencies.

RESPONSE TO WRITTEN QUESTION OF SENATOR CRAPO FROM MARY L. SCHAPIRO

Q.1. According to the American Banker, Annette L. Nazareth, a former SEC Commissioner, called the timetables imposed by the Dodd-Frank Act "wildly aggressive." "These agencies were dealt a very bad hand," she said. "These deadlines could actually be systemic-risk raising." Given the importance of rigorous cost-benefit and economic impact analyses and the need for due consideration of public comments, would additional time for adoption of the Dodd-Frank Act rules improve your rulemaking process and the substance of your final rules?

A.1. Implementation of the Dodd-Frank Act is a substantial undertaking. The Act's requirements that a significant number of Commission rulemakings be completed within 1 year of the date of enactment poses significant challenges to the Commission. Throughout, the staff and Commission have been diligent in working to implement the requirements of the Act while also taking the time necessary to thoughtfully consider the issues raised by the various rulemakings.

We recognize that many of our new rules may have near term market implications and costs and important long-term benefits. We must carefully consider these implications, including by engaging in a robust cost-benefit and economic impact analysis. As a result, we are providing market participants with sufficient time to understand the obligations that may apply to them as well as the potential costs and benefits, and economic implications, of those obligations.

While we are eager to get these important rules in place, it is critical that we get the rules right, and that we promulgate the rules in a timely fashion, taking into account the complexities of the markets being regulated and the number of rulemakings involved.

To help keep the public informed, we have a section on our Web site that provides detail about the Commission's implementation of the Act. We also are taking steps to gather additional input on our implementation process where appropriate, such as the joint round-table held on May 2 and 3 with the CFTC regarding the implementation of derivatives rules under Title VII. We value, and are committed to seeking, the broad public input and consultation needed to promulgate these important rules.

Q.2. Chairman Bair's testimony was unclear regarding whether the FSOC has the authority to issue a revised rule on the designation of nonbank financial institutions. She and others indicated some type of guidance might be issued instead. Is it in fact the case, in general, that the FSOC does not have authority to issue rules under Title I that have the force and effect of law? If the FSOC has the authority in general to issue such rules on designation, why specifically would the FSOC be precluded from re-proposing a rule that is currently pending? Is there additional authority the FSOC would need from Congress to issue such rules or to proceed with re-proposing its NPR on designation? If yes, what specific authority would the FSOC need from Congress for the FSOC to have the ability to proceed?

A.2. Like the FDIC, the Commission has not conducted its own independent legal analysis of this issue, but as discussed at the hearing, members of the FSOC have sought guidance from the Department of the Treasury, Office of the General Counsel. We understand from the Treasury Department that the FSOC has the authority to issue its proposed regulations on designations, and to re-propose those rules for further public comment. The FSOC has already exercised its rulemaking authority to release a notice of proposed rulemaking on the designation of nonbank financial companies to be supervised by the Federal Reserve. The FSOC plans to seek further public comment on guidance regarding its approach to designations of nonbank financial companies, and release a final rule that will reflect the input received on the proposed rule and guidance.

Q.3. In an August speech at NYU's Stern School of Business, Treasury Secretary Geithner outlined six principles that he said would guide implementation, and then he added, "You should hold us accountable for honoring them." His final principle was bringing more order and integration to the regulatory process. He said the agencies responsible for reforms will have to work "together, not against each other. This requires us to look carefully at the overall interaction of regulations designed by different regulators and assess the overall burden they present relative to the benefits they offer." Do you intend to follow through with this commitment with some form of status report that provides a quantitative and qualitative review of the overall interaction of all the hundreds of proposed rules by the different regulators and assess the overall burden they present relative to the benefits they offer?

A.3. We have been working closely, cooperatively, and regularly with our fellow regulators to develop the new regulatory framework and we are committed to continuing to do so.

We meet regularly, both formally and informally, with other financial regulators. SEC staff working groups, for example, consult and coordinate with the staffs of the CFTC, Federal Reserve Board, and other prudential financial regulators, as well as the Department of the Treasury, on implementation of the Dodd-Frank Act. Our objective is to establish consistent and comparable requirements, to the extent possible, taking into account differences in products, participants, and markets, and this objective will continue to guide our efforts as we move forward.

Finally, because the world today is a global marketplace and what we do to implement many provisions of the Act will affect foreign entities, we are consulting bilaterally and through multilateral organizations with counterparts abroad. The SEC and CFTC, for example, are directed by the Dodd-Frank Act to consult and coordinate with foreign regulators on the establishment of consistent international standards governing swaps, security-based swaps, swap entities and security-based swap entities. We believe that the recently formed IOSCO Task Force on OTC Derivatives Regulation, which the SEC co-chairs, and other international fora, as well as bilateral discussions with international regulators, will help us achieve this goal.

_____

RESPONSE TO WRITTEN QUESTIONS OF SENATOR VITTER FROM MARY L. SCHAPIRO

Q.1. Dodd-Frank set forth a comprehensive list of factors that FSOC must consider when determining whether a company posed a systemic risk and deserves Fed oversight. The council, in its advanced notice of proposed rulemaking, sets forth 15 categories of questions for the industry to comment on and address. However, the proposed rules give no indication of the specific criteria or framework that the council intends to use in making SIFI designations—other than what is already set forth in Dodd-Frank. As a result, potential SIFIs have no idea where they may stand in the designation process. Will the council provide additional information about the quantitative metrics it will use when making an SIFI designation?

A.1. As Department of the Treasury Under Secretary Goldstein noted in his letter to Senator Shelby:

> The Financial Stability Oversight Council (FSOC) recognizes the importance of a public review of its decisionmaking criteria and is working diligently to provide the public with greater detail on the process and framework for making designations. One of the FSOC's key guiding principles is transparency and openness, as demonstrated by our deliberate emphasis on continued public input in the rulemaking process.

> The process of determining which companies pose a potential risk to U.S. financial stability is not an easy task, but it is imperative that the FSOC get it right. The FSOC continues to work toward an approach that will allow the financial industry to assess whether they are candidates for designation while maintaining flexibility as the nature of institutions and markets change. Of course, ultimately the decision to designate a company will be based on an assessment of the unique risks that a particular firm may present to the financial system. The FSOC plans to seek public comment on additional guidance regarding its approach to designations.

> In addition to public comments from industry participants, the FSOC will also rely on the expertise of its members and their agencies' staff. These individuals have expertise that spans all aspects of the financial services industry. Any designation decision will draw on this experience.

Q.2. Would the council agree that leverage is likely to be the one factor that is most likely to create conditions that result in systemic risk? If so, how will the council go about identifying which entities use leverage?

A.2. Leverage is an important element of the systemic risk analysis and is identified as such in the criteria for making a SIFI determination under the Dodd-Frank Act. Leverage may be the factor that is most relevant for some institutions, but other factors may predominate for other firms. FSOC is pursuing the identification of specific metrics that could be used for different types of firms, including metrics with respect to leverage.

Q.3. One of the first steps in the systemic designation process, as outlined in the proposed rule, is that after identifying a nonbank financial company for possible designation the FSOC will provide the company with a written preliminary notice that the council is considering making proposed determination that the company is systemically significant. Is receipt of such a notice a material event that might affect the financial situation or the value of a company's shares in the mind of the investors? If so, wouldn't it need to be disclosed to investors under securities laws?

A.3. There are currently no specific "line item" requirements to disclose that a company has been notified that it is being considered for possible designation or if it has been notified and not designated. However, a company would need to review its description of its regulatory status and requirements to determine whether its disclosure requires updating. The company and its advisors would need to determine whether being notified that the company may be systemically important (and, once a determination has been made with regard to designation, the outcome of that determination) is material information that must be disclosed to investors. The test for materiality is whether there is a substantial likelihood that the disclosure of the omitted fact would have been viewed by the reasonable investor as having significantly altered the total mix of information made available. Whether a contingent or speculative event is material requires a balancing of both the indicated probability that the event will occur and the anticipated magnitude of the event in light of the totality of the company activity.

If material, the company would need to disclose the possible designation and/or the final determination as to designation, for example, in an annual or quarterly report. The possible designation and/or the final determination as to designation are more likely to be material if FSOC designations have had a material effect on other companies' stock prices. The materiality determination also would be affected by the consequences of being designated systemically important, such as capital requirements and limitations on business activities.

RESPONSE TO WRITTEN QUESTIONS OF SENATOR TOOMEY FROM MARY L. SCHAPIRO

Q.1. One of the first steps in the systemic designation process, as outlined in the proposed rule, is that after identifying a nonbank financial company for possible designation the FSOC will provide the company with a written preliminary notice that the Council is considering whether to make a "proposed determination" that the company is systemically significant. Is receipt of such a notice a "material event" that might affect the financial situation or the value of a company's shares in the mind of investors? If so, wouldn't it need to be disclosed to investors under securities laws?

A.1. There are currently no specific "line item" requirements to disclose that a company has been notified that it is being considered for possible designation or if it has been notified and not designated. However, a company would need to review its description of its regulatory status and requirements to determine whether its disclosure requires updating. The company and its advisors would need to determine whether being notified that the company may be systemically important (and, once a determination has been made with regard to designation, the outcome of that determination) is material information that must be disclosed to investors. The test for materiality is whether there is a substantial likelihood that the disclosure of the omitted fact would have been viewed by the reasonable investor as having significantly altered the total mix of information made available. Whether a contingent or speculative event is material requires a balancing of both the indicated probability that the event will occur and the anticipated magnitude of the event in light of the totality of the company activity.

If material, the company would need to disclose the possible designation and/or the final determination as to designation, for example, in an annual or quarterly report. The possible designation and/or the final determination as to designation are more likely to be material if FSOC designations have had a material effect on other companies' stock prices. The materiality determination also would be affected by the consequences of being designated systemically important, such as capital requirements and limitations on business activities.

Q.2. As FSOC considers how to determine the systemic relevance of the investment fund asset management industry, wouldn't it be more appropriate for FSOC to look at the various individual funds themselves, of which there may be several under one advisor, rather than focus on the advisor entity?

- Isn't it true that each of those funds may operate with separate and distinct investment strategies, each with its own unique risks?
- Isn't it the case that the vast majority of the assets are located at the funds and not at the adviser entity?

A.2. It is true that each of these funds may operate with separate and distinct investment strategies, each with its own unique risks. But a manager could advise several funds (and even separate accounts) with similar or identical investment strategies in a parallel or similar manner. These advisers may aggregate the trades for many funds for execution and then allocate the securities among the various funds. For example, an asset manager could engage in same trading strategy (which can be of systemic relevance) across several of the funds it manages. While the assets may be owned by individual funds, their trading may be done jointly. Thus in assessing systemic risk we recognize that it is important to engage in robust process and examine the issue holistically.

Q.3. What additional protection/supervision could the Fed provide for mutual funds that the SEC isn't already providing? Do we really need to subject this industry to an additional layer of regulation, especially a "systemic risk" regulation?

A.3. Under Title I, The Federal Reserve would have authority to impose enhanced prudential regulation over individual nonbank financial companies that are designated for oversight by two-thirds of the FSOC. However, one factor FSOC is required to consider when determining whether to designate any nonbank financial company for supervision by the Federal Reserve is "the degree to which the company is already regulated by one or more primary financial regulatory agencies." We believe, therefore, that FSOC will consider whether designation is appropriate for firm after considering current regulation as well as the other factors the Dodd-Frank Act requires that FSOC consider before designating any nonbank financial company. It's also important to note, that while the SEC has significant legal *authority* in this area; (1) the SEC's historic mission has been one of 'investor protection' rather than systemic risk; and (2) the SEC far fewer staff to perform examinations and oversee firm's activities.

Q.4. Can you share with us what the FSOC, OFR, FDIC and Fed are contemplating by way of fees that they may assess on SIFIs?

A.4. I understand that such fees would be considered and adopted by the Federal Reserve Board as part of the authority assigned it by the Dodd-Frank Act to supervise SIFIs, rather than by FSOC or the Commission.

International Competitiveness

Q.5.a. It is critical for the continued competitiveness of the U.S. markets that a regulatory arbitrage does not develop among markets that favors markets in Europe and Asia over U.S. markets. Will the FSOC commit to ensuring that the timing of the finalization and implementation of rulemaking under Dodd Frank does not impair the competitiveness of U.S. markets?

A.5.a The FSOC was created by Title I of the Dodd-Frank Act. Under the Dodd-Frank Act, Congress has given FSOC the following primary responsibilities:

- identifying risks to the financial stability of the United States that could arise from the material financial distress or failure—or ongoing activities—of large, interconnected bank holding companies or nonbank financial holding companies, or that could arise outside the financial services marketplace;
- promoting market discipline by eliminating expectations on the part of shareholders, creditors, and counterparties of such companies that the Government will shield them from losses in the event of failure (*i.e.,* addressing the moral hazard problem of "too big to fail"); and
- identifying and responding to emerging threats to the stability of the United States financial system.

The FSOC has 10 voting members, including the Chairman of the SEC. The SEC is charged with regulating, among other areas, the security-based swaps markets, and in doing so we consider the potential impact on the global competitiveness of U.S. markets. To this end, we have been carefully considering the potential consequences of certain provisions of Title VII and our proposed rulemaking for domestic and foreign market participants—in particular the impact on the ability of U.S. market participants to compete effectively with foreign market participants that may not be subject to the Dodd-Frank Act. In fact, we are required to take into account potential burdens on competition when engaging in rulemaking, including rulemaking under the Dodd-Frank Act. Our goal is to establish a level playing field for all market participants while adhering to the regulatory requirements and objectives of the Dodd-Frank Act, and we are considering how to promulgate regulations in a way that accomplishes this goal.

The SEC has been working closely with the CFTC, the Federal Reserve Board and other Federal prudential regulators who also are members of FSOC, in developing a harmonized approach to implementing the statutory provisions of Title VII to the extent practicable.

As we move from the proposing stage to implementation, we recognize that part of balancing regulatory concerns with competitiveness concerns involves establishing an implementation process for derivatives regulation that permits market participants sufficient time to establish systems and procedures in order to comply with new regulatory requirements without imposing undue implementation burdens and costs. We also are cognizant of the timing of legislation, rulemaking and implementation in other jurisdictions.

To this end, we have been discussing with our fellow regulators and with market participants what timeframes would be reasonable for the various rulemakings, and what steps market participants will need to take in order to comply with our proposed rules. Further, in addition to our consultation and coordination with the CFTC and other U.S. authorities, we have been engaged in ongoing bilateral and multilateral discussions with foreign regulators and have been speaking with many foreign and domestic market participants in order to better understand what areas of derivatives regulation pose such arbitrage opportunities. We have solicited and welcome comments on our proposed rulemakings regarding the potential impact they may have on the position of the U.S. security-based swap markets, especially comments that offer suggestions for mitigating regulatory arbitrage opportunities while achieving the goals of the Dodd-Frank Act.

As Dodd-Frank implementation proceeds, we expect to continue working closely with the other FSOC agencies.

Q.5.b. How will FSOC ensure that U.S. firms will have equal access to European markets as European firms will have to U.S. markets?

A.5.b. Many foreign jurisdictions, including the European Union, are in the process of adopting derivatives legislation and implementing regulations, and are at much earlier stages of development in their efforts than is the United States. While there are a range of views internationally on the appropriate level of derivatives regulation, the SEC has been actively engaged in ongoing bilateral and multilateral discussions with foreign regulators regarding the direction of international derivatives regulation generally, and the SEC's efforts to implement Title VII's requirements.

For example, the SEC, along with the CFTC, the United Kingdom Financial Services Authority, and the Securities and Exchange Board of India, is co-chairing the International Organization of Securities Commissions Task Force on OTC Derivatives Regulation ("Task Force"). One of the primary goals of this task force is to work to develop consistent international standards related to OTC derivatives regulation. In addition, on behalf of IOSCO, the SEC, along with the European Commission and an international organization of central banks, co-chairs the Financial Stability Board's OTC Derivatives Working Group ("FSB Working Group"). The CFTC and Federal Reserve Board also are members of the FSB Working Group.

These and other bilateral and multilateral efforts serve to keep the SEC informed about emerging similarities or differences in potential approaches to derivatives regulation and provide us with an opportunity to work with our counterparts in other jurisdictions in order to foster the development of common frameworks and coordinate regulatory efforts as much as possible with a view to mitigating systemic risk and preventing regulatory arbitrage.

The SEC expects to continue to work closely with the other members of the FSOC and recognizes that the FSOC can help bring agencies together to exchange information.

Q.5.c. How will FSOC ensure that Basel III will be implemented in the United States in a manner that is not more stringent than in Europe, making U.S. firms less competitive globally?

A.5.c. The Basel standards relate to bank capital adequacy and liquidity. The U.S. prudential regulators, including members of the FSOC have jurisdiction under Dodd-Frank for promulgating rules for capital and margin requirements for banks, and accordingly will utilize the Basel III agreement. The SEC has responsibility for promulgating capital and margin requirements under Dodd-Frank for nonbank security-based swap dealers.

The SEC has been carefully considering the potential consequences of certain provisions of Title VII and our proposed rulemaking for domestic and foreign market participants—in particular the impact on the ability of U.S. market participants to compete effectively with foreign market participants that may not be subject to the Dodd-Frank Act. In fact, we are required to take into account potential burdens on competition when engaging in rulemaking, including rulemaking under Title VII. Our goal is to establish a level playing field for all market participants while adhering to the regulatory requirements and objectives of the Dodd-Frank Act, and we are considering how to promulgate regulations in a way that accomplishes this goal.

Q.6. Is a broker/dealer that is not self-clearing less likely to pose systemic risk because it receives the financial backing and risk management attention of its clearing firm which already performs extensive monitoring of risk for the broker-dealers and which in all likelihood will itself be a SIFI?

A.6. Broker-dealers that are not self-clearing (otherwise referred to as an introducing broker-dealer), as a general matter, are less likely to pose systemic risk than do clearing firms because they do not maintain custody of customer assets and usually do not have proprietary positions in substantial size such that their failure would result in exposure to other large firms or result in market impacts from the liquidation of assets.

Whether a clearing firm would ever be a SIFI will depend on the approach taken by the FSOC to the designation of SIFIs. At a minimum, in order to be designated as a SIFI, any firm would first need to be evaluated by the FSOC with respect to size, leverage, concentrations, and other relevant factors. Under Commission rules, an introducing broker-dealer is required to enter into a contract with a clearing broker-dealer who agrees to both settle trades and maintain custody of customer assets. Further, under the Commission's financial responsibility rules, a clearing broker-dealer must monitor all introduced accounts and take appropriate actions, including taking capital charges, in the event those accounts do not have sufficient assets to be able to "self-liquidate." The failure of an introducing broker-dealer that handles a large number of customer accounts could create disruption resulting from the need to transfer those accounts to one or more other introducing firms, but generally speaking it should not result in systemic effects of the type that might accompany the failure of a large clearing firm.

Q.7. Titles I and II of Dodd-Frank references an entity's "asset threshold" or "total consolidated assets" several times. Are such calculations to be made in accordance with generally accepted accounting principles (GAAP)?

A.7. The terms "asset threshold" and "total consolidated assets" appear in a number of places in Title I and Title II, but the Dodd-Frank Act does not define them. While the terms appear in connection with the work of FSOC, they do not arise directly in connection with the Commission's responsibilities. FSOC is considering what definitions or interpretations of such terms may be required.

RESPONSE TO WRITTEN QUESTION OF SENATOR MORAN
FROM MARY L. SCHAPIRO

Q.1. Regarding this initial consultation phase which will occur prior to designation, should we assume that the markets and public will know to whom such notices are sent? Do you believe that public companies are obligated to disclose receipt of such a notice in their filings? What would happen if a firm that disclosed having received a notice was not designated as systemically significant? Is there a possibility that the markets would react to that news?

A.1. There are currently no specific "line item" requirements to disclose that a company has been notified that it is being considered for possible designation or if it has been notified and not designated. However, a company would need to review its description of its regulatory status and requirements to determine whether its disclosure requires updating. The company and its advisors would need to determine whether being notified that the company may be systemically important (and, once a determination has been made with regard to designation, the outcome of that determination) is material information that must be disclosed to investors. The test for materiality is whether there is a substantial likelihood that the disclosure of the omitted fact would have been viewed by the reasonable investor as having significantly altered the total mix of information made available. Whether a contingent or speculative event is material requires a balancing of both the indicated probability that the event will occur and the anticipated magnitude of the event in light of the totality of the company activity.

If material, the company would need to disclose the possible designation and/or the final determination as to designation, for example, in an annual or quarterly report. The possible designation and/or the final determination as to designation are more likely to be material if FSOC designations have had a material effect on other companies' stock prices. The materiality determination also would be affected by the consequences of being designated systemically important, such as capital requirements and limitations on business activities.

RESPONSE TO WRITTEN QUESTIONS OF SENATOR SHELBY
FROM GARY GENSLER

Q.1. You mentioned in your written testimony that it is important for "people who want to hedge their risk to do so without concentrating risk in the hands of only a few financial firms." How much concentration of the market in the top firms is too much? Are you concerned that the aggressive approach that you have taken with respect to swap dealer regulation will cause the field of dealers to narrow, not broaden, thus further concentrating the swap dealer business?

A.1. The Dodd-Frank Act brings essential reforms to the swaps markets that will benefit the American public and end-users of derivatives. While the derivatives market has changed significantly since swaps were first transacted in the 1980s, the constant is that the financial community maintains information advantages over their nonfinancial counterparties. When a Wall Street bank enters into a bilateral derivative transaction with a corporate end-user, for example, the bank knows how much its last customer paid for similar transactions. That information, however, is not generally made available to other customers or the public. The bank benefits from internalizing this information. The Dodd-Frank Act brings sunshine to the opaque swaps markets. The more transparent a marketplace is, the more liquid it is, the more competitive it is, and the lower the costs for hedgers, borrowers and their customers.

In implementing the Dodd-Frank Act, the Commission is adhering closely to the statute with the intent to comply fully with its provisions and Congressional intent to lower risk and bring transparency to these markets.

Q.2. You state that end-users will enjoy better pricing on derivatives transactions because of the rules that the CFTC is putting into place. Has your agency conducted economic analysis to support your conclusion that end-users will pay less for derivatives transactions under the Dodd-Frank framework?

A.2. Economists and policymakers for decades have recognized that market transparency benefits the public. There are two types of transparency that Congress, through the Dodd-Frank Act, sought to bring to the swaps markets. The first is transparency to the regulators, which will include swap data repositories that will provide data to regulators. The second is transparency to the public.

There are three phases that a swap transaction goes through that will be more transparent under the Dodd-Frank Act. The first occurs before the transaction takes place by moving standardized swap transactions onto exchanges or swap execution facilities (SEFs).

These exchanges will allow investors, hedgers and speculators to meet in a transparent, open and competitive central market. The Act includes exceptions from this requirement for block trades and transactions involving commercial end-users.

The second phase occurs immediately after the transaction takes place, when pricing data is made public in real time. Congress also has been very specific that market participants and end-users should benefit from such real-time reporting. This post-trade transparency—other than for block trades—must be achieved "as soon as technologically practicable" after a swap is executed, which will enhance price discovery. This requirement applies to both cleared and uncleared swaps.

The third phase occurs over the lifetime of the swap contract. The Dodd-Frank Act requires that swaps be marked to market every day until they expire and that such valuations be shared with market participants. If the contract is cleared, the clearinghouse will be required to publicly disclose the pricing of the swap every day. If the contract is bilateral, swap dealers will be required to share mid-market pricing on a daily basis with their counterparties.

In implementing the Act, the Commission is adhering closely to the statute.

Q.3. Judging from the proposed rules we have seen, the CFTC's rulemaking to date has not been particularly well-coordinated with the SEC's rulemaking. Are you willing to take your disputes to the Council for resolution before you move to the adopting stage, or are you planning to proceed with your preferred approach ahead of the SEC and hope that they will follow suit?

A.3. See response to question 4.

Q.4. Your agency is deeply engaged in rulemaking regarding over-the-counter derivatives. Judging from the proposed rules we have seen, your rulemaking to date has not been particularly well-coordinated. Are you willing to take unresolved disputes to the Council for resolution before you move to the adopting stage, or are you planning to proceed with your preferred approach before the SEC acts and hope that the SEC will follow suit?

A.4. Throughout the Dodd-Frank rule-writing process, the Commission is consulting heavily with both other regulators and the broader public. We are working very closely with the SEC, the Federal Reserve, the Federal Deposit Insurance Corporation, the Office of the Comptroller of the Currency and other prudential regulators, which includes sharing many of our memos, term sheets and draft work product. CFTC staff has held over 600 meetings with other regulators on implementation of the Act. Our rule-writing teams are working with the Federal Reserve in several critical areas. With the SEC, we are coordinating on the entire range of rule-writing, including swap dealer regulation, clearinghouse regulation and swap data repositories, as well as trading requirements, real-time reporting and key definitions. So far, we have proposed two joint rules with the SEC as required by Congress. We will continue to work closely together through the implementation process.

Q.5. Under Dodd-Frank, swap data repositories, before sharing any information with a regulator other than their primary regulator, must obtain an indemnification agreement with that other regulator. Will this requirement adversely affect regulators' ability to obtain a comprehensive view of the swaps markets?

A.5. Under the provision, domestic and foreign authorities, in certain circumstances, would be required to provide written agreements to indemnify SEC and CFTC-registered trade repositories, as well as the SEC and CFTC, for certain litigation expenses as a condition to obtaining data directly from the trade repository regarding swaps and security-based swaps. Regulators in foreign jurisdictions have raised concerns regarding the potential effect of the provision. However, I believe that the indemnification provision need not apply when a foreign regulator, acting within the scope of its jurisdiction, seeks information directly from a trade repository registered with both the CFTC and the foreign jurisdiction. Under the CFTC's proposed rules regarding trade repositories' duties and core principles, foreign regulators would not be subject to the indemnification and notice requirements if they obtain information that is in the possession of the CFTC.

Q.6. One of the Council's purposes is to monitor systemic risk and alert Congress and regulators of any systemic risks it discovers. What are the most serious systemic risks presently facing the U.S. economy?

A.6. Under section 112 of the Dodd-Frank Act, the Council must provide an annual report to Congress that sets forth what it believes are potential emerging threats to the financial stability of the United States. This annual report represents the Council and its members' analyses of emerging threats to financial stability and potential systemic risks to the economy. The report is prepared by both prudential and market regulators and identifies both the most serious risks to the U.S. economy as well as developing risks that may become more dangerous in the future.

———

RESPONSE TO WRITTEN QUESTIONS OF SENATOR CRAPO FROM GARY GENSLER

Q.1. According to the American Banker, Annette L. Nazareth, a former SEC Commissioner, called the timetables imposed by the Dodd-Frank Act "wildly aggressive." "These agencies were dealt a very bad hand," she said. "These deadlines could actually be systemic-risk raising." Given the importance of rigorous cost-benefit and economic impact analyses and the need for due consideration of public comments, would additional time for adoption of the Dodd-Frank Act rules improve your rulemaking process and the substance of your final rules?

A.1. The Dodd-Frank Act provides the Commission with ample flexibility to phase in implementation of requirements. The CFTC and SEC staff held roundtables on May 2 and 3, 2011, and have solicited comments from the public regarding such concerns. This important input informs the final rulemaking process.

We've also reached out broadly on what we call "phasing of implementation," which is the timeline for rules to take effect for various market participants. This is critically important so that market participants can take the time now to plan for new oversight of this industry.

Next month, it is my hope that we vote on two proposed rulemakings seeking additional public comment on the implementation phasing of swap transaction compliance that would affect the broad array of market participants. The proposed rulemakings would provide the public an opportunity to comment on compliance schedules applying to core areas of Dodd-Frank reform, including the swap clearing and trading mandates, and the internal business conduct documentation requirements and margin rules for uncleared swaps. These proposed rules are designed to smooth the transition from an unregulated market structure to a safer market structure.

Q.2. Chairman Bair's testimony was unclear regarding whether the FSOC has the authority to issue a revised rule on the designation of nonbank financial institutions. She and others indicated some type of guidance might be issued instead. Is it in fact the case, in general, that the FSOC does not have authority to issue rules under Title I that have the force and effect of law? If the FSOC has the authority in general to issue such rules on designation, why specifically would the FSOC be precluded from re-proposing a rule that is currently pending? Is there additional authority the FSOC would need from Congress to issue such rules or to proceed with re-proposing its NPR on designation? If yes, what specific authority would the FSOC need from Congress for the FSOC to have the ability to proceed?

A.2. The FSOC's proposed rule concerning nonbank financial institutions described the framework that the Council would use to determine whether an entity should be designated as systemically important. In response to concerns that have been expressed, the FSOC is considering a variety of ways in which it may be able to provide greater guidance and more clarity. FSOC member agencies are collaborating to develop further guidance to be provided in a manner consistent with statutory requirements and are also considering the appropriate form that updated guidance should take.

Q.3. In an August speech at NYU's Stern School of Business, Treasury Secretary Geithner outlined six principles that he said would guide implementation, and then he added, "You should hold us accountable for honoring them." His final principle was bringing more order and integration to the regulatory process. He said the agencies responsible for reforms will have to work "together, not against each other. This requires us to look carefully at the overall interaction of regulations designed by different regulators and assess the overall burden they present relative to the benefits they offer." Do you intend to follow through with this commitment with some form of status report that provides a quantitative and qualitative review of the overall interaction of all the hundreds of proposed rules by the different regulators and assess the overall burden they present relative to the benefits they offer?

A.3. The Commission is committed to consultation with fellow regulators here in the United States as well as in other countries. Throughout our rule-writing process, the Commission has shared term sheets and draft proposals with other regulators and sought their feedback. This coordination has helped to promote consistent and comparable standards. As we consider final rules, our teams are reviewing the proposals from other agencies as well to see how they interact with the Commission's proposals. As part of our significant outreach with other regulators, CFTC staff has met more than 600 times with other regulators on Dodd-Frank implementation.

RESPONSE TO WRITTEN QUESTIONS OF SENATOR VITTER FROM GARY GENSLER

Q.1. Dodd-Frank set forth a comprehensive list of factors that FSOC must consider when determining whether a company posed a systemic risk and deserves Fed oversight. The council, in its advanced notice of proposed rulemaking, sets forth 15 categories of questions for the industry to comment on and address. However, the proposed rules give no indication of the specific criteria or framework that the council intends to use in making SIFI designations—other than what is already set forth in Dodd-Frank. As a result, potential SIFIs have no idea where they may stand in the designation process. Will the council provide additional information about the quantitative metrics it will use when making an SIFI designation?

A.1. I expect that the council will provide additional information in this regard.

Q.2. Would the council agree that leverage is likely to be the one factor that is most likely to create conditions that result in systemic risk? If so, how will the council go about identifying which entities use leverage?

A.2. Leverage may very well be a factor that the FSOC considers in assessing the systemic risk arising from a firm's activities. Leverage is traditionally a measure of the relationship between a firm's total assets and its equity.

Q.3. One of the first steps in the systemic designation process, as outlined in the proposed rule, is that after identifying a nonbank financial company for possible designation the FSOC will provide the company with a written preliminary notice that the council is considering making proposed determination that the company is systemically significant. Is receipt of such a notice a material event that might affect the financial situation or the value of a company's shares in the mind of the investors? If so, wouldn't it need to be disclosed to investors under securities laws?

A.3. This question is more appropriately answered by others on the panel.

RESPONSE TO WRITTEN QUESTIONS OF SENATOR TOOMEY FROM GARY GENSLER

Q.1. Can you share with us what the FSOC, OFR, FDIC and Fed are contemplating by way of fees that they may assess on SIFIs?

A.1. The FSOC recently received a briefing concerning appropriate enhanced prudential standards generally, including discussion of systemically important financial institutions. These matters are also being considered at the international level as prudential regulators seek to ensure the development of consistent standards, particularly with respect to global systemically important banks. The Federal Reserve and the Federal Deposit Insurance Corporation have taken the lead on these matters.

International Competitiveness

Q.2.a. It is critical for the continued competiveness of the U.S. markets that a regulatory arbitrage does not develop among markets that favors markets in Europe and Asia over U.S. markets. Will the FSOC commit to ensuring that the timing of the finalization and implementation of rulemaking under Dodd Frank does not impair the competitiveness of U.S. markets?

A.2.a. As a member of FSOC, I believe we should be aware of the competitive implications of FSOC decisions. I look forward to working with my fellow members on these issues as we move toward the finalization and implementation of Dodd-Frank rules.

Q.2.b. How will FSOC ensure that U.S. firms will have equal access to European markets as European firms will have to U.S. markets?

A.2.b. It is important that the FSOC consider not only how the regulatory structure in the United States affects both U.S. and foreign institutions, but also how foreign regulatory structures affect those institutions. As a member of FSOC and Chairman of the CFTC, I regularly review foreign regulatory standards and proposals and how those standards and proposals will affect U.S. firms.

Q.2.c. How will FSOC ensure that Basel III will be implemented in the United States in a manner that is not more stringent than in Europe, making U.S. firms less competitive globally?

A.2.c. As a member of the FSOC, I consult with prudential regulators concerning these matters in any way that proves helpful and will continue to do so going forward.

Q.3. Is a broker/dealer that is not self-clearing less likely to pose systemic risk because it receives the financial backing and risk management attention of its clearing firm which already performs extensive monitoring of risk for the broker-dealers and which in all likelihood will itself be a SIFI?

A.3. As a member of the FSOC, when deciding whether to designate an institution as a SIFI, I would consider the potential systemic risk that the firm's activities may create, consistent with the statutory framework. I also would consider any factors that might mitigate such systemic risk.

Q.4. Titles I and II of Dodd-Frank references an entity's "asset threshold" or "total consolidated assets" several times. Are such calculations to be made in accordance with generally accepted accounting principles (GAAP)?

A.4. As a member of FSOC, I look forward to working with my fellow members to determine how best to apply these statutory terms to different types of institutions, consistent with the statutory framework and Congressional intent.